TOTAL
Impact

TOTAL

STRAIGHT TALK
FROM FOOTBALL'S
HARDEST HITTER

RONNIE LOTT
WITH
JILL LIEBER

Impact

DOUBLEDAY

NEW YORK   LONDON   TORONTO   SYDNEY   AUCKLAND

PUBLISHED BY DOUBLEDAY
a division of Bantam Doubleday Dell Publishing Group, Inc.
666 Fifth Avenue, New York, NY 10103

DOUBLEDAY and the portrayal of an anchor with a dolphin are trademarks of
Doubleday, a division of Bantam Doubleday Dell Publishing Group, Inc.

"This Is It"
(Kenny Loggins, Michael McDonald)
© 1979 Milk Money Music & Tauripin Tunes
All Rights Reserved. Used by permission.

Library of Congress Cataloging-in-Publication Data

Lott, Ronnie.
    Total impact : straight talk from football's hardest hitter / by
    Ronnie Lott with Jill Lieber.—1st ed.
        p.   cm.
      1. Lott, Ronnie.   2. Football players—United States—Biography.
    3. San Francisco 49ers (Football team)—History.   I. Lieber, Jill.
    II. Title.
    GV939.L68A3   1991
    796.332'092—dc20
    [B]   91-21558
                                                              CIP

ISBN 0-385-42055-2

Printed in the United States of America

October 1991

First Edition

For my mother and father. I love you very much.

—RONNIE LOTT

For my family, who always believed that a little girl could grow up to write about football. And for Jerry, my heartmate, soulmate, lifemate, and teammate.

—JILL LIEBER

CONTENTS

TOTAL
Impact

1

INTRODUCTION: MONDAY NIGHT MADNESS

MONDAY NIGHT MADNESS

Five hours before we played the New York Giants, I was standing outside the restaurant at the airport hotel. I was totally relaxed. My mind was consumed with the game. Suddenly Jim Burt, our nose tackle, grabbed me by the arm. He was sweating. His eyes were bloodshot. Burt was already on another planet. Giants games did that to him.

"Ronnie, I've got to tell you something!" Burt said.

For weeks he had been pumped up for this game. You would see him in the locker room constantly clenching his fist and proclaiming, "We've gotta beat these guys!" I figured Burt was about to deliver another one of his pep talks, and I didn't want him to break my concentration.

"What is it?" I asked.

"I just talked to Phil Simms on the telephone," Burt said.

"So what?"

"Ronnie, you won't believe what he said about you. It even made *me* mad."

"Why would Phil Simms waste time talking about me?" I asked. "Look, Jim, I really don't want to talk about it."

We were so close to kickoff. I just didn't want to be bothered. Forget the mudslinging. Forget the outrageous remarks. The *middle* of the week is the time to engage in verbal warfare.

"I gotta tell you! I gotta tell you!" Burt said. "Simms said you're overrated, that you haven't done shit. He says you're washed up, that you're turning down hits. He claims you don't want to hit anybody anymore."

Burt's words smacked me across the chest like a sledgehammer. No teammate had ever said anything so explosive to me on

3

game day. I had absolutely no reason to doubt what Burt had told me. He had been with the Giants for eight years before signing with the San Francisco 49ers in 1989 as a Plan B free agent. It was my understanding that Simms, the Giants' thirty-five-year-old starting quarterback, was one of Burt's closest friends. Why wouldn't two friends talk trash?

"Ronnie, I'm telling you, Phil's going to go after you," Burt added as we entered the restaurant for the pregame meal. "He's going to embarrass you."

My stomach started to burn. What did Simms have against me? I had never publicly criticized him, although I had had several chances throughout the bitter, physical Giants–49ers rivalry of the 1980s. I hadn't said one word after Simms' 1988 comment that San Francisco "lays down like dogs," and I held my tongue during a 1984 encounter following the 49ers' 31–10 victory on Monday Night Football. In that game, I had sprained my big toe and was replaced in the first quarter by Dana McLemore. Walking off the field after the game, I had seen Simms and called out, "Good game."

"What happened to you?" Simms replied. "I could have thrown on you all day."

I was stunned. At first I thought Simms was joking, but when he didn't add anything else, I concluded he was dead serious. People simply don't say that kind of stuff to your face after a game. This guy's a trip, I thought, but I left the comment alone.

Well, after digesting Burt's words, I could barely swallow my cantaloupe and croissant. This time I wouldn't ignore Simms' cutting remarks. Washed up? Overrated? Haven't done shit? Afraid to hit people? Who does Simms think he is? I've got to get off tonight, I told myself. I've got to have a hell of a game. This is judgment day for Ronnie Lott.

The next time I bumped into Burt, he was speaking to one of his New York buddies in front of the hotel. I was waiting for my jeep to be retrieved from valet parking. Offensive tackle Steve Wallace and I slid into the vehicle for the fifteen-minute drive to Candlestick Park, and Burt asked if he could ride along. By now, he was more worked up than he had been at breakfast.

"These guys are going to try to embarrass us," Burt said. "They hate us. They absolutely hate us! I'm telling you guys, we're going to have to fight. Really fight. Kill them! Steve, they're going to come after you."

"I'm going to block my butt off," Wallace promised. "I'm ready for them. I'm ready for them."

Then Burt dogged me even more, delivering the most painful blow of all.

"Simms told me he doesn't think you were ever any good," he said. That did it.

"I've never done anything to that guy," I said, shaking my head. "I don't understand this. Why doesn't he just worry about his own game?"

To say I had never been anything was insulting. At that moment, I didn't give a damn about winning or losing. The Giants game was going to come down to something more precious. *Respect.* As I pulled into the players' parking lot, I made a pact with myself to knock the crap out of every Giants player every chance I got. Before the night was over, I was going to make sure that I got respect.

Even without Burt's revelation, I still would have been plenty motivated for this showdown with the Giants. Never in my ten years with the 49ers had I experienced so much pregame hype for a regular-season game. Some of our Super Bowl games hadn't had this kind of buildup. Starting in early October, everybody—the media, the fans and even some of my teammates—was talking about the December 3 Giants–49ers game on Monday Night Football. For weeks, friends bugged me for tickets. The game was being promoted as a battle between the NFL's only unbeaten teams. And though the Giants had lost to the Philadelphia Eagles, 31–13, and the 49ers had lost to the Los Angeles Rams, 28–17, on the preceding Sunday, the hubbub at the 49er offices was similar to the chaotic atmosphere of a playoff game. More than 300 credentials were issued to the media from across the United States, as well as reporters from Japan, Germany and Great Britain. The 49ers tightened security throughout our Santa Clara, California, facility, and our practices were closed to out-of-town media. The security crew and public relations department officials patrolled the grounds with walkie-talkies to keep the players sealed off from the media and fans. During the lunch hour—our designated time for media interviews—most of my teammates made themselves scarce, hiding in the off-limits area of the locker room.

Both the Giants and 49ers had 10–1 records, but some of the teams that we had beaten—Atlanta, Cleveland, Green Bay, Dallas, and Tampa Bay—were not NFL powerhouses. This game would give us a true indication of how good the 49ers were and how we measured up against one of the best teams in the NFL, the New York Giants.

There was no escaping the immensity of this game. On Sunday morning, while I was lounging around the house, there on my television screen appeared former 49er coach Bill Walsh, who is a commentator for NBC Sports. He said that Ronnie Lott would have to be one of the keys to a 49er victory. For San Francisco to win, Walsh said, "Number 42 has to make the big plays. Game of the year for Ronnie Lott." He said that Lott would have to make "ten big stops on those great running backs from out of that middle." Deep down, I knew he was right, and I laughed when I heard Walsh make his proclamation. He always did know how to inspire me. Just issue your challenge, Bill.

At about 2 P.M., Wallace, Burt, and I entered our locker room. I took a whirlpool to soothe my left hamstring, watched some soap operas, then chatted with quarterback Joe Montana and third-string Giant quarterback Matt Cavanaugh, a former 49er who had dropped by. The three of us talked about old times and our families. I didn't even bother to ask Cavanaugh about Simms. I would settle that score in my own way—on the field.

While putting on my uniform, I thought about a good friend of mine, Ed Givens, a middle-aged car detailer from San Jose who had died of a heart attack a few days earlier. Givens had grown up playing football on the dirt fields of Texas, but whenever we got together over the past several years, we spent hours talking about life and religion. We were together so much that the employees at the detailing shop thought we were related. I wrote ED in tiny black letters on the back of my helmet and dedicated the game to him.

I noticed that most of my teammates were unusually quiet. However, there were a few exceptions. Burt paced in front of his locker, muttering to himself. Outside linebacker Charles Haley ranted on about racism, and some of the other defensive players acted annoyed that he wasn't talking about the Giants. I wasn't fazed. The more Haley vented his opinions before games, the better he played.

"Hey man, chill. Just chill," I said. "Let them have tight buttholes. You and me, we've got to win this motherfucker."

"We gotta party tonight," replied Haley.

The most focused group in our locker room was the defensive secondary. Ray Rhodes, our defensive backs coach, had undergone an emergency appendectomy three days earlier and was under doctor's orders to watch the game on television from his hospital room. Rhodes would be hooked up to the coaches' booth via telephone and his observations relayed to cornerback

Eric Wright on the sideline. I would direct the defensive backs on the field. It was hard to imagine a game without "RayBob" Rhodes on the sideline offering his words of inspiration. A former wide receiver and defensive back with the Giants, Rhodes had been my motivating force since I joined the 49ers in 1981. We had always stood together during the singing of the national anthem on a yellow line several feet behind the rest of the guys. Just the two of us. I phoned Rhodes from the locker room.

"We're going to win this one for you, RayBob."

"Ronnie, make sure you've got everybody doing everything right," Rhodes said. "Keep your composure. Don't act crazy. I want you to get after the Giants. You know what it means to me to beat those guys."

Since I have always had a tendency to flare up at the slightest mistake on defense, several of my teammates also reminded me that it was imperative that I maintain my composure. At first I was irritated that they felt they had to tell me to stay calm, but soon after the opening kickoff I realized it was a good thing they had. The electricity generated by the 66,092 fans packed into Candlestick Park—the largest crowd for a 49er game in stadium history—reverberated through my body, and the game quickly escalated into one of the most physical defensive battles I have ever been involved in. The hitting was fierce. It felt as if somebody had closed down Rome, and we were in the middle of the Coliseum with the Giants. Two teams of ancient gladiators.

Right from the start both defenses made their presence known. On the Giants' second series, third-and-six from our 30, Haley made a big play, nailing running back Dave Meggett for a 4-yard loss that knocked the Giants out of field goal range. Then, on the next Giants' possession, Simms completed a 9-yard pass to tight end Mark Cross, and I popped him hard. While the officials were measuring for a Giants first down, Simms tried to strike up a conversation with me: "Hey, R.L." I didn't respond. I was so angry at him I told myself to stay focused and not be drawn into any dialogue. By holding my tongue I wasn't letting Simms become a distraction.

The Giants' defense also did a good job of stopping our offense. We had one really bad stretch. On our first two possessions of the second quarter we were able to complete only one of seven passes and Mike Cofer missed a 43-yard field goal. Something inside me said that winning the game would rest on the shoulders of our defense.

With about four minutes to go in the first half, Simms marched the Giants to our 3-yard line. Our goal-line defense rose to the occasion, allowing the Giants only one yard in three plays, and they had to settle for Matt Bahr's 20-yard field goal.

In the days before the game, the media had raved about the Giants' special teams. They were excellent, and nobody disputed it, but our special teams players felt they weren't getting the respect they deserved. To get their juices flowing, they nicknamed themselves the Dogs of War. Underneath their jerseys, our special teamers wore T-shirts with the face of a snarling, bloodthirsty pit bull. Following the Giants' field goal, one of our top Dogs of War, Spencer Tillman, returned the kickoff 30 yards to give us great field position at our own 37. Five plays later we scored the only touchdown of the game. Montana pump-faked to flanker Jerry Rice, holding off cornerback Everson Walls, and split end John Taylor broke free from cornerback Mark Collins on a post pattern for a 23-yard touchdown with 1:30 left. We led 7–3 at halftime. I went into the locker room satisfied.

Because I had been instructed by my coaches and teammates not to holler at the other defensive players, I found myself better able to concentrate on my job. I noticed that yelling at players to get them in the proper positions and flaring up at their mistakes diluted my aggressiveness. Tonight, by minimizing my blowups, I was releasing all of my emotions into every hit.

With less than five minutes remaining in the third quarter, running back Ottis Anderson pitched the ball back to Simms on the flea-flicker, and Simms connected with wide receiver Mark Ingram on the left side for a 22-yard gain and a first down on the San Francisco 35. On the next play, I stung Giant tight end Mark Bavaro with a brutal shot, driving my shoulder and forearm high into his chest. The force of my hit snapped his neck back. Bavaro, who had been concentrating on catching the ball, had no time to brace himself for the blow and the pass fell incomplete. Slowly picking myself up, my head felt like it was filled with cobwebs. I had to pause for a moment to catch my breath. I looked back at Bavaro, and he was already on his feet. I was surprised to see him standing up. I gave him my best shot and he still got up.

All I could think of was the movie *The Terminator*. Arnold Schwarzenegger is a mechanical man sent from the future to kill a woman who will one day give birth to the leader of the rebel force. Schwarzenegger chases her for almost two hours and then, near the end, she turns the tables and tries to kill him. Schwarzenegger is crushed, incinerated, and blown up, but the Terminator never dies because underneath his human exterior he is made of metal. Bavaro, the Giants' version of the Terminator, sure demonstrated a lot of heart on that play. I could almost hear Schwarzenegger delivering his famous line as Bavaro walked back to the huddle. *I'll be back.*

The defensive struggle raged into the fourth quarter with the 49ers still leading 7–3. On the Giants' first possession of the quarter, first down from their own 31, Simms completed a 14-yard pass to Bavaro across the middle. As I threw my shoulder into Bavaro's chest, my right thigh rammed against a 49er tackler who was on the ground, and the impact drove my foot sideways. When I stood up, there was pain in my right knee. I finished the series and then walked to the sideline, where I asked our trainer Lindsy McLean to examine me.

"Goddamm it! I think my right knee is loose," I told McLean.

"How does it feel?"

"Wobbly."

"I'd better get the doctor," McLean said.

"Hurry! Hurry!"

Dr. Michael Dillingham, the 49er orthopedic surgeon, appeared a little concerned while testing the stability of the right knee. Then, after checking the left one, he told me that both knees felt loose. Well, come to think of it, I had whacked my left knee against the ground early in the game. I hadn't told anybody because I had concluded it was only a bad bruise. Dillingham said there didn't appear to be any ligament damage in the right knee. Just a nasty sprain.

"All right Ronnie, we'll tape it," McLean said. "But you can only go back in the game if you feel you can play."

"Tape it up! Let's get some protection on there," I replied. "And hurry."

There was nothing McLean could say to keep me from reentering the game. All I cared about was stopping the Giants from scoring. I was so focused on that task that nothing else mattered. On the following series, the Giants had a third-and-nine from their own 36, when Simms completed a pass to wide receiver Lionel Manuel on a crossing pattern. Cornerback Darryl Pollard was out of position, and I ended up making the tackle. Manuel got 13 yards, and Pollard got a piece of my mind.

"Why were you playing zone?" I hollered.

"I didn't know we were in man-to-man," Pollard said. "I didn't hear the coverage."

"Everybody else heard the coverage!" I replied. "What happened to you?"

Two plays later, I was the one in the wrong place at the wrong time. Anderson plowed off tackle, and as I ran up to the line to stop him, defensive end Kevin Fagan dived into the pile of players. Fagan's helmet slammed into my left shin, knocking the leg back and hyperextending my knee. What were the odds of screwing up both knees on successive series? I shook my left leg, hoping to reduce the pain, but that was futile. I attempted to walk it off but could barely stand up.

"Number 42, are you going off the field?" the referee asked.

"Get him off! Get him off!" Fagan shouted to the official. "He's hurt."

"No, I'm not," I said. "I'm not hurt."

"Ronnie, you're hurt," Fagan maintained. "Get off the field."

I managed to limp to the sideline. When I got there, I decided to stand right next to coach George Seifert. I wanted to hide from McLean and Dillingham because I knew that if they examined me again they would never let me back on the field.

"Are you all right?" McLean yelled out to me.

"Yes," I said, gritting my teeth and staring straight ahead. Experience had taught McLean that my failure to make eye contact meant I was in intense pain and needed to be left alone to focus on the injured area and block it out of my mind. I told Seifert I was ready to go back in, but he wanted me to wait. I thought, if I can't go back into the game I'll die. I understood the risk factor in continuing to play. If I got hit on the left knee, I could possibly tear the ligament completely. But I didn't care about that at this point. My only concern was that the Giants were now lining up on our 9-yard line. "Okay Ronnie, get back out there!" Seifert said.

In the huddle, inside linebacker Matt Millen was spouting positive reinforcement.

"We held them out of the end zone earlier, and we can do it again," he told the guys. "Let's keep them out of the end zone."

Then I spoke up: "We've each got to make a play. Take care of your responsibility. Make something happen."

On first-and-goal, Simms fired to wide receiver Stephen Baker in the end zone but the pass fell incomplete. Okay, we got that one, I told myself. Now how are we going to stop them? Where are they going to line up? What play are they going to run? On second down, cornerback Don Griffin broke up a pass intended for Ingram in the corner of the end zone. Simms and Ingram had scored a touchdown against Griffin on the same play a couple of years ago.

"Way to shut 'em down, Griff," I shouted.

When the ball was snapped on third down, I reacted by reading Simms' eyes, and he looked directly at Bavaro. I broke to the ball as Simms released the pass, pushed off my injured knees and, diving as far as I could, knocked the pass down with my left hand. Millen wildly hugged me and tapped his helmet against mine.

"Great play," he yelled. "Great play."

There was 3:59 remaining in the game. Would Giant coach Bill Parcells go for a field goal to cut our lead to 7–6? No. I was surprised that he didn't. Fourth-down situations are crapshoots for the defense. No matter how many times a defense has practiced for them, there is really no way to anticipate what an offense is going to do. For the offense, it's do or die, now or never, and they might try anything. All you know for certain is that the offensive players will be so emotionally charged that the only way to stop them is by elevating yourself to match their level of intensity.

For the fourth straight down, the Giants decided to attack us in the air. Simms threw to Manuel in the end zone. The ball seemed to move in slow motion, and it was right on the money. Pollard, who was covering Manuel, had his back to Simms and couldn't see the pass coming. Oh, no! He's going to catch it. Just as I finished getting the words out, Pollard quickly turned his body, reached up with his hand and tipped the ball away.

I was so charged that I leaped straight in the air. That goal-line stand ranked among the top two or three I have ever been involved in. Yeah, we stopped 'em! Awwwwwwrrrighttttt! Out of the corner of my eye, I noticed Simms, and without thinking, I raced over and pumped my fists, imitating his celebratory touchdown gesture. Respect that, Simms! Then I started swearing at him. Simms acted genuinely surprised. I have never been known as a player who taunts others. Very quickly we were facemask to facemask, butting heads and cussing each other out. Simms was poking me in the chest. I called him all sorts of names. I was berserk. I can't remember half the things I said. A couple of players finally pulled us apart, and I ran to the 49er bench.

My knees started to throb, and I thought, "I hope we don't

have to go back out there, because I don't know if I can do it. . . .
If Simms throws a seam pass, I'm dead."

However, with 36 seconds remaining, the Giants got the ball
back at the San Francisco 44 for one last shot. We lined up in
our prevent defense and rushed only three linemen. Simms
dumped off two passes to Meggett that gained a total of 17
yards, giving the Giants a first down on our 27. With no
timeouts, Simms threw the ball to the ground to stop the clock.
There were now three seconds left.

"We've got to win this game," I told the players in the huddle.
"We've come too far to be denied."

On the final play of the game, Simms, from the shotgun
formation, dropped back to pass and barely managed to elude a
hard rush from Haley. I hope they get him, I thought as I
watched Simms escape from Haley and run upfield. Which way
is he going to throw? Which way is he going to throw? Fagan
caught Simms from behind and sacked him on our 28. Simms
was visibly upset. Time had expired. While on his knees, he
wound up and fired the ball to the ground.

We had beaten the Giants, 7–3, in the lowest-scoring game in
the NFL all season. This was the first time since 1985—not
counting the strike-shortened season of 1987—the Giants had
failed to score a touchdown in a game.

The Candlestick fans began chanting, "Defense! Defense!" but
before I celebrated, I wanted to explain my outburst to Simms.

"Look, man, the reason I said what I said is because Jim Burt
told me what you think about me," I told Simms.

"I can't believe you talked to me that way," Simms said. "I
can't believe you would say that kind of shit."

"Me say shit? What about you?" I shouted. "What about all
the shit you said about me?"

Then Burt interrupted.

"Phil, it's my fault."

"I can't believe you said that, Jim," Simms shouted, pushing
Burt out of his way.

"I'm sorry, Phil," Burt said. "I'm sorry."

Simms didn't pay any attention to Burt's apology and kept on
pursuing me. Someone reached over and pulled me back. From
behind I heard Giant linebacker Gary Reasons screaming,
"Leave it alone, Ronnie." But very little of this registered with
me because I was in such a rage.

Suddenly Simms and I once again found ourselves facemask
to facemask.

"I respected you more than anybody in this league," Simms yelled, shoving his chest into mine and pushing me backward.

Forty-niner nose tackle Michael Carter, who was trying to serve as a peacemaker, reached in and separated us. Bavaro pulled Simms away. But any hope of a civil conversation went out the window as photographers, television cameras, and microphones quickly swooped in and surrounded us. Several more of our teammates came running over. The pushing and shoving started to escalate.

"You knew I wouldn't say that," Simms screamed at me.

Then Burt came running over and said something to Simms. Reasons chimed in again. "Leave it alone, Ronnie!" he said. He was right. At this point, I probably should have left it alone, but I still wanted Simms to listen to my side of the story, and I wanted to show him a little class in this ridiculous episode.

"I'm sorry, man," I said. "I'm just telling you why I did what I did. Burt told me stuff . . ."

"I used to respect you," Simms interrupted. "But now I don't respect you at all."

That hurt. It hurt a lot. I shook my head in disbelief and walked away.

"Ronnie, it's my fault," Burt called out. "Phil, my fault."

But I had had it with Simms and Burt for the night. I limped off the field angry and dejected. For the first time after a big victory, I actually felt defeated. I couldn't believe how I acted. How could I lose my cool like that? In trying to apologize to Simms, I looked like an ass. The game had been played in front of 48 million people, the largest audience in the twenty-one-year history of Monday Night Football.

By the time I got to the locker-room door, I was emotionally drained. We gathered in a circle to say the Lord's Prayer, and as my teammates recited the words, tears streamed down my face. I was sobbing uncontrollably. Our owner, Eddie DeBartolo, Jr., put his arms around me and, in a comforting voice, asked if I was all right. I didn't answer. I just kept on crying.

All of my emotions had totally overwhelmed me. I was so mad at myself for losing control on the field. I was elated about our victory. I was disappointed Rhodes hadn't been on the sideline with me. I was sad Ed Givens had died and I hadn't said goodbye. I was absolutely petrified about my damaged knees. The pain was slowly intensifying. For the first time it dawned on me that I was at the crossroads of my career. I was scared. Everything just hit me at once.

Eric Wright and 49er general manager John McVay led me into a private area in the back of the training room to calm me down. I could barely speak. I felt so nauseous, I thought I was going to throw up. I couldn't quite grasp what was happening to me because I had never ever been in that state of mind before. My emotions kept spilling out.

About fifteen minutes later, I regained my composure. I felt as if I had dropped ten pounds, although I didn't feel washed out. Montana walked into the training room to check on me. I told him I was okay. Dillingham popped in to examine my knees, and reassured me that he didn't think there was any ligament damage, but told me I would have to undergo more tests the following day to be sure. McLean wrapped both knees in ice, and Dillingham ordered me to stay on crutches for the next two days.

While linebacker Keena Turner and I were discussing the game, the media began swarming toward the training room. Cameras and microphones were rushing in my direction, and guess who was at the front of the stampede? None other than Phil Simms. I couldn't believe it. I didn't have the energy to deal with this anymore.

"Hey man, are you all right? I see you got hurt pretty bad," he said, walking into the training room where I was sprawled on a table.

"Yeah, it's bad, but I'll be back," I responded. "How did you come out?"

"Oh, I came out all right," Simms said.

Enough small talk, I thought. Let's get serious.

"Look, I just want to apologize for what I did," I said. "But when Burt said that to me, all I could think of was the stuff you said to me in 1984—you know, how you could have thrown on me all day. And I just lost it."

"I never said that to you," Simms replied.

What? Hearing that answer, I wondered if perhaps my mind was playing tricks on me. "I swear to God, Phil, I would never make something like that up," I said. "I would never make it up."

"I didn't say that to you," Simms insisted.

I refused to believe him. But this time I maintained my cool.

"Well . . . whatever," I said. "I just want you to know that I have respect for you on the football field."

"I respect you, too," Simms said, and with that we both said goodbye, and he turned and walked away.

In the shower, I felt stupid. I had let down myself, my family, my coaches, and my teammates, and it had turned into an even stickier scene when Simms came parading through our locker room to have a last word with me. My knees burned. I hobbled back to the training room, and Ray Tufts, our assistant trainer, helped me get dressed. He slipped my sweatpants over my legs, pulled on my socks, and tied my sneakers. As I left the locker room on crutches, a man who identified himself as a friend of Parcells approached me in the tunnel. "Coach Parcells wanted to make sure you were all right," he said, "and he wanted me to tell you you're a hell of a player."

"Tell him thanks," I said.

In the parking lot, I instantly detected fright in the eyes of my fiancée Karen Collmer. She had seen me injured before but never this badly, and certainly she had never seen me so dejected after a victory. Eric Scoggins, a former college teammate from the University of Southern California who had flown in from Los Angeles for the game, helped me into my jeep and drove me home. I barely spoke. Scoggins understood what it was like to be battered and emotionally spent after a game. I didn't bring up the Simms incident, and he didn't ask me about it because he knew I would tell him when I was ready. Usually I analyze the game as I head home on the freeway, but this night I was just hoping I'd be able to fall asleep.

2

BORN TO KICK ASS AND TAKE NAMES

MY CHILDHOOD I discovered my first sports hero when I was four. He was playing in an intramural basketball game in a little gymnasium at Bolling Air Force Base in Arlington, Virginia. He wasn't particularly quick for a guard, and he didn't have spectacular leaping ability or great hands. Nobody ever referred to him as an outstanding defensive player. But his unorthodox jump shot always made me smile. He would curl both legs up behind him and then release the ball. The New York Knicks won the NBA title in 1969–70, and when I watched their guard Dick Barnett shoot his Fall Back, Baby, jump shot it reminded me of my basketball hero. To me, Roy D. Lott, my father, was the greatest basketball player in the world.

Dad spent twenty-two years in the Air Force, and when each intramural game was over he would climb up the bleachers to join the rest of the family—my mother Mary, brother Roy, and sister Suzie. Even though I didn't understand everything, Dad and I watched the other intramural games together. In the car on the way home, I listened intently as Dad talked more basketball. Eventually I became the water boy for his team. My favorite part of the job was watching games from the end of the players' bench. During timeouts, I used to inch myself inside the huddle to soak up the strategy. At halftime, I practiced free throws and imitated the moves of dad's teammates. While most of my friends were glued to their television sets, I was my father's tag-along pal.

Spending time with us kids was important to Dad. Soon after his birth in 1938 in Oklahoma City, his parents moved to Detroit. His mother was a domestic and his father a hospital corpsman. Both were very young and had little money, and they left Dad in Kingfisher, Oklahoma, to be raised by his mother's parents. Forced to work as a child, Dad swept the floor and shined shoes at a barbershop and helped his grandfather carry luggage at a hotel. Because he had felt deprived of nurturing from his parents, Dad went overboard with us. My brother and I begged him for bikes one year, and he came home with the most gigantic two-wheelers we'd ever seen. When Mom ironed his Air Force uniform in the kitchen, my brother and I stayed in the back room with Dad shining our shoes. We regularly visited the military barbershop together for our haircuts.

Three months after graduating from Kingfisher High School in 1956, Dad enlisted in the Air Force. He was just seventeen. When he returned from a tour of duty in Korea, Dad was assigned to Sandia (now Kirtland) Air Force Base in Albuquerque, New Mexico. One Sunday morning he and an Air Force buddy, Chuck Young, attended a service at the Rex Chapel Methodist Church. There he spotted a beautiful teenager in the choir. Later he introduced himself to Mary Carroll, and they soon began dating.

Mary, sixteen, had little interest in sports, but she showed remarkable patience for Dad's fanaticism. She detested her gym classes at Albuquerque High because the girls had to wear baggy green bloomers. When she and the other girls walked from the high school to the athletic field, the boys teased them, saying they resembled sacks of potatoes with legs.

After less than a year of courtship, my parents were married by a Justice of the Peace, and on May 8, 1959, she gave birth to me. The longtime family joke is that I'm smarter than my brother and sister because I attended my mother's high school graduation when I was only a few weeks old and weighed a little less than six pounds. Dad wanted my first name to begin with the initial R, so he chose the name Ronald. My mother claims she found my middle name—Mandel—in a book of baby names, but I suspect she really named me after Young's musical group, The Mandells, who recorded a hit song in 1961 called "Darling, I'm Home."

Young and his wife Eva are important people in our lives. He happens to be my godfather, and in some ways he is a second father. Over the years Young has been a good friend, and his sports knowledge is excellent. Mom and Eva have been best friends since they lived a few blocks from each other as kids. Dad and Chuck played on football, basketball, and slo-pitch softball teams at various Air Force bases throughout their military careers. They took all of their games very seriously. Chuck, more demonstrative than Dad, would rant and rave throughout the course of a game and madly pace the sideline. If Dad didn't know the answer to a sports trivia question, or he couldn't come up with an obscure baseball player's statistics, it would be on the tip of Young's tongue or easily dug up from the stacks of sports magazines he collected. I never felt left out of their sports talks. They let me watch games on television with them in the living room, and if they had an errand to run during the action it was up to me to give them the details when they returned.

Compared to many military families, we had a pretty stable family life. Dad was never separated from us. His assignments were always in the United States. I had to adapt to only two new environments. However, both were distinctly different, coming at critical junctures in my childhood, and they made me wary of forming close friendships. Each time, as the new kid on the block, I was thankful to have athletic talent because it allowed me to be more readily accepted. Sports made it easy for shy, quiet kids like me and my younger brother Roy to fit in. All we had to ask was, "Wanna play catch?"

In late August of 1963, when I was four, we moved from our quiet neighborhood in Albuquerque to a three-bedroom apartment on Southern Avenue, on the Maryland border of Washington, D.C. Dad had been transferred to Bolling Air Force Base, where his job was chauffeuring generals to and from the Pentagon. We rolled into town in our loaded-down car a few days before Dr. Martin Luther King, Jr.,'s historic Civil Rights March on Washington. Mom and Eva went down to the Lincoln Memorial to hear Dr. King's "I Have a Dream" speech. Our neighborhood was predominantly white but underwent constant change with white families moving out and blacks moving in.

For the first time, I became aware of the color of my skin. Although I attended an integrated school, I was the only black kid in my kindergarten class. During a meeting with my mother, the teacher, who was white, pointed out that whenever I colored or painted, I made everybody's face brown.

"That's not unusual," my mother explained to the teacher. "That's Ronnie's point of reference."

My mother also vividly remembers the afternoon I came running into the kitchen crying.

"What's wrong, Ronnie?" she asked, wiping the tears from my cheeks.

I told her that one of my best friends, a white kid, was moving out of the neighborhood.

"Why is his family leaving?" she wanted to know. "Did his father change jobs?"

"They've got to leave because niggers are moving into the neighborhood," I replied.

I didn't know what the word "nigger" meant.

The race riots in Washington, D.C., following Dr. King's assassination on April 4, 1968, were the scariest moments of my early years. I looked out my bedroom window one night and saw the 7-Eleven store across the street engulfed in flames. The next morning I woke to the sound of military vehicles. The National Guard was dressed in full riot gear and carrying rifles, and I worried that some sort of war had broken out. We lived under a curfew and had to be in the house before it got dark. I watched as looters ran in and out of the 7-Eleven with armloads of food and drinks, and a few days later some buddies and I tried to haul out baskets of candy from the store. As I was standing guard out front, a police officer stormed up on a motorcycle. I bolted, leaving my friends inside, and escaped down an embankment. The cop gave chase but couldn't catch me, and all I could think was, I sure hope he doesn't shoot.

My life in the nation's capital revolved around sports, and my elementary school years there were defined by playgrounds, parking lots, sidewalks, and kids of all ages, sizes, and cultures. Each and every one of them was out for blood. Once I was shooting a basketball through the monkey bars at the playground behind our apartment complex. When it came time to go home for dinner, I asked the other kids to return my ball. They refused.

"My dad wants me home by six," I said. "If you don't give me the ball, my dad's going to kick my butt."

"You can't have it," a tough kid said. "You can go home, but we're keeping your ball."

I went home and told my dad, and together we retrieved the basketball without a problem.

"Here you go, Mr. Lott, here's the ball," the kid said, tossing the ball with a smile.

Dad turned his back and walked toward our apartment. When he was out of earshot, the kid gave me an intimidating look and threatened, "Hey, next time we're keeping the ball. And we're going to kick your dad's butt, too."

If you could earn respect in the neighborhood, your age and

skin color didn't matter. I went to great lengths to prove I could hold my own against the older kids. I had to show them I could fight through injuries, pain, and adversity. One winter we all went sledding on Boone's Hill Road, a wooded area behind our apartment complex, and I slid face-first into a telephone pole. Luckily I escaped serious injury. Tough guy that I was trying to be, I went straight to the top of the hill and slid back down.

Another time, my brother and I were in the woods, hiding from friends, when we tripped and fell into a big nest of bees. Bees were all over us. They were in our underwear, our socks, and our baseball caps. That's how I found out I was allergic to bee stings. I had to go to the hospital for the next five years to get allergy shots.

And then there was that dog whose teeth looked like Dracula's fangs. Playing football in a friend's backyard, I was running up the side of the field when a huge German shepherd bit my left hip. Right through my clothes. I guess I had frightened him. Thank God he had had his rabies shots.

The playground taught me the most important lessons of life. Norris Jones, a neighborhood friend, taught me to believe in my convictions. I was playing football in a parking lot at our apartment complex and Jones broke the rules. After I called him on it, he belted me in the eye with his fist. I ran into the house and told Dad.

"Look what Norris did to me!" I said. "He was cheating."

"You'll be all right," he said. "Go back out there and stand up for yourself. Play your butt off and kick his butt in the process."

I learned not to buckle under to peer pressure in a neighborhood football game. I was getting roughed up by this one particular kid who was several inches taller than me.

"You can take him," my buddies baited me. "You can take him."

I quickly became overconfident. "Yeah, yeah," I said to myself, "maybe I can take him." I made a move to hit him, and he beat me up. He wore me out. That was the last time I listened to my friends.

I tried to get into games with kids who were older, bigger, and more talented. That challenge helped develop my skills more quickly, and the excitement of those games made me love sports even more. My first chance at playing with the big guys, I got hit with an elbow on the bridge of my nose, but I told myself not to quit or I might not get to play with them again.

Richard Walker was my favorite "big guy" to play with. He

and his younger brother Stanley were military brats. Richard was a few years older than me. On Sundays, when the Lotts and Walkers weren't watching football games together, both of our families would be at the movies. We took drives along the Potomac River, picnicked under the cherry blossoms, toured the monuments, the Smithsonian, and the White House, and visited the Tomb of the Unknown Soldier and President John F. Kennedy's grave. Whenever possible, we made our fathers drive past RFK Memorial Stadium, the home of our beloved Washington Redskins.

When we played football, I pretended I was Charley Taylor, my favorite Redskin. Taylor wore number 42, and that's the number I later wore in high school, college, and pro football. Richard Walker pretended to be (Dead Eye) Daryle Lamonica of the Oakland Raiders. Stanley Walker was Sonny Jurgensen of the Redskins, and my brother Roy thought he was Paul Warfield of the Cleveland Browns. We hated the Dallas Cowboys, especially their quarterback (Dandy) Don Meredith.

One Christmas, Roy and I begged for plastic Redskin helmets like the Walkers', and I pleaded for a pair of sneakers—P.F. Flyers—insisting that those particular shoes would make me run faster and jump higher than all of the other kids. Dad gave in on the sneakers, and to demonstrate how good they were, I jumped from our second-floor apartment window to the first-floor landing. I hit the four-foot-square cement block perfectly. As I was about to try it a second time, my mother caught me and gave me quite a spanking. Regardless, from that day, my P.F. Flyers became the most important part of my athletic gear.

At the time I was eligible for organized football, my father got a new job as an Air Force recruiter, and in 1968 we were transferred to San Bernardino, California, which is 60 miles east of Los Angeles. A year later, we settled in nearby Rialto. I had difficulty channeling my aggressiveness, developed through playing on the pavement with the big kids in Washington, D.C. During one recess, I clobbered a fifth-grade teacher with a kickball while making a tag and was ordered to write and illustrate a booklet on the history of basketball and the meaning of sportsmanship. This is what I wrote in my childlike scrawl:

Sportmanship

Sportmanship is one of the important rules of football, baseball, basketball, and hockey. If you have bad sportman-

ship they give you a warning and sometime they kick you out of the game. So you should always have good sportmanship in every game.

I dedicated the booklet to Dad, and he still keeps it on the nightstand beside his bed.

Fortunately, my new environment offered a variety of organized sports to absorb some of my energy. I persuaded my parents to let me try out for Little League baseball by promising I'd wash and iron my uniform. I talked my way into the Rialto recreational basketball league when I was ten. The day of the draft, I showed up at Eisenhower High School in Rialto and began shooting baskets. A white man approached me.

"We'd like you to play," he said, "but do you think you can play with white kids?"

"I'll play with anybody," I said.

I was the first pick of the entire draft.

For two years, I started at quarterback for a new Pee Wee team called the San Bernardino Jets. We were a tough bunch, a predominantly black team, and we surprised everybody in 1971 by winning all ten regular-season games. Seven were shutouts, and we outscored our opponents 377 to 22. The Jets became a family affair. Dad was the designated athletic director/administrator. Mom brought the hot dogs and hamburgers. Suzie was a cheerleader, and Roy played wide receiver.

I'll never forget the day of our showdown against the Redlands Terrier Pups for the Pee Wee championship. Our coach got so hyped up that he had us cross-body blocking each other during warm-ups. We were bruised and exhausted before the game even started. The stands were packed with rabid Redlands fans. Their vicious cheers began when we lined up for the opening kickoff.

"Beat 'em up!"

Clap. Clap.

"Beat 'em up!"

Clap. Clap.

"Beat 'em up!"

Clap. Clap.

And while you're at it, *clap, clap,* tear those little Jets apart, limb by limb.

Well, Redlands beat us up, all right. They ate us for breakfast. It was one of my worst days at quarterback. In the car, I cried all the way home. I was embarrassed and humiliated. It was my first big defeat. That day I became aware of how deeply sports affected me. I realized I was just as passionate about the games as my father had been. I started taking them even more seriously after that, reading *Sports Illustrated* and *The Sporting News*, and devouring every sports autobiography I could get my hands on. I wanted an insight into what made the legendary athletes so great. Statistics meant nothing to me. I needed to know how they grew up, the ways they developed their skills, and what was inside their hearts.

I read that former NBA great Oscar Robertson worked on his peripheral vision, so I worked on mine. Sitting in classes, I stared straight ahead but tried to concentrate on what was on either side of me. In order to buy the ankle weights North Carolina State's David Thompson wore while shooting baskets, I bought gum and candy before school each morning, then hustled the goodies at a profit to my junior high classmates. And after reading that Louisiana State's (Pistol) Pete Maravich dribbled his basketball everywhere he went, I bounced my ball through the streets of Rialto.

I studied every sport imaginable on television. Not only football, basketball, and baseball, but boxing, rodeo, wrestling, and bullfighting. I probably never would have made it out of junior high if we had had ESPN, the cable sports channel, back then. My brother and sister could stand inches from my ears, screaming bloody murder, and if I was transfixed on sports I still wouldn't acknowledge them. I was—and still am—too engrossed.

I even practiced my own sports medicine. I applied Ben-Gay all over my body, locked myself in the bathroom, and turned on the shower.

"Ronnie! Ronnie!" the folks would shout, pounding on the door. "We need to get into the bathroom!"

"No, you can't," I'd yell back. "I'm taking a steam."

When I got out on the field for my junior high football games, I was a terror, much too focused to smile. I hit so much harder than anybody else because that was the way my favorite pro football players did it. Tackling wasn't enough. I had to drive my helmet into an opponent's midriff, keep my feet moving, and lift him into the air. I never complained that running into people hurt.

My father never pushed me. He offered encouragement from the sideline. When I came off the field, he'd say, "Take your time. . . . Don't worry about it. . . ." Dad always understood my passion. In me he saw a kindred spirit.

ALL-AROUND ATHLETE   Most people in Southern California haven't a clue where my hometown of Rialto is located. To get there from Los Angeles, you drive east on Interstate 10 for about 50 miles. If you're not careful, you're liable to miss the Riverside Avenue Rialto exit. There are no other signs for the town, and no shopping malls or industrial parks to pull you off the freeway. Why, the only so-called landmark in the Rialto area is the Wigwam Motel on Foothill Boulevard. This unique-looking structure is made up of twenty Indian teepees. Each is a separate motel room. The Wigwam appeared on a postcard in the opening of the movie *National Lampoon's Vacation,* starring Chevy Chase.

I will always have a warm spot in my heart for Rialto. In February 1977, I hefted the first shovel of dirt at the groundbreaking ceremony for my high school's new 7,000-seat football stadium, and several years later I was the Grand Marshal of the Rialto Days Parade. The mayor proclaimed February 19, 1981, as Ron Lott Day in Rialto. My parents still live there in a small ranch house on the north side of town.

A quiet little community in the mid-'70s, much of Rialto's working population was employed by the military and at Kaiser Permanente Hospital in nearby Fontana. The student population at Eisenhower High School during my three years there reflected the Rialto community. Most of the kids came from middle to lower-middle income families and included a large number of black and Hispanic students. You have to work hard to fit in at a melting pot school, but I didn't have too much trouble because I was an athlete and I was also comfortable with being Ronnie Lott.

My friends came from a variety of cultural, religious and socioeconomic backgrounds. They called me Yellow Man because I was so light-skinned. We hung out together in study halls and gyms and at the baseball and football fields. After every athletic event, we wore our green Eagles letter jackets with the white leather sleeves at the Del Taco Mexican restaurant. Everyone knew who I was because my athletic nickname, Lott-T-Dott, was stitched across the back of my jacket.

In each of my three years I lettered in football, basketball, and baseball. No other athlete in Eisenhower history has ever matched that feat. I made the All-Citrus Belt League football team at wide receiver, safety, and quarterback. I had 21 career interceptions and was named to the prestigious Parade Magazine High School All-America team at the end of my senior year in 1976. As a guard on the Eagles basketball team I was All-CBL three years, had 589 career assists, and was selected to play with the best high school players from the Los Angeles area in the Olympic Development League the summers after my junior and senior seasons. My statistics in baseball paled in comparison. But I'll never forget the long home run I belted off Santa Monica High School right-hander Tim Leary, who went on to major-league baseball and now pitches for the New York Yankees. I also played first base in the Northern–Southern California High School All-Star game at Dodger Stadium.

Prior to graduating from Eisenhower on June 15, 1977, I received the Ken Hubbs Memorial Award as the area's outstanding athlete. Hubbs, the 1962 National League Rookie-of-the-Year with the Chicago Cubs, was killed two years later in a plane crash. Only twenty-two years old, he had been an outstanding four-sport star at nearby Colton High School.

Participating in three different sports helped make me the athlete I am today. I learned to appreciate and balance the contrasting emotions and different levels of concentration demanded by each sport. The physical strength and aggressiveness in football, the creativity and fluidity in basketball, and the patience and timing in baseball. Competition for college athletic scholarships and the big-money contracts in pro sports have caused three-sport high school athletes to go the way of the dinosaur. That's a shame. I can only hope that Bo Jackson, an All-Star in baseball and football in 1990, opened kids' eyes to the many benefits and beauties of exploring more than one sport. Although I barely had a chance to catch my breath between seasons, those years were some of the best of my life. Even my summers were busy. I had a job sweeping streets in Rialto from 8 A.M. until noon. Then I played American Legion baseball, drove to Cal State–Los Angeles for a summer league basketball game, and returned to Rialto to compete in a football-passing league.

Although I've never admitted this before, basketball came the easiest and was my most natural sport. It got me through the other two seasons. As for football, well, I enjoyed the contact, but I never dreamed of playing in the NFL. It took three men— my high school coaches—to lay the foundation and bring out the best in me. Without their motivation, inspiration, encouragement, and nurturing, who knows where I'd be.

The butterscotch-colored infielders glove smelled of new leather. I happily slipped it on my left hand and pounded the pocket with my right fist. The glove had been given to me in the late spring of my sophomore year by Mike Mayne, my baseball coach at Eisenhower. I was determined to be a good shortstop. I didn't want to disappoint Mayne. That summer I played sixty American Legion games and worked extra hard at turning the double play.

When I first reported to the Eagles baseball team earlier that spring, everybody was surprised that I had chosen baseball as my third sport over track and field. Almost every kid in Southern California who's involved in baseball plays year-round. Baseball was frustrating at times, but the challenge drove me. All the frustration and awkwardness in the world couldn't make up for the experience of playing for a winning team. During my three years, we won three consecutive CBL championships. In my junior season, we had a 25–5 record and were ranked among the top teams in the nation.

When I was a sophomore, the Eagles, who were loaded with talented seniors, were a confident bunch. Sitting on the bench as the backup right fielder, I found myself intimidated and overwhelmed by their skills. Even though I'd played football with most of them, I felt uncomfortable a lot of the time. The older kids hazed me and ordered me around. Pick up the balls! Retrieve our gloves! Drag the infield! At practice one day, I had finally had enough. One of the seniors had told me to drag the infield *again,* and I backed him into a corner of the dugout. "No more," I said, "I've had it with you. You're not going to do that to me anymore."

That episode helped me gain respect and acceptance. My junior year, I emerged as a team leader, and my on-field talents were best described as a shortstop with a football player's mentality. Aggressive. Relentless. Competitive. Mayne would send me to home plate with the lineup card. I'd shake the hand of the opposing coach and look him in the eyes. Years later, Mayne admitted that this was an attempt at intimidation, and he said that several of the CBL coaches had told him his ploy had worked.

In his two years as my coach, my sophomore and junior seasons, Mayne taught me more about baseball than any other coach ever taught me about any sport. He drilled and drilled us on fundamentals. As a tactician, Mayne, a physical education teacher, was the best. Detailed and patient. Whenever possible, I sat beside him on the bench to listen to him discuss strategy.

Mayne also taught me about team unity and the importance of togetherness. From September to February, he expected his players to help him maintain the varsity baseball field. This included hauling bags of seed, spreading fertilizer, and mowing the infield grass. The night before games, he and his wife held potluck suppers for the players at their home.

Basketball was my first love. I discovered the magical sound of a ball bouncing against a hardwood floor long before it ever occurred to me to look twice at a girl. If I could be any other professional athlete, I would be Magic Johnson for a day. I have had season tickets courtside at Golden State Warriors games since 1984—as stipulated in my 49er contract—and I regularly attend the NBA All-Star Weekend. I'm the kind of guy who would happily pay an outrageous amount of money to attend a Los Angeles Lakers fantasy camp. Just let me run the fast break one time. Give me a chance to go one-on-one with Magic Johnson or Kareem Abdul-Jabbar.

When I was in high school, I adored Philadelphia 76er forward Julius Erving. I read everything I could get my hands on about Dr. J, and my teammates teasingly called me Dr. Lott. Determined to follow in his footsteps, I considered transferring to nearby San Gorgonio High School before the ninth grade because San G. had a stronger basketball program than Eisenhower.

My dad talked me out of it. "You don't need to transfer," he said. "If you're going to be good, you'll be good anywhere. Eventually, you'll have to stand on your own two feet."

My varsity basketball coach, Dick Cardosi, liked to use a full-court press, and that suited me just fine. This time I was a *guard* with a football player's mentality. My teammates weren't spared my aggressiveness during drills at the end of practice. I'd bring up the rear, snapping a towel on the butt of the player in front of me, yelling, "Faster! Faster! Faster!"

I rode my brother Roy harder than any other teammate. When

I was a junior and MVP of the varsity basketball team, Roy was the MVP of the sophomore team. We played together on the varsity the following season, and I thought he was a better basketball player than me. I became upset when he didn't make the Olympic Development League team. Unfortunately, Roy was always "Ronnie Lott's little brother." Even when he played well. Roy, shy and laid-back, never showed the drive and intensity I did. Coaches, players, and other faculty members couldn't understand why he was so mellow. Sometimes they held that against him, and I'll tell you I was as much to blame as everybody else. It frustrated me that Roy didn't get more out of his basketball talent.

One of Roy's best games occurred on February 15, 1977, in a 67–60 victory over rival Redlands, which gave us our first ever CBL basketball championship. At the time, this was by far the biggest basketball victory in Eisenhower history. Roy scored 27 points and grabbed 5 rebounds. The local newspaper plastered a huge photograph of him cutting down the net across the top of the sports page. When reporters asked Roy if he had prepared in any special way, he said in characteristic fashion, "I just concentrated on the game a little more, I guess."

By the way, the Redlands game wasn't one of my shining moments. I had only 8 points and 7 assists. I didn't start because I had injured myself on a recruiting trip at the University of Utah and hadn't practiced that week.

But that's a story for later.

The Orange Show Stadium in San Bernardino doubled as our home football field. The show, which was held early each spring, drew thousands of Californians who displayed their finest jams and jellies. There were assorted livestock and farm exhibits and stage shows with country and western acts. At other times the fairgrounds hosted rodeos and stock car races. The promoters hauled in truckloads of dirt to create rodeo rings and stock car pits in the center of the track, and when they raked the dirt to produce a semblance of grass for our football games, they didn't do a very good job. It wasn't unusual to find automobile nuts and bolts on the field as you pushed yourself up off the ground after making a tackle.

My coach, Bill Christopher, made playing at the Orange Show Stadium an adventure. In the spring of my sophomore year,

1975, Christopher, then twenty-seven, was hired to rebuild the Eagles football program. He worked us so hard for two weeks straight, two grueling hours a day, that Reggie Tatum, our junior running back, threatened to quit the team. Tatum was angry that Christopher hadn't designated him a starter.

"Reggie, you can't let anyone see you quit," I said that day. "You're going to stick it out. You've worked too hard to come this far and quit."

"He's riding me hard, Ronnie," Reggie said. "Who does this guy think he is?"

"It's good for you," I replied. "He wants to win."

By the end of practice, Tatum agreed to stick it out.

What impressed me most about Christopher was his outgoing personality, positive attitude, warmth, and energy. Norm Daluiso, our former coach, was cold and brusque. A biker, Daluiso had been a regimented disciplinarian, distant and unyielding. Christopher, a former small-college offensive lineman, had a lot of ideas. They ranged from offensive play selection and coverages in the secondary to fund-raisers and team get-togethers. It all came at you a mile a minute, in a voice that was so loud he never had to carry a whistle.

I'm sure Eisenhower's athletic director hired Christopher for another reason, too. Christopher had been the defensive coordinator at Fontana, one of the CBL's powerhouse teams. When we played Fontana in my sophomore year, I had put a monkey wrench into Christopher's defensive strategy by trotting out for warm-ups camouflaged in a different-numbered jersey. All week long, Daluiso and his coaching staff had said that my sprained left knee would keep me on the sideline, and I had wanted to test my knee before the game without giving Christopher a chance to make wholesale changes in his game plan.

In his first full season as my head coach in 1975, Christopher was inspiring. At the opening of summer practice, he instituted a traditional sleep-over in the Eisenhower gym. Friday evenings before games, he held a team dinner at a hamburger or steak joint. Then we changed into our uniforms in the boys' phys ed locker room and boarded buses for the Orange Show Stadium or our opponents' stadium. Saturday mornings we all met at Christopher's house for scrambled eggs and doughnuts to watch game films. I'll never forget his pep talks. He had us lie on the floor with the lights off as he played a taped speech from the movie *Patton*. I can still hear the words of George C. Scott: "Americans don't tolerate losers. You've got to grease the guns with their guts." Those words fired me up. Our first league loss that year came against Chaffey, whose star player was 250-pound lineman Anthony Munoz, who later became a perennial All-Pro with the Cincinnati Bengals. We finished the year at 6–3, the first winning season Eisenhower ever had. I would have run through walls for Bill Christopher.

Instead, Christopher had to settle for me running through Reuben Henderson, the leading rusher at Fontana.

On a foggy Friday night, in front of 8,000 fans, I laid out Henderson in one of those bone-jarring hits every kid dreams of. Early in the first quarter, I saw Henderson read the hole. "He thinks he's going to hit the hole without somebody coming up to hit him," I said to myself. "Ha! I know where he's going."

I shot like a torpedo straight at Henderson's midriff, but I miscalculated and hit him in the kneecap instead. We were both knocked out, flat on our backs. I suffered a slight concussion, stumbled off the field, and argued with Christopher until he let me back in the game.

"Please, Coach," I begged through my tears. "Please let me back in."

Though Henderson claimed he was just slightly bruised, Fontana coach John Tyree used him solely on defense in the second half. Henderson, who went on to play at San Diego State and briefly at cornerback with the San Diego Chargers, was held to just 12 yards for the night. By the way, Christopher gave in late in the third quarter and allowed me to line up at wide receiver. Quarterback Fritz Robinson then connected with me on two passes, one a 32-yard touchdown with 10:22 left to close the gap, but we still lost 14–7.

Before my senior season in 1976, Christopher posted a list of "10 THINGS TO DO" by the wrestling room. The first four were outrageous: 1. Be CBL Champs; 2. Make the CIF Playoffs; 3. Have at least an 8–1 season; 4. Beat Fontana, Redlands, and Chaffey. Well, we accomplished almost everything. We shared the CBL title with Chaffey and Fontana, made the playoffs, had a 6–4 record, and beat Fontana and Redlands. And we did all that with me at quarterback.

To take advantage of my quickness, Christopher had moved me to quarterback and installed the veer offense, which gave me more opportunity to run with the ball. Initially I wasn't too crazy about the idea because I thought it might hurt my chances for a college scholarship. Following my favorite defensive backs every weekend—Dennis Thurman from the University of

Southern California and Jack Tatum of the Oakland Raiders—I was bound and determined to play that position at a major university. But whatever Christopher asked me to do, I did. I was a team player, first and last.

Defeating Redlands, the thorn in my side since Pee Wee football days, was like winning the Super Bowl. The Terriers had been programmed to win football games from as far back as I can remember. The week before the game my dad commented on how nervous I seemed. I couldn't concentrate in the classroom. My homework went by the wayside. I was obsessed with beating the Terriers just once in my Eisenhower career. My sophomore year they creamed us, 34–6. The next season we were annihilated, 32–0. We had to give them a dose of their own medicine and spoil their homecoming, leaving them in ruins on their beautiful University of Redlands field. When I finished with the Terriers that day, I'm sure they never wanted to see me again. I accounted for three touchdowns—49- and 24-yard TD passes and a 13-yard run—had 145 yards rushing on 14 carriers and ran for a two-point conversion. The final score: Eisenhower 32, Redlands 8.

After the game, I told the press how much we believed in ourselves and our coach, that we knew he would stick by us no matter what, and that we actually loved this man. I never really told Christopher face-to-face how I felt about him until I saw him on the sideline at Stanford Stadium before Super Bowl XIX. A friend of his worked security for the game, and knowing Christopher hadn't seen me play in person since I left Eisenhower, he offered my old coach a security job on the field. When I came out for pregame introductions, Christopher was standing near the tunnel. I was so happy to see him that afternoon, so thankful that he'd been my high school coach, that I wrapped my arms around him and said, "I love you, Coach."

There are two drawbacks to being a three-sport star in high school. You get three times as many letters and phone calls from college recruiters, and, when you are finally faced with narrowing it down to one sport, it takes three times longer than you thought it would.

The football recruiting blitz began in my sophomore year, when I received a letter from the Nebraska Cornhuskers. Enclosed was a questionnaire asking for my height, weight, and statistics. In a way, I'm sorry I cooperated. In return, I received letter after letter from what seemed like every Nebraska alum on the face of the earth. That was followed by phone calls or mail from Pittsburgh, Wisconsin, Minnesota, Arkansas, U.S. Air Force Academy, San Diego State, and Oregon.

None of this fazed me. By the fall of my senior year, I was inundated with close to forty letters a week from every major college west of the Mississippi. Air Force was the only school to promise me the opportunity to try out for all three sports. Because there was so much mail, Eisenhower's athletic director assigned me a mailbox in the faculty lounge to collect all the envelopes. Strangely, Nebraska never contacted me during my senior year.

I had read a number of newspaper and magazine articles about recruiting, and I honestly thought I could cope with it. I was wrong. It's something that you have to experience to appreciate, if that's the right word. The recruiters were like vultures. Our phone rang from 7 A.M. until midnight, and many times I'd peer out the front door and notice assistant coaches parked in the street, waiting for me to go outside. During the basketball season, I recall looking across the court from the bench and having UCLA football coach Terry Donahue and USC tailback Ricky Bell smile at me.

Most of the recruiters were just glorified salesmen. Ninety percent of what they told me was bullshit. They all used the same tiresome lines:

"My name is such and such. I'm from such and such. I've heard a lot about you . . . You've had a great high school career . . . You're at the top of my list . . . We need a quarterback/defensive back/wide receiver like you . . . You can be a starter for us as a freshman . . . Our campus is tremendous . . ."

And on and on and on. Until they finally delivered the standard punchline: "I know you'll just love our campus when you come up for a visit." That always got me. I wasn't being invited. I was being told. I almost never could get a word in edgewise with these guys, and many times I was reduced to hello and goodbye.

Recruiters underestimate high school kids, especially blacks. They figure you'll be impressed by the fact that somebody from a big university is coming to see you. They think they can win you over by referring to you as "man" or "partner." The biggest phonies are the white assistant coaches who talk as if they were brought up in the ghetto.

To keep from being overwhelmed by all of the attention and the hard sell, I made recruiting into a game whenever possible by playing hide-and-seek. One day I caught a glimpse of Jim Mora—a University of Washington assistant who is now the head coach of the New Orleans Saints—stalking the halls at Eisenhower in search of me. He hadn't told me ahead of time that he was coming, so I dashed to my car, hoping to avoid him. When Mora noticed me, he sprinted after me in the pouring rain.

"Check out this guy," I said to myself as I put the key in the ignition. "He's really serious."

"Hi, Ronnie, what are you doing?" Mora asked, as he tapped on my window.

"I gotta go to lunch."

"Can I talk to you when you get back?"

"Sure," I answered.

My recruiting odyssey began in earnest with a visit to the University of Colorado, and what a trip of firsts that turned out to be, starting with my first time on an airplane. This small commuter plane ride from Ontario to Los Angeles left me sweating bullets. Once we landed at the Los Angeles International Airport I almost got lost trying to find the right gate to board my flight to Denver. My mother had insisted I wear my dress shoes, which were so tight that I got a blister on the back of my heel. In Boulder, I made my first trip to a bar, where I sampled my first low-alcohol beer. It felt so cool to hang out with the older guys on the Colorado football team, players like Odis McKinney, Mike Davis, and Mark Haynes. The Buffaloes had just played in the Orange Bowl for the first time since 1961. I was infatuated with Colorado, probably because it was the first stop on my list.

Although I was captivated by the beauty of the Rocky Mountains, it wasn't until I made my trip to Utah that I actually slapped on a pair of skis. Can you picture snow-capped mountains and me, with two other black high school kids, on a ski lift? From the time I got off the chair lift, I fell. And fell. And fell. And fell. Until I finally reached the bottom of the hill. I was so exhausted, I begged out of a second run.

"Why don't I just take the skis off and meet you inside?" I said to a couple of the Utah football players. Taking off my boots, I discovered a large gash in my calf. I must have cut myself on the edge of one of the skis or poked myself with a ski pole. I was bleeding profusely.

"This looks pretty bad, son," the doctor at the local hospital said. "What are you doing here in town?"

"I'm on a recruiting trip to the University of Utah," I responded.

"Are you thinking about going to school here?" he said, eyebrows raised.

"Yeah."

"Well, are you a good black or a bad black?" asked the doctor, a white man in his early forties.

I was so taken aback I wasn't quite sure how to answer. "A good black, I guess."

"Then you won't mind it here," he said. "If you were a bad black, this isn't the area you'd want to live."

After he finished stitching me up, I phoned my dad, and when he was through chastising me he yelled at the coaches from Utah. That's the last contact I had with the Utes.

I must have been one of the few recruits in the country who wanted to play at Arizona State for Frank Kush, who had the reputation of being one of the toughest, if not meanest, coaches in college football. He reminded me of Vince Lombardi—a stern disciplinarian who demanded that players always be at their best. Before the season, Kush would take his team to camp for ten days in the White Mountains north of Phoenix. They called it Camp Kush. He had three practices a day instead of the usual two. I heard these workouts were brutal. Arizona State had a 12–0 record in 1975, the only unbeaten team in major college football, and ranked No. 2 nationally. Their 17–14 upset over Nebraska in the Fiesta Bowl that season put Arizona State on the map. But somebody who worked in the ASU athletic department pulled me aside on my recruiting trip to Tempe and said that the Sun Devil football program might be undergoing some changes. Kush isn't going to be your coach, I was told. The Sun Devils were coming off a dismal 4–7 season in 1976, and prior to that Kush had turned down a job to become the head coach of the Philadelphia Eagles.

They just blew this one, I thought. I wasn't going to sign with a school without knowing who my head coach was going to be.

It was on my Arizona State trip that I received the most unusual sales pitch. Jim Brock, the Sun Devils' baseball coach, told me: "I know you're interested in business. Reggie Jackson owns half of Arizona and if you want to, we can talk to Reggie and help you get started in business." Jackson had gone to Arizona State on a football scholarship and lettered at defensive back in 1965. Regardless, I wasn't impressed by the sound of Brock's proposal. Why would a teenager need to know about investments?

After visiting UCLA and USC on my own, I wasn't sure which school I liked better. I had attended a UCLA basketball game against Notre Dame in Pauley Pavilion, and I was mesmerized. Gee, I thought while watching the game, it sure would be great to play football *and* basketball for UCLA. Meanwhile, USC had told me I could wear the number 42 jersey that belonged to senior tailback Ricky Bell. Bell, the younger brother of singer Archie Bell, of Archie Bell and the Drells, had led the nation in rushing in 1975. Bell had helped recruit me, and I had the utmost respect for him. He was good-hearted and genuine, the nicest of all the Trojans. This wouldn't be just attaching a number to my name. It meant following in his footsteps. That was a big selling point.

I was so confused between the two Los Angeles schools that I devised a crazy plan for choosing which one I liked better. I would sign with the school that won the UCLA–USC football game. At the end of November I was glued to the TV, pulling for UCLA big time, until All-America safety Dennis Thurman picked off an interception, returning it 47 yards for a touchdown, to give USC a 7–0 halftime lead en route to a 24–14 victory. "Well, dang, I don't think I'm going to UCLA," I told my dad afterward.

What nixed UCLA for good was a visit I had with Bruin coach Terry Donahue. From the moment he walked into my family's living room, I didn't have good vibes. He seemed too old-fashioned, straitlaced and perfect, as if he had just stepped out of the TV show "Leave It to Beaver." I told him I wanted to be an option quarterback. "We never start freshmen," Donahue flatly stated. "Never." That was all I needed to hear. How could any coach put limitations on people he hadn't seen against his own players? Leave the door open. All Donahue had to say was, if you're good enough, you can start at UCLA, and I would have considered playing for him. A visit from USC coach John Robinson had been so enjoyable in comparison. He was honest, warm and funny. And, in a way, fatherly. Robinson belonged in our living room. With hard work and self-discipline, he said, the sky was the limit.

Still, when the time came to sign the national letter-of-intent in early February 1977, I waited two more weeks, holding out in case a school wanted to offer me a basketball scholarship at the last minute. There were no takers.

During that period I received a frantic call from Tom Osborne, the football coach at Nebraska. "Ah . . . Ronnie?" Osborne began, clearly embarrassed that he'd blown me off during my senior year. "We seem to have had problems with our mailing list. And I noticed you haven't signed yet. I was wondering . . ."

"Coach," I interrupted, "it's too late."

Utah also telephoned. "We hadn't talked to you since the accident," said a member of the Utes' coaching staff, "and we were wondering how you were."

"Thanks for calling, see you later," I replied.

Finally, one day I came home for lunch, and alone at the kitchen table I forced myself to decide between Colorado and USC. The challenge of playing with the USC Trojans would be enormous, I told myself, but at least I'd find out once and for all how good I really was. But before I could inform USC of my decision to go there, I got a phone call from a Colorado coach. When I told him I had made up my mind to go to USC, he began screaming.

"Wait a minute! Stay right where you are! I'm getting on a plane this afternoon! I'm flying out to see you!" the Colorado coach said. He paused for a moment.

"Ronnie, did you sign anything?" he asked.

I hadn't, but I told a little white lie. "Yes. Yes coach," I said. "I've signed. I've signed."

THE TROJAN WAY

Oh, my God, he's so huge! How am I going to block this guy?

Mario Celotto, a 6-foot-4, 230-pound senior linebacker, planted his tree-trunk-size legs in the turf, scratched the grass with his cleats, and dug in. An Elvis Presley look-alike with jet-black hair and steel-blue eyes, Celotto was what the USC football coaches called a physical specimen. His shoulders expanded to the wingspan of a 747 jet. His biceps bulged from his jersey sleeves. From the darkness behind his facemask, Celotto snarled at me.

It was my first week of practice at USC, and I was battling for a spot on the Trojans' special teams, hoping and praying to make the travel squad. Coach John Robinson had shown us a film of the greatest special teams hits in USC history. He told us that many of the Trojan superstars started their careers playing on special teams. We ooohed and ahhhed at each high-speed collision and ferocious hit. By the end of the film I was so worked up that I stormed out of the room and vowed to throw bodies all over the field.

On this August afternoon in 1977, we were practicing punt coverage. As the outside coverage man on the punt return team, it was my job to clear Celotto out of the way. "You can do this," I told myself. "All you have to do is jump outside of him. Yeah. That's it. Shove him to the inside, Ronnie."

The ball was snapped, and I hooked Celotto underneath his shoulder pads. He grabbed my facemask and yanked my helmet halfway around my head. "Oh, shit, Oh, shit," I said to myself. "I pissed this guy off." I straightened my helmet. Too intimidated to say anything to Celotto or for that matter, anybody else, I quietly shuffled to the sideline with my head down.

For the first time in my life, I found myself nervous and scared on the football field. And this was only practice. Intimidated by the size and stature of USC's upperclassmen, I wasn't sure I could hack it physically, mentally, or emotionally. USC practices were a test of survival. An exercise in pain and frustration. My teammates were ornery and scrappy. Every day it seemed as if we were playing for the national championship.

The thud drills—full-speed game simulation with less than full-force hitting—were taxing. Getting knocked to the ground by a forearm to the mouth was routine. Even the prized Trojan tailbacks had to endure punishing bag drills. They had to run through a gamut of defenders throwing rock-hard pillows at their legs.

My first few weeks at USC were overwhelming. Coming from Rialto, I was a bit of a hick. I wasn't street smart or sophisticated by any means. Although we lived a ninety-minute drive from Los Angeles, it might as well have been on the other side of the planet. I really felt out of place walking on campus in my blue jeans, T-shirts, and trademark Panama straw hat. USC, an expensive private school, has been nicknamed the University of Spoiled Children. There was an endless stream of rich kids dressed in brightly colored polo shirts, wearing Rolex watches, driving BMWs and small shiny convertibles. What the hell is a polo shirt? Who is Ralph Lauren?

At the same time I was wondering how, and if, I fit into the

USC student body, I was also faced with figuring out where I fit in with the USC football players. Could I measure up to their standards? How would my achievements compare? I remembered reading their names in the high school and college All-America lists in national magazines in previous years, and now here I was, standing beside them in the locker room and playing on the same field. It was frightening. The upperclassmen resembled grown men, and the freshmen seemed to be much better athletes than I was. I had made the Parade Magazine High School All-America team, too, but I was never quite convinced I was good enough.

On another level I had to figure out where I fit in with the black football players. Black athletes tend to size each other up more than white athletes. I think that happens because, unfortunately, black kids are more apt to come from single-parent homes. The lack of a male role model forces young black males to measure themselves against each other and to rely on their own dignity to get through life. One of my freshmen teammates, Dennis Smith, who is black and came from Santa Monica, remarked that he had taken it for granted before meeting me that I was white, since I was from the boondocks. The inner-city guys figured that because I had come from a middle-class, suburban environment I hadn't had as hard a life as they had. There were many days that I felt some of my black teammates didn't think I was tough enough.

Meanwhile, the other freshmen were faced with racial adjustments of their own. Steve Busick, a white linebacker from Torrance, California, matter-of-factly stated that he had never played with blacks before. Eric Scoggins, a black defensive back from Inglewood, California, admitted he wasn't comfortable relating to whites. Apparently I had the ability to transcend racial barriers, to walk comfortably on both sides of the fence, and that made Scoggins curious.

"How do you speak to white people?" asked Scoggins, who had attended a predominantly black high school.

"I talk to them just like I talk to anybody else," I replied. "I don't really think about it."

"But Ronnie, you can always deal," Scoggins said. "You can always flip the cards."

"It's not a matter of flipping the cards," I told Scoggins. "It's a matter of the experiences in your life. If I had to cross a street I've never crossed before, I'd question it. I'd make sure I wouldn't get hit. I look at a person for who he or she is. I ask myself, 'Is he a good person or a bad person?' And then I act on my gut feeling."

Freshman fears brought Scoggins, Smith, and me together almost from the moment we first slipped on our cardinal-and-gold uniforms. Our bond was strong and unyielding. Safety in numbers. Our relationship blossomed when we embarrassed ourselves during the annual freshman talent show. We stood up in front of the entire football team and belted out "Three Blind Mice." From that moment on, we were inseparable. If you saw us in my little cardinal-and-gold sports car my father had bought me for a high school graduation present, you'd find Scoggins in the passenger seat and Smith folded in the hatch-back, his legs hanging out a window. We lived in the same dorm. In fact, Smith and Scoggins were roommates. We enrolled in the same classes and studied together. On road trips, we sat side by side on the team buses and planes.

I was the most philosophical of the Three Blind Mice, conscientious to a fault. Scoggins and Smith laughed at my small-town paranoia and named me "Jethro" after the character of the dense, naïve son on "The Beverly Hillbillies." Scoggins, loud and funny, was the talkative one. He attributed that to his inner city background. He drove a beat-up green 1968 Plymouth Roadrunner and answered to "Wimpie," a nickname that grew out of his love for hamburgers.

Smith was the athlete, graceful with amazing speed. Away from football, however, we had to take his pulse to make sure he was still among the living. He was mellow and quiet. Smitty answered to "Kojak," a nickname he picked up in high school for wearing his hair in tight curls. At USC, Smith and Scoggins wore bushy Afros, and I had a short haircut with mutton-chops. Even back then, my hair wouldn't grow, and I was always fidgeting with some concoction to slow down my baldness.

There were eerie moments when I felt as though I had known Smith and Scoggins for years. Because of the moving I had done as a kid, I had been wary of developing close relationships. I opened up to them. They become my first best friends. We never had arguments or disagreements. Football was our passion. Our goal was to be the best. We competed against each other on the practice field, although we never articulated it, and we shared our fears openly. We listened to the words of wisdom from our coaches and picked the brains of the older players.

Bob Toledo, our defensive backfield coach, taught from a unique viewpoint. Because he had always been on the offensive side of the ball, first as a second-team All-America quarterback at San Francisco State and then as head coach at the University of California–Riverside, he instructed us with an offensive mentality. He told us to give two different looks at the line of scrimmage, so the quarterback would never know what the pass coverage was until the ball was snapped. He explained the kind of formations we were looking at and which offensive players we should key on.

A stickler for detail, Toledo drilled us for hours on the fundamentals. When he joined Robinson at USC in 1976, he and the other defensive coaches waded through reel after reel of the Pittsburgh Steelers' Steel Curtain defense. Robinson, who had been an assistant with the Oakland Raiders in 1975, had great respect for the Steelers. The USC staff wound up installing 57 combinations of defensive coverages, more than any college team in the country.

The best defensive backs, according to Toledo, kept their weight low as they ran backward. Making their break with receivers, and turning to sprint stride for stride upfield, defensive backs had to maintain their balance, as well as keep their motion fluid and their bodies on the same plane. In the latter stages of games, Toledo drummed into us, defensive backs wind up standing more and more erect. Their legs get fatigued from all the backpedaling. He felt that body language gave quarterbacks and receivers a distinct advantage.

Running backward is the most unnatural movement in sports, and no athlete does it more than a defensive back, so Toledo instructed us to train our legs by duckwalking. We would crouch, our hands scraping the ground, and walk backward across the field, slowly, seriously, accentuating every step. Of course we looked absolutely ludicrous, but Toledo said it was the best way to develop the quadriceps, hamstrings, and buttocks. When Scoggins, Smith, and I heard that, there wasn't enough hours in the day for the Three Blind Mice to duckwalk.

Dennis Thurman, a 5-foot-11, 173-pound senior All-America safety, noticed our desire to excel and our craving for knowledge, and took us under his wing. He tutored us in the finer points of football strategy, which helped us to mature more quickly. Thurman had been recruited as a flanker out of Smith's alma mater, Santa Monica High School, and in his first two seasons at USC, under coach John McKay, he had played on both offense and defense. Immerse yourself in football, Thurman advised us, know the responsibilities of every defensive player. His favorite saying was "It's Rose Bowl or no bowl."

Thurman become our mentor. We watched him hold court on the team bus for the defensive players. He would designate himself the Judge, make cases against any player who had acted like a jerk or dressed like a slob, thoroughly embarrass him, then hand down a sentence. We spent a ton of time with Thurman, listening to how he became an All-America and learning the three most important goals of Trojan players. Beat Notre Dame. Beat UCLA. And win the Rose Bowl. Whenever we went anywhere or wanted to try anything, we felt we had to have Thurman's permission. He was our father figure. His approval was important to us.

One of Thurman's most inspirational pep talks still fires me up. It's about USC defensive line coach Marv Goux who played center and linebacker for the Trojans in the early '50s and coached there from 1957 to 1982. Goux injured his back as a sophomore while making an interception against Notre Dame. Three years later he had spinal surgery to fuse several vertebrae. Season after season, the week of the Notre Dame game Goux would lift up his shirt to reveal a long, ugly scar on his back to motivate the USC players.

"They ruined my fucking back!" Goux would cry. "They are the reason I walk funny."

Goux would then name the entire 1952 Fighting Irish team because he held every single one of them responsible for putting him in the hospital.

"The best trophy you can win isn't the one on the mantel in your living room or the plaque on the wall in your den," Goux would say. "The best trophies are your scars. Those are the ones you'll remember because you'll carry them with you forever."

Thurman would imitate Goux's battle cry: "We're going to kick ass and take names! Burn their barns! Pillage the town! Hide the women and children! We're the men of Troy. We'll take no prisoners! Get one of them before they get you!"

Kick ass.
Take names.
Take no prisoners.

The Three Blind Mice were the only freshmen to make the travel squad, and as luck would have it, I was the first to start a game.

That memorable moment came in the fourth week of the 1977 season in the Los Angeles Memorial Coliseum against Washington State and the nation's leading passer, Jack (The Throwin' Samoan) Thompson. I'd gotten the nod when starter Larry Braziel was sidelined with an injury.

The day before the game, the Trojan Marching Band danced onto the pratice field and began jamming. The players shimmied and shook, and even the coaches were swinging and bopping with the band. If only you could have felt the thumping of my heartbeat. I could barely sleep the night before the game and eating was practically out of the question. By game time, I was in such a buzzed state, I'm still not sure what came over me on one Washington State play, a sweep to my side. I nailed the ballcarrier for a loss. "What did I do?" I asked myself.

The hit took place in front of the USC bench, and it was the hardest blow my teammates had ever seen me deliver. The coaches and players were jumping up and down, and when I returned to the defensive huddle, Thurman looked at me peculiarly. His eyes seemed to ask, Who was that guy who smoked the running back? It couldn't have been one of those Three Blind Mice. "Be cool now, Ronnie," Thurman said as we broke the huddle. "Be cool."

I could barely control my emotions the rest of the game. We crushed the Cougars, 41–7, and it seemed as if the band played our fight song, "Fight On," a hundred times. Our mascot, Traveler, the sleek white horse that galloped around the Coliseum after every USC score, almost had to be airlifted from the field when the game was over because he was so pooped out.

The following Saturday against Alabama I only played on special teams, but that didn't dampen my enthusiasm. USC was ranked No. 1 in both wire service polls, and our 15-game winning streak was the longest in the nation. We were on national television, and before the game started I found myself staring across the field. On the other sideline was the man they called The Bear. Legendary Alabama coach Paul (Bear) Bryant, wrinkled and grizzly at sixty-four, was dressed in his trademark hound's-tooth hat. He was in his twentieth season as the coach of the Crimson Tide. I wondered, what would it be like to play for him?

On punt coverage that day, my goal was to hit somebody as hard as I could. My parents were in the Coliseum stands, and I wanted them to say, "That's my son out there." Once I chased downfield after Ozzie Newsome, who later played thirteen years with the Cleveland Browns, and just as I got ready to tackle him somebody gave me a wake-up call. "You're going to be all right, Ronnie," Robinson said when I came to the sideline. Later, I *did* level an Alabama player. And this time Robinson told me, "Ronnie, you're going to be a great player." I repeated that to myself the rest of the afternoon.

The wily ol' Bear dipped into his offensive bag of tricks and used a variety of plays from the wishbone, the I, and slot-I formations. He threw in tight-end reverses, halfback passes, and option pitchouts. We scored with 35 seconds left on Lynn Cain's 1-yard touchdown run, cutting Alabama's lead to 21–20.

Should we kick the extra point to tie? Should we go for the victory with a two-point conversion?

Robinson decided to go for the victory, and it failed. In his postgame speech Robinson didn't apologize or make excuses, which taught me a valuable lesson. That is, you lay it all on the line. Leave a piece of yourself on the field. When you walk into the locker room after the final gun, you shouldn't have any energy left. If you don't win, it doesn't mean you're a loser. It just means your best shot wasn't good enough. By playing hard, you earn the respect of your opponents.

"I don't want anybody making any excuses," Robinson said. "When somebody beats us at USC, we keep our heads up. You walk out feeling good because you gave 110 percent. I won't make excuses, so you won't either. If the press asks you why you lost, you tell them you lost, plain and simple. Then you send them to me. We're all in this together."

Our 49–19 loss to Notre Dame in South Bend was a disaster for the team and a rude introduction for the Three Blind Mice. Prior to the debacle, USC had beaten the Fighting Irish nine out of the last ten years. Playing in South Bend can be an intimidating experience. You stay in a little hole-in-the-wall hotel. And you don't see or hear anybody. It's all pretty low-key.

Until you get to the stadium. Then you wonder where everybody came from.

In the pregame warm-ups, Toledo noticed something out of the ordinary. Notre Dame players were wearing socks with green stripes. It looked strange with their traditional gold helmets, dark blue jerseys and gold pants. He pointed it out to our other coaches, but nobody knew the significance of the socks. The Irish retreated to the locker room after warm-ups, and when they reappeared on the field before the opening kickoff, the capacity crowd of 59,075 erupted. Notre Dame coach Dan

Devine had dressed his players in shamrock-green jerseys. It had been fourteen years since the Fighting Irish had last worn them.

For all I cared, they could have been dressed in purple. I hated Notre Dame to begin with, and after three hours on the same field I detested the Irish even more. A man named Joe Montana, who had started the season as a third-string quarterback, passed for two touchdowns and ran for two others, and linebacker Bob Golic blocked a punt to set up another Fighting Irish TD. In the fourth quarter, with the game out of control, our defensive coordinator Don Lindsey threw the Three Blind Mice into the game. Lindsey wanted to expose us to big-time college football. At USC, either you learned quickly or you missed the show.

Unfortunately, we missed the show.

All three of us froze. We ran around in circles. We didn't cover anybody. But instead of criticizing us, Lindsey made light of the situation. "I'm going to rename that coverage, 'Cover Sieve,' " he said, laughing, which was a little out of character.

Lindsey, who had been at USC for seven years, had a deep, gravelly voice and a fiery temper. He was a perfectionist, and if our defensive players made the slightest mistake, he hollered on the sideline. He graded the defense on loafs. In other words, if you weren't flying to the ball as though you were the last man on the field, it was considered loafing. Lindsey taught me how to compete with myself. After watching me try to one-up Smith time and again on the practice field, he called me into his office and sat me down. Lindsey said, "Ronnie, I want to ask you something. Who did O.J. Simpson compare himself to?"

"I don't know," I replied.

"He was the best, right?" Lindsey said. "Could he have compared himself to anybody?"

"No," I said.

"If Dennis Smith does something well, you turn around and try to do it better," Lindsey said. "And if Dennis tops that, you try to outdo him again. Ronnie, that's not giving your all. Try to top yourself. That's the only way you'll get the most out of your talent."

Nobody had more pride than Lindsey. Before the Stanford game in my freshman year, he told us how badly he wanted to beat Bill Walsh, who was in his first season as the Cardinal coach. As a longtime NFL assistant and self-proclaimed offensive wizard, Walsh had once lectured at a coaching clinic Lindsey attended, and his words didn't sit well. Walsh boasted that college defensive coaches didn't know how to defend against him. As hard as they tried, they just couldn't. In our pep talks that week Lindsey announced, "Men, you're going to shut these guys out. This coach thinks nobody can stop his offense. This guy thinks his shit doesn't stink."

Our blood pressure rose even more when we stepped onto the field at Stanford Stadium. The Stanford students and alumni were waving dollar bills and credit cards, poking fun of our reputation as a private school for rich kids and calling us the University of Second Choice, claiming that most USC students had been rejected by Stanford.

We demolished Stanford 49–0, holding their star receiver James Lofton to only two receptions for 15 yards and Darrin Nelson to 22 yards rushing. Because Lindsey wanted to prove that Walsh's offense could not only be stopped but shut out, the Three Blind Mice sat on the bench. Lindsey wasn't the kind of coach who only showed up to play. He came to win.

Yes, win at all costs, even if it meant reducing me to tears against our most hated opponent, the UCLA Bruins. You won't find a more heated rivalry in Los Angeles than the USC–UCLA game. That's all anybody talks about. When the game rolled around, you wore blue and gold or you wore cardinal and gold. If you were dating a girl from UCLA, she let you know it. Our band members dangled Bruin teddy bears from their tubas, with nooses choking their fuzzy little necks.

Against the Bruins I played strong safety but was yanked in the first quarter because I wasn't aggressive enough. Lindsey yelled at me on the sideline and replaced me with junior Willie Crawford. "I blew it," I told myself. "I'm not getting in this game the rest of the day."

In the fourth quarter, with USC leading 26–20 and the Bruins threatening to score, we called a timeout. Thurman walked to the sideline to confer with Lindsey, and they motioned me over.

"I need somebody who can cover the tight end," Lindsey said. "You're bigger than Willie, so I'm putting you back in. All I want you to do is cover the tight end. That's all I want you to do."

"Fine, put him in," Thurman said. "Ronnie can do it."

On the next play, we blitzed Bruin quarterback Rick Bashore. Instead of covering the tight end, I started chasing Bashore. As I was getting ready to sack him—I mean, I was close enough to smell his breath—Bashore threw a 1-yard touchdown pass to tight end Don Pederson. Frank Corral's extra point put UCLA ahead, 27–26, with less than three minutes to play. When I came to the sideline, Lindsey avoided me, and Thurman kept his distance. To this day, that play still bothers me. Fortunately, Frank Jordan booted a 38-yard field goal with two seconds left, giving us the victory. By winning, we knocked UCLA out of the Rose Bowl and put the Washington Huskies in.

Walking off the field, I had tears in my eyes. Not even Scoggins and Smith spoke to me. But by the next morning, when I walked into Lindsey's office before our film meeting, I had a smile on my face.

"What are you smiling about?" Lindsey barked.

"We won," I said.

"Ronnie, I can't believe you. I put you in the game and you screw up. And now you come in here smiling? You could have cost us the game. I need to apologize to Willie [Crawford] right now. I took him out in a crucial situation, and he thinks I don't have confidence in him."

At that moment, as if on cue, Crawford walked into Lindsey's office.

"Willie, I want to apologize to you," Lindsey said. "I put this guy in, and he didn't take care of the job. I'm sorry. I made the wrong decision."

I slumped in my chair and kept my head down. I couldn't look at Crawford. He might have been USC's toughest defensive back. Each time the ball was snapped in practice, Crawford bolted off the line. Whenever we split up in teams for tackling drills, we carefully positioned ourselves so we wouldn't have to face him. Although I was bigger and stronger, Crawford always knocked the shit out of me.

"Willie," I would remind him after each breathtaking blow, "this is only practice."

That morning in Lindsey's office, I decided I had to push myself as hard as I possibly could to redeem myself and win the starting strong safety job from Crawford the following season. Every day during that summer before my sophomore year, I stood in front of an imaginary tight end on the practice field at Eisenhower High School. I made believe I was covering him in each of our defenses. It was just me against the invisible tight end on an empty football field. That's how embarrassed I felt by my UCLA blunder. I told myself I'd never make that mistake again.

THE COACH OF LIFE

Heritage Hall, home of the USC Athletic Department, is a shrine to the school's sports supremacy. Staring me in the face each time I walked in the front door were the Heisman Trophies won by tailbacks Mike Garrett (1965) and O. J. Simpson (1968). I couldn't miss the national championship trophies. Commemorative medallions honoring the most outstanding athletes in USC history spread like ivy across the handrails on the second floor.

On Thursdays at Heritage Hall, coach John Robinson gave his big pep talk of the week. He would build his words to an emotional crescendo then pretend to stutter. Pausing, he'd laugh and ask, "Did I just say that twice?" We always busted up, and then he'd jump back in where he left off, stopping again for strategically placed wisecracks.

"You know [UCLA coach] Terry Donahue is over there telling his guys they can win this one," Robinson liked to say before our showdowns with UCLA. "The guys at UCLA walk around with mean faces, and you guys are over here laughing. You know why? Because you're going to win it. Their buttholes are too tight."

If Robinson ever felt any pressure, he never let us know it. During my four years at USC, he certainly had the weight of the world on his shoulders. First of all, he was following in the footsteps of John McKay, who had won four national championships. Secondly, from 1978 to 1980—the sixth week of my sophomore year until late in my senior season—we had the nation's longest unbeaten streak. It was stopped by Washington at twenty-eight games (twenty-six wins and two ties). And, finally, because we had one of the largest pools of talent in college football, the USC alumni expected nothing less than a victory in the Rose Bowl.

In my sophomore year in 1978, we finished with a 12–1 record, beat Michigan in the Rose Bowl, and shared the national championship with Alabama, which created a lot of controversy. USC was voted No. 1 in the United Press International poll of coaches, edging out the Crimson Tide by five points, UPI's closest race for the title in twelve years. Alabama finished first in the Associated Press poll of the sportswriters and broadcasters. It was frustrating to share No. 1, knowing that we had beaten Alabama 24–14 in the third game of the season and played our asses off the rest of the way. Robinson didn't say too much about it as I recall, but I thought at the time, the hell with the polls. Let's get together with Alabama in a playoff game to determine the national championship.

Robinson's biggest accomplishment as a coach was his masterful job of putting together all of the extraordinary pieces of the giant jigsaw puzzle that was our 1979 team. We were everybody's preseason pick for No. 1. A few sportswriters called us "the team of the century" and "the third best team in the country behind the Dallas Cowboys and the Pittsburgh Steelers." What talent we had! It was a team for the ages. A total of forty players from this team were selected in either the NFL or United States Football League draft. Twelve would become first-round draft picks in the NFL: Anthony Munoz, Brad Budde, and Charles White in 1980; Keith Van Horne, Dennis Smith, and myself in 1981; Chip Banks, Marcus Allen, and Roy Foster in 1982, and Bruce Matthews, Joey Browner, and Don Mosebar in 1983. Our offense may have been one of the most prolific in the history of college football. We scored 389 points and generated a school record 5,655 yards in total offense. We defeated Ohio State in the Rose Bowl to finish 11–0–1. A 21–21 tie to unranked Stanford—although we were beating them 21–0 at halftime—cost us the national championship.

Robinson never cracked under the daily rigors of USC football. He thrived on challenges. He insisted we play hard, but he wanted us to have fun. And he had a sense of humor. He got such a chuckle out of me when I joined the Trojan basketball team after the football season my junior year. And why not? "Ronnie Lott is the reason the NCAA made the glass backboards thicker," said Stan Morrison, the Trojan basketball coach. "What a touch! When he went to the free-throw line, it was kind of guess-and-be-golly." In my debut against Oregon State, I shot an airball on my first free throw and almost broke the backboard on the second. I fouled out in nine minutes against UCLA at Pauley Pavilion and didn't dare ask Robinson for his reaction to that performance.

I've never had a coach as easygoing as Robinson. The bigger the football game, the more stakes that were on the line, the looser he appeared. "If I have a tight butt hole," he liked to say, "then everyone else will have a tight butt hole."

In the locker room before kickoff, Robinson never wore a

game face. If we dared wear one, he pounced on us like a cat on a canary. "What's your problem, son?" Robinson would ask, then quickly slip in a joke to break the tension. On the sideline, even if all hell was breaking loose the calm expression on his face rarely changed. He seldom cursed or whined at the officials, choosing to deal with them in his own way. "No, that's not the call!" he'd shout. "That's not the call! Oh, all right. But come back and give me a better one next time."

Robinson was always optimistic. My junior year, the day before we were to play LSU in Baton Rouge, we arrived at Tiger Stadium for practice and were greeted by, without exaggeration, what must have easily been 5,000 crazy fans. They chanted, "Tiger meat . . . Tiger meat . . . Tiger meat . . ." That wasn't nearly as intimidating as the screaming 78,322 nut cases who packed the stadium on game day. Early in the fourth quarter, with the Tigers leading 12–3, Robinson caught me moping on the sideline. I was depressed. Hanging my head. Our hopes for a national championship down the drain.

"Hey, Ronnie, we're going to win this game," Robinson said. "We're going to win. Trust me."

"Sure, Coach," I replied, unconvinced. "Whatever you say."

We went on to score two touchdowns, the game winner with 32 seconds remaining, to go home with a 17–12 victory. In the locker room, Robinson's face glowed with contentment, not relief. I wondered if I ought to bow to him. Was this guy the Messiah? From that point on, whenever we took the field, we were already up seven points as far as I was concerned.

Positive energy flowed through Robinson's veins. Writers continually asked him how the Trojan tailbacks could keep running 28 Pitch, better known as Student Body Right, the power-I version of the old single-wing power sweep. Wasn't USC's offense too obvious to opponents? Robinson laughed in their faces and kept telling us that with the proper execution and—more important—the undying desire to do it better than anyone else time and time again, we could run 28 Pitch all day and never be stopped.

"In the fourth quarter, we're going to get even better," Robinson promised us. "We'll run it, and we'll wear them down. We'll win this sucker."

Sometimes coaches panic and take out the frustrations of losing on their assistants, but Robinson was protective of his staff and almost never ripped into them. Lindsey told me a story about Robinson's first game at USC in 1976, a disastrous 46–25 loss to Missouri in the Coliseum. Not only was the USC defense unable to stop the Tigers, but it couldn't even slow them down. Late in the afternoon, Robinson strolled over to a depressed Lindsey, put his arm around him, and slowly grinned. "Have you got anything that can stop them?" Robinson asked.

It was one of the few times Lindsey, Mr. Intensity himself, actually chuckled during a game, and he told me it helped him keep football in perspective.

After the defeat, Robinson called all of USC's assistants into his office. "It was a tough day, and I'm sure the papers are going to eat us alive tomorrow," he told the coaching staff. "Don't you worry about that. I'll handle it. You're my staff. I don't think any less of you today than when I hired you." Lindsey never forgot that, and he admired Robinson for not turning practices the following week into blood baths.

During my four years at USC, Robinson was obsessed with how we *played*, not whether we won or lost. It was more important that we give an honest effort than go through the motions and run off the field celebrating victory. In turn, he was straightforward with us, the most sincere man I've played for and one of the most honest I've ever known. He stressed education, claiming that athletes ought to get better grades than ordinary students because they had been programmed to compete. As a freshman, I made a pact with myself to graduate in four years, and though I had to go to summer school to achieve that, I got my degree in Public Administration in 1981, just as I had planned.

Robinson was approachable, a real down-to-earth guy, much like his childhood friend John Madden, the former coach of the Oakland Raiders. They had known each other since the fifth grade at Our Lady of Perpetual Help in Daly City, a suburb of San Francisco, and Robinson was best man at Madden's wedding. Robinson's office door was always open, and I knew that I could call him at home if I needed to. Today Robinson is coach of the Los Angeles Rams and when we speak on the field before games, he'll always say, "If you ever get some free time, give me a call. We'll have a beer." I was honored that Robinson came to my wedding on March 2, 1991, in San Jose.

Robinson never treated us like kids. He had two sacred rules: Do not embarrass the university, this football program, or your teammates, and do not steal from your teammates. The third-team scout players were treated the same way as the superstars. He wasn't about to kiss anybody's butt, put up with arrogant attitudes, or allow guys to break the rules. And he wouldn't allow his assistants to be patronized either. The year before Charles White won the Heisman Trophy, he and two of his San Fernando buddies, all wearing shades, sauntered into the office of running back coach John Jackson.

"All right," said Jackson, an ex-Marine, "just turn around and walk out that door and don't come back until you can act like real people."

I also remember the time that White rubbed defensive line coach Marv Goux the wrong way.

"Charlie, I need to talk to you," Goux said, a few weeks after White won the Heisman Trophy in 1979.

"I'll be over there in a minute," White replied and kept right on talking to some of the other players.

"No, Charlie," Goux said. "I need to talk to you now."

A little while later, White finished his conversation and leisurely walked over to Goux.

"Just because you won the Heisman doesn't mean you're better than me," Goux said. "I don't think you're any more special a person because you've got this fucking trophy. I've seen a lot of great players, and I respected them because they respected me."

Respect was an important word at USC. Robinson explained that we didn't necessarily have to like each other. That was downright impossible for ninety-some guys. But on the field and in games, he said, we had to respect one another. "You've all got to think about one thing, winning," he explained. "You should be so focused, so single-minded about your goal, that you could play anywhere against anybody at any time."

Players weren't allowed to display inflated egos. Robinson kept me humble through a summer job at a steel mill in central Los Angeles prior to my junior and senior seasons. In a steamy warehouse the size of an airplane hangar, I placed sheets of steel into a big machine that rolled them into coils and cut them. I'll never forget the sounds. *Eroooo ppshunk. Eroooo ppshunk.* Dressed in steel-toe boots, a hard hat, and blue jeans, which quickly turned black from all the grease, I banded steel from 7 A.M. to 3 P.M. Then I returned to campus to lift weights and run until 5:30, grabbed a quick bite, and attended summer school classes that evening.

One day, while banding steel with Oscar, a slightly built Hispanic fellow, I learned to treasure my USC football experience even more.

"You know, I'm a hell of a pool player," Oscar said. "But I'll never know how good I can truly be because I can't quit my job and play pool. I have to support my family. If I could make the money you're going to make in pro football, I swear I'd be the best pool player on earth because I'd work hard at it every day. You're real lucky. You've got a chance to be the best at what you're doing. Don't give up this opportunity for anything. Make the most of it."

Robinson never became self-absorbed either. He realized he was only as good as the players around him, and the only way to make them good players was to motivate them. In practice, he was a hands-on, enthusiastic instructor with an enormous amount of patience.

"Son, that's how you did it at your high school," he'd say, putting his arm around a freshman, "but if you want to get it done here, you're going to have to compete harder."

Instead of barking orders from a tower like other college football coaches, Robinson instructed on the practice field, working at eye and gut level. He ran from drill to drill, chatting with everybody. "By God," he'd holler, "that's the way you play USC football!" His assistants would laugh when they saw him coming, and oftentimes they positioned their bodies between Robinson and their players so he wouldn't take over the drill.

"Get up that field, Charlie [White]," he'd coax. "Come on! Come on! Get up that field."

"That was great, Ronnie!" he'd shout. "But I know you can give me a little bit more."

I felt Robinson wanted me to be a leader in practice, and sometimes I think he even motivated the team through the Three Blind Mice. My sophomore year, the Monday before the season opener against Texas Tech, he announced that I had beaten out Willie Crawford for the starting strong safety job. Smith got the start at free safety, and Scoggins was set to start at his new position, outside linebacker. From then on, Robinson pushed us to turn it up a notch, in practice and in games. Smith was reckless. He threw his body into piles. I put a beam on guys and ran right through them. Lindsey, afraid that we'd hurt the receivers on the practice field, regularly told us to back off.

The Three Blind Mice put out contracts on Trojan offensive players who thought they were cool or tough. We warned the players at the beginning of practice, and when it came our turn to face them in pass coverage, we started talking trash. Once they were distracted, we knocked their heads off. Marvin Williams, for example, came out of high school believing he was the tailback of all time. We put so many contracts out on him, he switched to defensive back. Every week, we targeted wide receiver Kevin (Bug) Williams. Williams, an itty-bitty 5 feet 8, 155 pounds, had a mouth that moved as fast as his feet. He was the lead-off runner on USC's national championship 400-meter relay teams in 1978 and 1979. Tailback Marcus Allen couldn't escape the wrath of the Three Blind Mice, either. When Allen arrived at USC in 1978, he played defensive back. Robinson made Toledo choose between Allen and me as to which one of us would move to tailback. Allen never lost his defensive player's heart. He'd fight if he had to. We loved to light him up because we knew he could handle the punishment.

I'll always remember December 6, 1980, the last afternoon I spent in the Coliseum with Robinson. It was the final game of my USC career. We beat No. 2-ranked Notre Dame, 20–3, in front of 82,663 fans, handing the Irish their first loss of the season and ruining their hopes of a national championship. Robinson called it "the greatest defensive effort I've ever seen" as we limited Notre Dame to 120 yards in total offense, one first down in the first half, and stopped them on two goal-line stands.

Afterward, Robinson introduced the outgoing seniors to the Coliseum crowd and cited each of the players' contributions to Trojan football. It was his way of sending us off. When it came time to talk about me, he told the USC fans how much he was going to miss me, and I remember telling him later that evening that I was going to miss him, too. His passion for football. His deep feelings for his players. All the fun we had together.

Because Robinson believed in me as a person, I was inspired to be more of a man.

I loved him.

MY ROOKIE YEAR In July of 1981, after days and days of intense negotiations for my first NFL contract, I received a surprise telephone call from 49er owner Eddie DeBartolo, Jr. Training camp was only a few days away.

"What's the problem?" DeBartolo asked. "Why aren't you signed?"

"I just want my fair market value," I countered.

"Well, we don't need you!" DeBartolo screamed. "The 49ers will get along fine without you."

I was devastated. My brain felt like scrambled eggs from the emotional and seemingly endless contract negotiations, and now my stomach was churning. I wondered what I had done to deserve that attack from DeBartolo. I had never spoken to him in my life. Why, I hadn't even known who he was when he first called. When I hung up the phone, I sat on the floor in my empty Los Angeles apartment and cried.

Just three months earlier life was wonderful. On April 28, 1981, the 49ers had made me their No. 1 pick. I was the eighth player chosen overall and the second defensive back behind Kenny Easley, an All-America safety from UCLA, who had been taken by the Seattle Seahawks with the No. 4 pick.

When 49er public relations assistant Delia Newland called me on draft day at 7:50 A.M. to officially inform me I had been selected by the 49ers, I was like a kid on Christmas Eve, bursting with joy and anticipation. Growing up, I'd never had a goal of becoming a professional football player, yet I had traveled a magical yellow brick road throughout my athletic life, culminating with being named a consensus All-America as a senior at USC and being honored as the Trojans' Most Valuable Player and Most Inspirational Player. And now I had become only the third defensive back in 49er history to be selected in the first round. Since San Francisco wasn't exactly the NFL's promised land, coach Bill Walsh took an apologetic approach in our initial conversation.

"We've got a young team," he told me on draft day. "We are going to build and get better and better. Our time will come."

The 49ers were a pathetic franchise, having gone more years without winning a championship than any other team in pro football. San Francisco's record from 1978 to '80, was atrocious: 2–14, 2–14, and 6–10, respectively. In 1980, the 49er defense allowed 29 touchdown passes. They used 32 defensive backs from the May minicamp through the end of the season. Walsh joked that the only way he knew who the guys were was by reading the name on the back of their jerseys.

DeBartolo had bought the 49ers in 1977 for about $17 million, when he was only thirty, and he selected Joe Thomas as his general manager. After two dismal seasons, DeBartolo let Thomas go and hired Walsh, who had a 17–7 record in two seasons at Stanford, as his head coach and general manager, entrusting him with all player personnel decisions. As a long-time NFL assistant with Oakland, Cincinnati, and San Diego from 1966 to '76, Walsh had proved to be a master at working with quarterbacks. In his first two 49er seasons, Walsh put his time in with the offense. He drafted Notre Dame quarterback Joe Montana in the third round in 1979, in spite of scouting reports that claimed he was inconsistent and couldn't throw long. Then in the 1980 draft Walsh concentrated on defense, selecting end Jim Stuckey, linebackers Keena Turner, Bobby Leopold, and Craig Puki, and safety Ricky Churchman.

The 49ers desperately needed me in training camp in Rocklin, California, in a couple of days, but the front office was playing hardball. Management had criticized my agent, Leonard Armato, a young San Diego attorney who was representing his first athlete and negotiating his first NFL contract. The 49ers claimed Armato had no idea how financial packages were put together. The front office also tried to scare me by floating stories of a trade with the New England Patriots. The rumored deal involved myself and right tackle Keith Fahnhorst for Patriots tackle Brian Holloway, who had played for Walsh at Stanford, and a defensive back. And if all that wasn't enough to make me crack, the 49er management applied additional phone pressure.

"Eddie D just wanted me to give you a call and talk to you about things," said running back O. J. Simpson, who played with the 49ers in 1978–79. "I don't want to get in the middle of this. I'm not saying Eddie's right or wrong, or you're right or wrong but . . ."

"Juice," I interrupted. "I'm just trying to do what's right. I just want a contract in the neighborhood of Easley's." (Easley had signed a four-year contract valued at a reported $1 million.)

"Eddie's a good guy," Simpson said. "You've got to work on getting this done."

A few days after training camp started, I received a call from agent Mike Trope, who had negotiated the deal for my USC roommate Dennis Smith, the fifteenth pick in the draft. At one time I considered having Trope represent me, but had rejected him because I felt he had too many clients. Thanks to Trope, Smith had left for the Denver Broncos' training camp in a brand-new blue Mercedes, and now here I was moping around watching soap operas.

"I talked to the Niners, and I know the numbers you're asking for," Trope said. "I can get them for you. The salaries. The bonus. The whole deal."

"You can get me this contract?" I asked. "You're sure?"

"I know I can," Trope said. "I just got off the phone with the Niners."

By this time I was confused. And very pissed off. I was furious with the 49ers for letting me dangle so long. I was angry with Armato because he hadn't been able to hammer out a contract. Why couldn't he get it done? After an earful from Trope, I phoned Armato at his San Diego office, fully intending to fire him.

"Goddamm it, Leonard," I said. "Trope said he can get me the money. Why can't you get me the numbers?"

"Trust me," Armato said. "I can get it for you if you go the distance with me. Trust me."

Since I'd come this far with him, I decided to stick it out. On July 19, after missing five days of training camp, I finally signed four one-year contracts worth approximately $850,000. I had to take a little less money than Armato had planned on, but at least I would be a 49er. I immediately set out to prove that DeBartolo, Walsh, and the 49er front office made a mistake in putting me through an emotional contract hassle and, most important, for having rated Easley higher in their predraft reports.

The first day of practice after my holdout, I slammed a blocking sled during drills, prompting defensive backs coach George Seifert to rave to the press: "He picks it up off the ground. Nobody else does that." I batted down a pass from quarterback Steve DeBerg to running back James Owens. "A lot of guys get in position and figure they've done their job," Seifert told reporters. "That's when he accelerates—right at the critical moment."

Ray Rhodes, our assistant defensive backfield coach, who had been hired in mid-July after playing seven years in the NFL as a wide receiver and cornerback, pulled me aside. "I don't want you at the back of the line for any drills," Rhodes said. "I want you to stand up front. We're going to need you for leadership."

No way am I stepping in front of this line, I thought. I don't want to step on any toes.

"Please, Ronnie," Rhodes said. "Step in front."

Walsh and Seifert felt I was the most versatile athlete in the secondary, and they switched me from safety to left cornerback, the toughest position on defense because that's the side where the NFL's fastest receivers line up. I looked at the position change as a challenge, and psyched myself into believing I had an advantage over receivers because at 6 feet, 200 pounds I was bigger and more physical than most cornerbacks.

Eric Wright, a 6-foot-1, 180-pound safety from Missouri and a 49er second-round pick, would start at right cornerback. Carlton Williamson, a 6-foot, 204-pound third-round pick from Pittsburgh, would play strong safety, and Dwight Hicks, signed as a free agent in 1979, started at free safety. Hicks had been working in a Detroit health food store when the 49ers called to offer a tryout. Lynn Thomas, a 5-foot-11, 181-pound fifth-round pick from Pittsburgh, came in as the fifth defensive back on passing downs.

There was very little time for grooming, polishing, and perfecting our positions. Defensive coordinator Chuck Studley had just put in a new 3–4 defense used by the Philadelphia Eagles the preceding season, and nobody, including the coaches, had mastered it. Seifert just threw us right out onto the field. None of the other defensive backs had had the exposure to as many different defensive coverages that I had come in contact with at USC. Wright found the move from safety to cornerback particularly difficult because he had never played that position at Missouri.

In our preseason games, the rookie starters worried too much about making mistakes, and it showed. We repeatedly blew coverages and missed tackles. I found out about life in the NFL against the San Diego Chargers in our second exhibition game. The Chargers' quarterbacks—Ed Luther and Dan Fouts—completed 28 of 33 for 358 yards and two touchdowns, and I was burned by wide receiver Charlie Joiner. One time I grabbed Joiner's arm and pulled it down, but he simply reached out with the other arm and snared the football one-handed.

"I just covered the hell out of this guy, and he still caught the ball," I said. I don't feel so bad now, knowing that Joiner spent eighteen years in the NFL and finished as one of the top receivers in pro football history, but at the time I thought, This is going to be a long year. My God, is this how it's going to be the rest of my career?

Our third preseason performance, against the Seattle Seahawks, turned into a comedy of errors. On one unforgettable play, Seahawk backup quarterback Sam Adkins scrambled upfield, and as Williamson and I were closing in to make the tackle, he eluded us. We smashed into each other, and Adkins gained 44 yards in the process. Talk about an embarrassing moment. Another laugher came when a Seahawk running back easily broke through five tackles for a long gain.

At halftime Seifert pulled the rookie defensive backs aside in the locker room and attempted to calm us down. "Hey, would you please relax and have fun out there?" Seifert pleaded. "I don't care what you do. Don't think. Just have fun." We followed his instructions and in the second half we flew around the field, playing football the way we had in college. With 15 seconds left, Wright picked off Seahawk quarterback Jim Zorn and returned the interception 48 yards for the game-winning touchdown in a 24–17 victory. That gave us the confidence we needed, and it was the start of something big.

Seifert was the Taskmaster of defensive backs. He was the living, breathing Bull Meecham character, straight from the pages of Pat Conroy's book *The Great Santini.* Seifert was the spit and image of Meecham, the fighter-pilot father nicknamed The Great Santini, who ruled his family with an iron fist. Seifert treated the rookie defensive backs the same way The Great Santini treated his oldest son, Ben, a talented athlete whose best was never good enough for his old man. No matter how hard we tried, we could never satisfy Seifert. God, how we despised him. He constantly rode us. He demanded we watch game film during our lunch break. He forced us to stay on the field at least half an hour after practice for more drills, and then he ushered us into the meeting room for a few hours of extra film work. Many a night the janitorial crew would arrive before we would leave for dinner. Studley worried that we might not be able to absorb all of Seifert's information, but Walsh, a perfectionist, found the cram sessions rather amusing.

To us, Seifert was a straitlaced egghead whose previous head coaching experience had been at Westminster College in Salt

Lake City, Utah, and at Cornell University in 1975–76, where he was fired after posting a 3–15 record. His .167 winning percentage is still the lowest of any coach since the Big Red started playing football in 1894. Seifert joined the 49ers in 1980 after coaching the secondary at Stanford for Walsh. A man of few words, Seifert worked in his cubbyhole office all day, drawing up elaborate defensive coverages. The defensive backs figured that he hadn't had the physical ability to make it as a player so he chose to take out his frustrations on us.

Seifert quizzed us endlessly about our responsibilities on defense, and whenever he drew a play on the blackboard, he repeated himself like a tedious college professor. If one of us didn't use the proper terminology, he drilled that person until he got it right. Seifert used to pick on Wright, who wound up getting so flustered when called on that he would change his correct answers to the wrong ones.

"Darn it, Eric," Seifert would say in disgust. "What technique do you have on this coverage?"

"That's my man," Wright would say.

"No, Eric, it's *read* technique. You *read* the quarterback and then go to your man," Seifert would reply.

Then in answer to the next question Wright would say, "I've got the third."

"No! Eric, the *deep* third of the field," Seifert would yell.

Wright knew what to do, and we all realized that. We would whisper under our breaths, "Give him a break, George." I contemplated jumping Seifert and tying him up. Hicks advised him to coach in a more positive manner. Finally one day Williamson couldn't take it anymore. "Hey, stop picking on Eric!" he screamed.

On the practice field Wright nearly came to blows with Seifert. While practicing our goal-line defense one afternoon, the tight end kept beating Wright. Seifert harped on him until he became so confused he couldn't concentrate. We had to restrain Wright from punching out Seifert's lights.

By my estimation, the Taskmaster has worn out a dozen film projectors since he has been with the 49ers, and Lord only knows how many VCRs he has destroyed. Seifert was notorious for running a play over and over—eight, nine, and ten times.

"See that? . . . See that? . . . See that?"

Okay, we see that.

"No, no, no!" Seifert would continue. "Look! See this right

here. Check out your backpedal. Analyze your roll. Notice where your hands are."

We would study a quarterback's handoff for ten minutes before we even got to see what happened in the secondary. From time to time we would fall asleep, and he would catch us. But that's as far as we dared to test his patience. Seifert was the Gestapo. He was so strict that he wouldn't let us bring food into the meeting rooms, and on Mondays when the rest of the team had beer and soda after practice, we weren't allowed to join in the fun.

The Saturday morning prior to a game, Seifert gave us three-page tests on personnel and formations. We had to know opponents' numbers, defensive calls, and audibles that were predicated by formations. He stood over us as we took the tests, then he would correct them and run through the answers on the blackboard. On game day, he hit us with umpteen questions in the locker room. There were so many times we wished we could have told him to get out of our faces.

On Monday afternoons, while the rest of the 49ers underwent a light workout, the Taskmaster, who ran several miles a day, subjected us to his training runs. We whipped through the neighborhoods of Redwood City resembling children tagging along with the Pied Piper. We kept thinking, "He's got to turn back soon," but then he would turn up another residential street and climb farther into the hills. Williamson and I always matched him stride for stride down the back stretch, but we never beat him.

When Seifert wasn't pushing us, we were torturing ourselves. We were gluttons for punishment. Often we ate dinner with each other to discuss opponents or to review practice. Each week I would speak with my former USC mentor, defensive back Dennis Thurman, who was in his fourth season with the Dallas Cowboys. Thurman gave me tips on receivers and opposing offensive systems. Then I would share this information with the guys. Anything that would help.

On the practice field, the rookie defensive backs portrayed invincibility. We refused to let anybody catch a pass on us. We forced our best receivers, Dwight Clark and Freddie Solomon, to fight for the ball.

"Pull out the blanket," Thomas would spit out in his stutter.

"The bank is closed," added rookie defensive back Saladin Martin. "You ain't making any deposits today."

Solomon always wanted me to cover him, even if it wasn't my turn. "I want the best," Solomon joked. "Send him out."

In my mind, practices were played under game conditions, although we had to abide by one Walsh rule that defensive backs couldn't hit the receivers. There were so many times I stretched the Walsh rule. I pushed and shoved Solomon up and down the field, knocked down passes, intercepted balls, grabbed his jersey.

In our more civilized moments after practice, Solomon showed me the many ways receivers might set me up. Together we worked on techniques I could use to counteract them. I learned to recognize routes within the first five yards a receiver came off the ball. Solomon taught me how to focus on my man and pointed out tendencies I had that could tip off receivers to zone or man coverage.

"Freddie, tell me more," I begged.

"Champ, I can't," he said.

"Why can't you tell me, Freddie?" I pleaded.

"Champ, then when you have to cover me, I won't be able to beat you," he said, laughing. "And I'll be out of a job. Can't give up all my secrets."

I was thankful that linebacker Jack (Hacksaw) Reynolds was willing to give up some secrets. Reynolds was signed as a free agent by the 49ers in June after failing to reach agreement on a contract with the Los Angeles Rams. He knew everything about defense and had an uncanny knack for being able to call out plays before they happened. A master of detail, Reynolds spent hours watching film, then shared his intricate findings with the whole defense so we'd all be on the same page. Reynolds kept copious notes, toting them around in a bulging, battered briefcase. If a coach contradicted himself in meetings, he'd point it out from the scribbles on his notepads.

To get inside the coaches' minds, Reynolds lived at the 49er offices, piling his locker full of essentials like pencils, pencil sharpener, pads of paper, film projector, and shoes. He borrowed clothes from anybody he could, scarfed down the coaches' catered dinners while hanging around late to watch films, and then caught a few hours of sleep in his small apartment nearby.

Reynolds, a twelve-year veteran and the oldest player on the team at thirty-four, was a lovable eccentric. He earned his nickname, Hacksaw, during his senior year at the University of Tennessee in 1969. After the Volunteers lost to Mississippi, 38–0, knocking themselves out of a berth in the Sugar Bowl,

Reynolds took out his frustrations on a 1953 Chevrolet. He sawed it in half using a cheap hacksaw he had bought at K Mart. It took him eight hours and thirteen blades.

At pregame breakfasts. I would find Reynolds drinking pots of coffee while poring over our game plan. Amazingly, he would be dressed in his complete uniform, from eye black to cleats. Even his ankles and shoes were taped. He could have tackled one of the busboys. I always said to myself, "This guy means business." After breakfast, Hacksaw would put on his 49er helmet and drive to Candlestick Park in his gold 1970 Lincoln Continental with its rattling engine and smoke coming out the tailpipe. What a crazy old turkey he was.

By game time, Reynolds' own motor was so revved up that he would jump all over teammates for making mistakes. He disagreed with assistant coaches on the sideline, often smashing his portable chalkboards in his rage. Inspired by Reynolds' fire, I mimicked him, yelling and screaming on the field and body-slamming opponents.

"Ronnie, Ronnie, you're a wildman," Reynolds would say. "Cool it. You're a rocket, a human projectile. When the guy breaks the line of scrimmage, just tackle him around the legs. You're inflicting pain, but you're hurting yourself more."

Walsh communicated with Reynolds more than any other player except tight end Charle Young, who was traded from the Rams to the 49ers in 1980. Reynolds and Young were the only 49ers who had Super Bowl experience. Walsh used to call Reynolds up to his office and pick his brains about the offensive game plan.

"Do you think this will bother them?" Walsh wanted to know.

"Three receivers in the backfield? Of course, Bill," Reynolds replied sarcastically.

Reynolds' passion for football played a major role in driving the 49er defense in 1981. After losing our opener to Detroit, we came back the following week and defeated the Chicago Bears, 28–17. Our defense forced running back Walter Payton to lose two fumbles, which matched his total for all of 1980. One time Reynolds put a vicious hit on Payton, just leveling him, and I dived into the pile after them. There on the ground, much to my surprise, I found Reynolds and Payton laughing at each other. This is what pro football's all about?

Two weeks later I made my first interception, returning an Archie Manning pass 26 yards for what proved to be the game-winning touchdown. We beat the New Orleans Saints, 21–14. It was the first time since October 1, 1978 that the 49er defense had scored a touchdown, and it was a taste of things to come. We won the next three games over Washington, Dallas, and Green Bay, with the defense making seven interceptions and allowing only one touchdown pass.

It was against Washington that the secondary came to be known as Dwight Hicks and His Hot Licks. Zeroing in on Redskin running back Terry Metcalf, who was running a sweep, my helmet cracked against the football as he came around the corner. The ball popped straight up, and Hicks lunged forward to grab the loose ball, which he took 80 yards down the sideline for a touchdown. Hicks also had a 32-yard interception return for a touchdown in the game. When we arrived home, a sportscaster asked if our secondary had a nickname. That hadn't even occurred to us. He suggested Hicks and His Hot Licks. We loved it.

About a week before our sixth game, we acquired defensive end Fred Dean from the San Diego Chargers. We gave the Chargers our No. 2 draft pick in 1983 and also agreed to exchange No. 1 picks that same year. Dean was the final piece to the puzzle that would eventually propel us to the Super Bowl. He solidified our defense. We didn't have a superstar until we got him. Now we finally had the biggest guy coming off the bus. Dean was the sergeant at arms, the commissioner, the hammer.

At 6 feet 2, 227 pounds, his trademark was brute force. Raw energy. Solid as an oak. He called it "farm-boy strength," developed by baling hay and hauling logs as a kid growing up in Ruston, Louisiana. He'd never lifted weights. Dean feasted on quarterbacks, the kind of pressure the 49ers had lacked since 1976 when they featured defensive ends Tommy Hart and Cedrick Hardman. Offensive linemen would stare over to our bench to see if he was coming into the game, and when he stepped onto the field, you could actually see their bodies sink in dismay. In the huddle, I couldn't take my eyes off him. He was calm. As cold as ice. He never tired.

Dean loosened up the locker room. He brought the offense and defense together by buying Kentucky Fried Chicken for lunch. Every day.

"Deano, are you going to get chicken?" I would ask.

"Yeah, man, I've got to have some of those pimp yard dogs," Deano would respond.

I questioned him constantly about everything from paying fines to what it took to be an All-Pro. It meant so much when he told me he admired the way I hit, and I liked making him laugh at the end of each week. After the game plan had been laid out, I'd yell, "And we're going to kick ass." I stood next to him during the national anthem, hoping some of his All-Pro strength and wisdom would rub off on me.

On October 11, Dean had an awesome debut against the Dallas Cowboys. He blew past a 250-pound tackle named Pat Donovan, sacking quarterback Danny White twice and forcing a third. We crushed the Cowboys, 45–14, handing them their worst loss since 1970. I intercepted White twice, returning one 41 yards for a touchdown, and the other 32 yards to set up a field goal. I also recovered a fumble on the Dallas 6-yard line. Both Dean and I received our first 49er game balls.

Two weeks later, against the Los Angeles Rams, who had beaten us ten times straight at Candlestick Park, Dean continued his rampage. Ram quarterback Pat Haden was sacked six times, and Dean was responsible for four and a half of them in a 20–17 49er victory. I had never seen a pass rusher like that in my life. So quick when the ball was snapped. So fast.

No game was more important to the 49ers in 1981 than our meeting with the Pittsburgh Steelers at Three Rivers Stadium on November 1. We had a 6–2 record, with a two-game lead in the NFC West Division, but we were still such a naïve group. The Steelers were four-time Super Bowl champions who hadn't lost at home to an NFC team in ten years. They had tough men on defense like Mean Joe Greene, L. C. Greenwood, Jack Ham, Mel Blount, and Jack Lambert. I remember my reaction after seeing Lambert in warm-ups. He looked so formidable dressed in black that I thought he was Darth Vader, that he could reach into my chest and rip out my heart. While loosening up, Steeler wide receiver Lynn Swann, who wouldn't be playing that day because of an injury, sauntered over to me.

"I'm sure sorry I'm not playing you guys today," Swann said. "I probably would have had a great day." I thought of Swann's arrogant remark later, after Carlton Williamson destroyed Pittsburgh receivers Calvin Sweeney and John Stallworth with ravaging blows. Both were knocked out and unable to return to the game. I looked over to the Steeler bench and wondered if Swann still wished he had been well enough to play. Williamson also recovered a fumble to set up a field goal, and his 28-yard interception off quarterback Terry Bradshaw in the fourth quarter led to the game-winning touchdown in a 17–14 victory. We had snapped the Steelers' Three Rivers Stadium winning streak at fourteen games.

I didn't do much celebrating afterward because I had given up my first touchdown pass of the season on a 22-yard toss to Jim Smith. Instead of covering Smith, I had kept my eyes on Bradshaw in the backfield. Bradshaw noticed me peeking and hit Smith for the score. That was the last time I peeked that season.

I made very few mistakes in 1981. Keena Turner still says that he has never seen a rookie defensive back have such an incredible season, and Eric Wright refers to it as "a blessing from the sky." In all, I had 89 tackles and 7 interceptions. Three of them were returned for touchdowns, matching the rookie record set in 1967 by Lem Barney of the Detroit Lions. No one has broken our record. I finished second in voting for NFL Rookie–of–the–Year behind linebacker Lawrence Taylor of the New York Giants, and I finished third in voting for the NFL's Most Valuable Player. Montana won that award, and Taylor was the runner-up.

My only other glaring mistake happened in the NFC Championship Game on January 10 against the Dallas Cowboys. You might remember that game because of the play they call The Catch. But I remember that game because of two pass interference calls against me that led to 10 Dallas points. The first penalty came after I knocked down a pass intended for wide receiver Drew Pearson. The referee said I was bumping Pearson, but to this day I believe he was bumping and pushing me. The Cowboys were "America's Team," so they got the calls. We got no respect. In newspaper stories the week of the game, Ed (Too Tall) Jones, the Cowboys' 6-foot-9, 275-pound defensive end, had said that he didn't even know most of our names and probably wasn't going to bother to learn them. That became a burr in our saddle. I'll never forget Montana on a naked bootleg to his left, faking out Too Tall. He shouted to Jones, "Respect *that*, mother-fucker!"

To be perfectly honest, I don't think The Catch was the most important play in 49er history. The entire series of plays leading to The Catch was important. If you ask Montana and Dwight Clark, they'd say the same thing. The most important player on the field during that drive was a little-known halfback named Lenvil Elliott. We called him Rat Daddy. A tenth-round pick out of Northeast Missouri State, Elliott had played six years with the Cincinnati Bengals before being released in 1979. He played for the 49ers in 1980 and underwent knee surgery after the season. Walsh promised Elliott, then thirty, another chance if he could get his legs in shape. He liked Elliott's dependability and the way he followed his blockers. When running back Paul Hofer went down with a knee injury in the fifteenth game of the year, Walsh activated Elliott instead of defensive tackle Pete Kugler or special teamer Ricky Churchman.

With 4:54 left to play, Dallas led 27–21. The 13-play drive began at our 11-yard line. Elliott got us rolling on three of the first five plays, charging up the middle for six, sweeping right for eleven and running left for seven more. Seven plays later, Elliott's 7-yard sweep took us to the Dallas 6, and Walsh called a timeout. We were facing a third down from the 3-yard line with 58 seconds left. After huddling with Bobb McKittrick, the offensive line coach, Walsh opted to go with the "sprint right option," the same play we had used to score our first touchdown. Under a heavy rush from Jones and Larry Bethea, Montana rolled right, looking for Freddie Solomon, his primary receiver, who was covered. Clark, meanwhile, sprinted along the back of the end zone, toward Montana's roll. Montana pumped once, then threw the ball off the wrong foot. It sailed high over Clark's head, but he leaped to make a miraculous catch. Touchdown. Ray Wersching kicked the extra point, putting us ahead 28–27.

"You've just beaten America's Team," Jones said to Montana as they lay on the turf.

"Well, you can just sit home with the rest of America and watch the Super Bowl," Montana snorted.

There was pandemonium on the sideline. Studley motioned for the defense to cease celebrating and gather around him in front of the bench.

"Let's play sound football," Studley said. "Don't miss any tackles. Don't give up any big plays."

With 38 seconds left, White connected on a post pattern to Drew Pearson for 31 yards. I charged Pearson, but took the wrong angle and ended up bumping into Hicks. I tumbled to the turf, and my heart fell with me. Pearson's so good at shaking tackles I thought as I pounded the ground, but I don't think there's any way he can outrun Eric Wright.

Sure enough, Wright caught up to Pearson, and with one hand grabbed him by the jersey, snagging him down at the San Francisco 44. I call that play The Stop. In my mind, that's the most important play in 49er history. If Wright hadn't made that play, the Cowboys would have been in a position to score. And we might have stayed home for the Super Bowl.

OUR FIRST
SUPER BOWL

United Airlines Flight 5073, the charter that would transport the 49ers to Detroit for Super Bowl XVI, boarded from an inconspicuous cargo hangar at the San Francisco International Airport on Sunday January 17, 1982. Painted on the fuselage in red and gold were the words "49er Liner." About a hundred of our faithful fans who managed to locate this secluded area were kept under control by cops dressed in helmets and riot gear. "Dee-fense!" they shouted, while waving their sponge rubber 49ers No. 1 fingers. "Dee-fense!"

Coach Bill Walsh had an informal dress code for road trips, and it was interesting to observe how many of the getups reflected the relaxed mood of the team. Linebacker Jack (Hacksaw) Reynolds looked comfortable in his nylon jogging suit. Tight end Charle Young exuded confidence in his brown derby hat and matching three-piece suit. Wide receiver Dwight Clark acted like a kid in his ten-gallon cowboy hat. I was ready for the Winter Olympics with my ski jacket, cowboy hat and leather gloves. I had fur-lined snowboots and wool sweaters packed in my suitcase.

As usual, I was the last 49er player to board the plane. "I'm late! I'm late!" I announced, waltzing to my seat ten minutes before our scheduled 2:25 P.M. departure. "But I'm ready to play right now!" Everybody was on board except Walsh, who was in Washington, D.C. being honored as Coach of the Year by the Washington Touchdown Club. Taxiing to the runway, it was fun to listen on our headsets to the dialogue between the control tower and the other planes: "This is Eastern . . . We yield to the 49er Liner . . . This is Delta . . . We yield to the 49er Liner . . . This is American . . . We yield to the 49er Liner . . ." Until we were No. 1 for takeoff.

From time to time during the four-hour flight, the pilot interrupted to relay good luck and best wishes from the control towers in several cities we flew over. We dined on slabs of roast beef, and for dessert we were served cake with "49ers—Super Bowl XVI" inscribed on a chocolate wafer on top of each piece. Instead of a movie, we watched the videotape replay of our NFC Championship Game victory over the Dallas Cowboys. There was a feeling of excitement that afternoon. I had read about the hype of Super Bowls and had some knowledge secondhand from Dennis Thurman, who was a rookie on the Dallas Cowboys team that lost to the Pittsburgh Steelers, 35–31, in Super Bowl XIII in Miami. But that still wasn't enough to prepare me.

When the 49er Liner landed at Detroit's Metropolitan Airport, the pilot announced that the temperature was minus 7 degrees. Out the window, the landscape was a sea of white covered with what seemed to be a foot of snow. This weather was better suited for our opponents, the Cincinnati Bengals. They had beaten the San Diego Chargers, 27–7, in the AFC Championship Game the preceding weekend, with a wind-chill factor of minus 59 at Riverfront Stadium. Their head coach, Forrest Gregg, a former All-Pro tackle with the Green Bay Packers, had played in the Packers' 1967 NFC Championship Game victory over the Dallas Cowboys in 16-below zero temperatures at Lambeau Field. As our bus crawled the 20 miles of treacherous roads to our hotel in Southfield, Michigan, I could console myself knowing Super Bowl XVI would be played indoors at the Pontiac Silverdome, where the thermostat was set to 72 degrees.

Getting off the bus at the hotel, I trudged toward the lobby with my head down to shield my face from the bitter cold.

"Can I carry your bag sir? Can I help you?" asked a bellhop, reaching for my bag.

"No thanks," I said, yanking my luggage tightly to my side.

I later learned that the bellhop was actually Walsh in disguise. He had flown in earlier that afternoon from Washington, D.C. and had given the real bellhop twenty dollars to borrow his uniform. Only a few of the players recognized Walsh—it was so damn cold, no one bothered to stop and look at the bellhop's face—and for sure, nobody tipped him.

That Walsh would pull such a prank didn't catch me by surprise. He relied on his sense of humor and a touch of sarcasm to keep the team loose in 1981. And it worked. When we first started winning, he used to tease us. "I can't believe this," he would say in team meetings. "The media keep saying, '. . . when the 49ers lose that will be devastating . . .' The oddsmakers in Las Vegas keep predicting, 'This will be the week the poor 49ers lose. Bet against them.' Men, don't you feel sorry for those poor 49ers?" Walsh's nonchalant approach was perfect. Hidden underneath our youthful enthusiasm was a layer of insecurity. Like the oddsmakers, we had all wondered how long our luck would last. By making fun of the pressure, Walsh made the players feel as though we could just enjoy winning and ride the wave of the fantasy.

The week of Super Bowl XVI, Walsh used every opportunity to turn problems and distractions into jokes and jabs to keep us from worrying too much about the game. When the 49ers were assigned the morning practice session at the Silverdome, which translated into dreadful 6 A.M. wakeup calls—3 A.M. San Francisco time—Walsh laughed at the absurdity of the situation. Why were the Bengals, who lived in the Eastern time zone, allowed to get a few more hours' sleep and practice later in the morning? On the first day, naturally several of our players and coaches overslept. And then the bus driver couldn't find his way from the hotel to the Silverdome so practice had to be delayed. Crises? Not really. Walsh didn't act concerned. Instead, he told us that the NFL was against the 49ers, that Commissioner Pete Rozelle wanted the Bengals' seventy-three year-old owner Paul Brown, one of the pioneers of the league, to win his first Super Bowl. All week I kept telling myself, the NFL is screwing us. The league wants to make it difficult for the 49ers to win.

Walsh used the same premise to prevent us from focusing on how miserable and isolated we felt in our hotel. The frigid weather made us reluctant to go out, although one night some players braved the elements to attend a Diana Ross concert. Most of the time we just left our doors unlocked, walked from room to room, and wound up playing cards and watching TV together. The Thrill-of-the-Week Award went to Clark and quarterback Joe Montana who performed "donuts" in a rental car, when they spun circles in an icy shopping center parking lot. The air in our hotel rooms was so dry and overheated that many players had problems breathing and sleeping. To inject some moisture into the air, James Klint, one of our team doctors, advised us to run the shower before going to bed and to fill up our sinks and tubs with water.

On Thursday Walsh tried another psychological ploy, but this time it was directed at the Bengals. While practicing a sideline pass pattern, I collided with wide receiver Freddie Solomon, who was our deep threat. Solomon suffered a sprained medial collateral ligament when I fell on his knee. Walsh made the injury sound worse to the media than it really was and went so far as to lament that I might have to replace Solomon as the punt returner. I hadn't returned punts all season. After I stepped on the right foot of Jim Miller, our barefooted punter, while practicing kickoff returns, Walsh once again worried out loud about the "injury." What he failed to emphasize was that Miller, who grew up on a farm in Ripley, Mississippi, and learned to kick sticks and rocks barefooted, had been wearing shoes when I stepped on his foot.

Make no mistake, Walsh would have done anything to beat the Bengals. He had been their quarterbacks and receivers coach for eight years. Walsh left Cincinnati after the 1975 season disappointed, because Brown had named Bill Johnson, another longtime Bengal assistant, to succeed him as the head coach. Walsh learned he had been passed over for the job when a local sportswriter called for his reaction to the hiring. Although he didn't verbalize his feelings to us, it was obvious that Walsh was obsessed with showing up Brown in Super Bowl XVI. Our practices were insanely intense. Walsh demanded precision. If anybody made the tiniest mistake he insisted we run the play over until we got it right, and he didn't care how long it took.

That practice approach sounds a lot easier than it was. Every day Walsh seemed to add a new wrinkle, until the offensive game plan grew to more than 120 plays. Typically, Walsh's game plans totaled between 85 and 95 plays. Montana has since told me that it was the most complex and detailed game plan he had ever seen. In fact, the game plan for Super Bowl XVI had become so massive by the end of the week the 49er offense hadn't even practiced a third of the plays. The defense wasn't spared Walsh's meticulousness and obsessiveness, either. During our week off following the NFC Championship Game, he had scrutinized films of Bengal quarterback Ken Anderson, a former pupil and Walsh became concerned by what he saw. Anderson, thirty-two, the NFL's Most Valuable Player, was hurting defenses with his scrambling. He had the mobility to elude a pass rush, Walsh said, as well as the speed to run for important yardage in key situations. He thought we had to pressure Anderson from the inside, so he instructed Chuck Studley to create more blitzes. One was called the Nickel Blizzard, in which Carlton Williamson blitzed from his strong safety position. Studley also designed a formation featuring defensive end Fred Dean, the best pass rusher in the NFL. He placed five players on the line—three linemen in the middle to occupy the guards and center, and two linebackers playing in the down position on the outside to take care of the offensive tackles. Dean became the middle linebacker, blitzing wherever he could find an open lane. The day Studley unveiled the formation, Dean salivated.

"What should I call it, Fred?" Studley asked. "I want something with real impact."

"Call it Cobra."

On Thursday night, our team leaders, tight end Charle Young and right tackle Keith Fahnhorst, called a players-only meeting to remind everybody to remain focused for the final days. I was the only rookie to talk. I mentioned the importance of not deviating from the pregame schedules we had kept throughout the season, something I had learned from coach John Robinson at USC. The 49er coaching staff had been debating whether players should sleep with their wives and girlfriends the nights preceding the game. Sam Wyche, our quarterback coach, had argued against it, while the players were divided about the issue.

"Do whatever it takes to win," I told the team, in what was one of my first pep talks ever. "Do the same things you've been doing all year long. If you've been screwing all night the night before games, then you screw all night. If you like to have two beers the night before, you go out and have your two beers. Don't treat this game any differently. Don't change anything now."

Fahnhorst, our offensive captain, gave an emotional speech about what it meant to him to finally reach the Super Bowl after eight years.

"You rookies who've made it right off the bat, have no idea how lucky you are or what an accomplishment this is," Fahnhorst said. "The older guys went through a couple of tough years here, trying to turn this thing around. We bled for this moment."

The morning of Super Bowl Sunday there was little hot water at the hotel, and some of the 49ers, including owner Eddie DeBartolo, Jr., were forced to take ice-cold showers. Luckily, I wasn't one of them. As the day wore on, I decided not to take the team bus to the game, because I wanted to be at the Silverdome at least four hours before kickoff. I went in a limousine, and I'm glad I did. About twenty minutes before we were scheduled to go on the field for warm-ups, I looked around and saw that there were only about fifteen players in the locker room. It turned out that our No. 2 team bus was delayed in traffic a half mile from the Silverdome due to the motorcade of Vice President George Bush. On the bus were Walsh, DeBartolo, Montana, Reynolds, and two dozen other players. Instead of panicking, Walsh laughed at our predicament. Fahnhorst and guard Randy Cross volunteered to play on both offense and defense. Equipment manager Chico Norton said he would be available as a running back. Trainer Lindsy McLean offered to fill in at quarterback. Solomon and Clark, our starting wide receivers, told me they would join me in the secondary.

Back on the bus DeBartolo grew impatient and along with O. J. Simpson, who was his guest, scaled snowbanks and a couple of hills to reach the Silverdome. Trying to keep everybody calm, Walsh grabbed the microphone next to the bus driver and cracked, "Well men, one thing is certain. They can't start without us." Then he pretended to be a radio play-by-play announcer, "Lindsy McLean on the quarterback sneak for a touchdown. The 49ers are up, 7–0. . . . Roy Gilbert [the 49er ticket distributor] grabs the pass and rambles 20 yards. . . ."

When the group finally walked into the locker room about a quarter to three, you would have thought we were hosting a surprise party. They were greeted by resounding laughter. The banter went back and forth. "Hey, nice of you guys to show up. You gonna play today?" "Aw, we've been ready to go for hours. We just stopped at the refreshment stand for some beers and a couple hot dogs." Even Walsh was relaxed. Although he had never permitted music to be played out loud in our locker room, he asked Montana to turn on his cassette tape player. The hit song "This Is It" by Kenny Loggins and Michael McDonald boomed from the big box. "Turn it up!" Walsh yelled each time the song ended. "Let's hear it again! Turn it up!"

> . . . *This is it!*
> *Make no mistake of where you are.*
> *This is it!*
> *Your back's to the corner.*
> *This is it!*
> *Don't be a fool anymore.*
> *This is it!*
> *The waiting is over . . .*
> *For once in your life, here's your miracle*
> *Stand up and fight!*
> *This is it! . . .*

With less than two hours until kickoff, neither the coaches nor the players had time to overanalyze what was about to happen. The curtain was going up too quickly for anybody to get sweaty palms. Seeing Walsh so self-assured kept me relaxed. When I walked onto the field for warm-ups, there was a nasty haze of gray cigarette smoke hanging above the field but that didn't bother me. If anything, I felt disappointed. I longed for the wide-open, grandiose feeling of the Rose Bowl. Not even the Super Bowl could compare to the excitement generated by a crowd of 100,000 at the Rose Bowl. It was obvious—just with the noise level alone—that there were 20,000 fewer people in the Silverdome. My butthole wasn't tight at all. I had that old USC attitude: Take no prisoners.

The story in the first half was Cincinnati turnovers, Walsh's surprise plays, and the precision of our placekicker Ray Wersching. Those elements helped us to build a 20–0 lead, which at the time was the largest halftime margin in Super Bowl history. On the Bengals' opening possession of the game, 49er free safety Dwight Hicks intercepted Anderson's pass at the San Francisco 5 and returned the ball to the 32. The 49er offense then drove the length of the field, aided by a new Walsh play called the Triple Pass which he had borrowed from Paul Brown. On that play, which picked up 14 yards, Montana handed off to running back Ricky Patton, who handed off to Solomon, who pitched back to Montana, who threw downfield to Young. Six plays later, Montana dived over the middle from the 1 to put us ahead 7–0.

On the Bengals' first possession of the second quarter, cornerback Eric Wright stripped the ball from wide receiver Cris Collinsworth. Defensive back Lynn Thomas recovered on our 8-yard line. Montana then marched us 92 yards, climaxed by an 11-yard touchdown pass to fullback Earl Cooper on another Walsh innovation called Fox-Two Special. Montana faked a handoff to Cooper. Solomon and Mike Shumann, the receivers who had lined up on the left side, ran their routes to the inside, and Cooper snuck out behind them, beating Bengal linebacker Reggie Williams. The 49ers went up 14–0. Wersching added 22- and 26-yard field goals, the last one coming only two seconds before halftime. Perhaps Wersching's biggest contributions were the squib kickoffs that he and Walsh had developed in Tuesday's practice. The squib kicks bounced and slid on the hard Astro-turf, driving the Bengal kick returners crazy and keeping Cincinnati in poor field position.

The Bengals came out fired up for the second half, and Anderson scored on their first series with a 5-yard touchdown run. That made the score 20–7. We punted on our next two possessions. With less than seven minutes left in the third quarter, the Bengals took over at midfield, and seven plays later found themselves with fourth-and-one on the San Francisco 5. Studley called for our goal-line defense. Madly rushing to get the right personnel in and out and lined up, nobody bothered to count the number of players on the field. Bengal fullback Pete Johnson plowed up the middle for two yards and a first down to the 3. All of a sudden I heard several players yelling for line-backer Keena Turner. "Keena. Keena. Where the hell is Keena?"

Sure enough, Turner had missed the preceding play. He hadn't heard Studley calling for the goal-line defense. Turner had assumed it was a short-yardage situation, in which he wasn't required to be on the field. None of us could get too angry at Turner. After all, he still had a case of the chicken pox. Shriveled to 207 pounds and lacking stamina, Turner felt sicker than a dog. We practically had to carry him onto the field for the NFC Championship Game. Trainer Lindsy McLean woke him up, told him it was time to put on his uniform, then pushed him out the locker-room door. Turner missed a play in that game, too, and Cowboy running back Tony Dorsett scored a touchdown.

Turner's blunder was followed by one of the most exciting goal-line stands in Super Bowl history. In our goal-line defense we used six linemen, four linebackers, and myself as the defensive back. On first-and-goal from our 3, Johnson exploded into the line. John Choma, a seldom-used offensive guard, wrapped his arms around Johnson's gigantic thighs, slid to his ankles and dragged the 249-pound fullback to the turf at the 1. Dan Bunz assisted on the tackle. Choma will always be remembered in 49er history because of this play. One of the team's least-known players, he had signed as a free agent at the beginning of the 1981 season, after being cut by both San Diego and Kansas City. He was our backup right tackle and right guard, and he played on the kickoff return, extra-point, and field-goal attempt teams. We didn't have enough defensive linemen for goal-line situations. Choma had become a starter on the goal-line team after making a touchdown-saving tackle on Chicago Bear running back Walter Payton in the second game of the season. With all his other duties, it was nearly impossible for Choma to find time to work on the goal-line defense. He would join us for a few plays in practice but that was all. Studley had basically talked him through this play in each of the seven days before Super Bowl XVI.

With a second-and-goal on the 1, you would think Johnson would have scored easily, running behind the strength of the offensive line on the left side behind tackle Anthony Munoz and guard Dave Lapham. However, Bunz held his ground against lead blocker Charles Alexander, a running back, which enabled Reynolds and tackle John Harty to pop Johnson with devastating blows. While studying Cincinnati game films, Reynolds had discovered that Johnson often tipped off his running plays. When Johnson got into his stance, he would put his left wrist on his hip, with the arm tight to his chest in anticipation of the handoff. Reynolds also noticed tendencies in goal-line situations. When Johnson ran to the left, Alexander would always move up closer to the line than Johnson, thus becoming the lead blocker. The Reynolds hit certainly inspired us. All week, the media talk was that nobody could stop Johnson, and now we had accomplished this feat on consecutive plays.

On third-and-goal from the 1, Anderson rolled to his right and tossed a pass to Alexander in the flat. Bunz, another unlikely 49er hero, was in position. One of the four remaining draft picks from the reign of former general manager Joe Thomas, he had lost his starting linebacker job to Craig Puki at midseason. Supposedly, Bunz wasn't aggressive enough, but I believed Bunz had too much personality for Walsh. A free spirit with long blond hair, he was never afraid to say what was on his mind. As Alexander caught the ball, Bunz drove his helmet into his back, slamming him to the carpet at the 1. Without a doubt it was the defensive play of the game.

The Bengals then called timeout. Studley pulled the defense over to the sideline and told us to watch for several plays: the quarterback bootleg, the inside trap, etc. By the time we lined up, our heads were swimming. Cincinnati kept it simple. Anderson handed off to Johnson, who followed Alexander to the right side of the line. Bunz stopped Alexander, and Reynolds led the swarm of 49ers that smothered Johnson.

When Reynolds came off the field, he was so excited that he not only caused himself to cramp, but he felt as though he was going to wet his britches. "I've got to take a piss," Hacksaw moaned. I remember him motioning wildly for our defensive players to make a circle around him near the bench. Reynolds unzipped his uniform pants and pissed right on the sideline. That still ranks as one of the craziest things I have ever seen in pro football. Afterward Walsh kidded Reynolds that he should have raised his hand and asked the head coach for permission.

The goal-line stand ate up six valuable minutes, but it didn't assure us the victory. The Bengals scored on their next possession, and Wersching had to add two more field goals later in the fourth quarter to put the game out of reach. I didn't relax until Clark recovered an on-side kick at our 48 with 14 seconds left. The 49ers had won, 26–21, and I began hugging everyone in sight. These guys symbolized what the word team was all about. There were no big egos. Just a humble bunch of overachievers who sacrificed bodies and individual goals to win. We loved each other. Enthusiasm and inspiration carried us to the Super Bowl.

During the bus ride back to the hotel for our postgame victory celebration, I sat next to defensive backs coach George Seifert—the Taskmaster.

"Ronnie, do you know what's really great?" Seifert asked, with a big smile on his face. "We get to try to do this again next year."

Give me a break, George.

After hearing that comment, I knew that pro football would never be the same for me, and I figured the 49er organization would change, but I wasn't sure how. I realized we'd never be able to capture the beauty and innocence of our first Super Bowl Championship. We were so oblivious to fame and fortune that we almost forgot to take the Super Bowl XVI trophy home with us. Long after we had cleared out of our locker room, our equipment manager, Chico Norton, noticed the huge sterling silver Lombardi Trophy on the floor next to a TV platform. Everyone on the team had had his picture taken with the trophy, but nobody remembered to haul the damn piece of hardware back to San Francisco. Norton put the trophy into a laundry trunk with the sweaty uniforms and dirty towels.

When we landed at the San Francisco International Airport on Monday afternoon, the entire city embraced us. We boarded buses in a freight hangar and, led by a police motorcycle escort, sped up Highway 101 to downtown. Near Pier 50, we switched to ten motorized cable cars with our names on the side for our victory parade through the streets of San Francisco. A few policemen guessed the crowd at 50,000, but when we turned toward the financial district it was clear they had grossly underestimated the turnout. There was a mass of humanity for as far as I could see. A half million people, at least. Everybody was delirious. Cheering loudly, waving wildly, 49er fans were hanging from lampposts and windows. They piled on top of cars and phone booths. While I was waving to the crowd, several fans rushed up to the street car to shake my hand, and they ripped a gold bracelet from my wrist. It didn't matter. At City Hall, Mayor Dianne Feinstein presented Walsh with the keys to the city. The whole experience choked me up. I had tears in my eyes for most of the afternoon. It was my real-life fairy tale.

3 | KAMIKAZE FOOTBALL: THE ELEMENTS OF MY GAME

HARD HITS

I've always thought if I could only hit as hard as former heavyweight champion Mike Tyson, if I could only generate the same velocity and reproduce his emotional and thought processes, then I would truly be the hardest hitter in the NFL. I've studied the way Tyson throws his punches. He's not just hitting his opponent. As I see it, he's literally punching through the guy's face and out the back of his skull. And he does that with so much style.

Watching Tyson perform in the ring arouses my emotions. The violence turns me on. Intrigues me. I've studied Tyson's face right before he delivers the blow. His eyes are alert—flashing and happy. His grimace is powerful. Tyson looks as if he puts every emotion imaginable into his hits. What do his punches feel like? I can only compare it to being popped in the face in a football game. Even with a facemask on, if you're tackled and hit in the face, it hurts like hell. There aren't any muscles to shield you from the powerful fist.

According to some boxing experts, Tyson's speed and quickness are his greatest attributes. But I admire the explosion in his legs. Tyson reminds me a lot of 325-pound Michael Carter, who is the 49ers' nose tackle and one of the biggest men on the team. Carter resembles an enormous block of granite, yet his vertical leap is something you'd expect from a lean basketball player. I witnessed him jump up on tables that were three feet high. I concentrate on Tyson's legs every time he throws a punch. His legs uncoil as if he's jumping off the canvas. That's why he is able to leave brains sloshing.

Tyson brings it from his toes all the way up through his heart and out his fist. That's the way I approach football. While I enjoy having the reputation of the NFL's hardest hitter—and I think Lawrence Taylor of the New York Giants, Mike Singletary of the Chicago Bears, and Vaughan Johnson of the New Orleans Saints are devastating hitters, too—I believe it's my *style* of tackling that makes me different from everyone else in the game. Most of the big guys just throw people to the ground. But I accelerate through my opponent. I visualize a spot on the other side of him and run full speed, straight through, to get there. People think you're supposed to stop there. No way. I keep moving. My knees fly forward into a receiver's helmet. My arms or hands whip into his facemask.

Too often TV commentators cite these movements as Ronnie Lott's intimidation tactics. That's nonsense. If that's going to intimidate a football player, we're all in trouble. Why do those same TV commentators always say, "Look at that determination!" when an offensive player is crawling all over a defensive player? There shouldn't be a double standard here. I'm only fighting to hold the guy back. Just as he's fighting for extra yards. I keep my entire body moving through the tackle until I'm sure he's securely down. If I don't tackle this way, I think he'll slip out of my grasp and be gone.

The most important lesson I learned from watching Tyson fight is that whenever you do something—say you're going to hit somebody and you plan on taking him down—well, you can't do it halfway. Either you do it or you don't. You've got to take it all the way to the end. All the way to the mat. When Tyson throws a punch, he's not just throwing a punch to make contact. He's throwing punches to knock you out.

That's how I explain running full force right through my own teammates to bring down enemy ballcarriers. In my decade with the 49ers I clobbered linebacker Keena Turner in the back more times than he cares to remember. He will tell you that I came out of nowhere. I know he wondered if I even saw him. Well, I didn't. I was too focused. On these backswiping tackles, Turner usually gave me one of his looks of Whose side are you on anyway? I would shoot back with a glare of If you would just get the hell out of my way! Inside I laughed at the absurdity of the situation and giggled about those zany outer limits my passion for football drove me to.

In Charles Haley's first two seasons with the 49ers in 1986 and 1987, I gave him one nasty hip bruise after another. (In training-room lingo, they're known as hip pointers.) Haley would tangle with an offensive lineman, trying to throw him to the side so he could get to the running back, and I'd blast into both of them at the same time, like a human bowling ball. *Kaboom!* Once he wised up to how I played the game, Haley made sure to counsel the newcomers to the 49er defense: "If you see Ronnie coming, back off your man. Get out of his way!"

Picking a point on the other side of the opponent and running through him is taught in Football 101. It's a basic lesson you learn in Pee Wee and Pop Warner football. Still, it's one thing to talk about the technique and another to do it. If you run through a person it's going to hurt. And, besides that, you know you're not going to be right the next couple of plays afterward. Don't believe all those guys who say, "I love to hit." The physical contact may be a turn-on for some people, but nobody looks forward to running full force into—much less through—a 250-pound bulldozer like former Houston Oiler running back Earl Campbell. The eighth all-time rusher in NFL history and a 1991 inductee into the Pro Football Hall of Fame, he was the player I had the most trouble tackling. I never was able to bring him down. If I tried to run through him, I ricocheted off his barrel chest, and if I attempted to wrap my arms around him, they wouldn't begin to encompass his wide body. Once in a Pro Bowl game, where players usually take it easy, I ran up to tackle Campbell, and he straight-armed me, knocking me back three yards on my ass.

Right before impact, my adrenaline rises. I can actually feel it surge. I can taste it. It's the same rush a person gets when he lifts something heavy. It's the feeling a mother has when she sees her baby pinned underneath a car, and she hoists the front end to pull the child out. It's the sensation that occurs when you can't get the cap off the ketchup bottle. Something inside says, PUSH! TWIST! H-A-R-D-E-R!!! An inner force tells me to push harder. Something deep inside says, "Let everything go into this hit. Bring it from your toes!"

Why do I believe in mystical powers? Because my legs had to be the scrawniest and skinniest on the 49ers. (Joe Montana ran a very close second, by the way.) Great quarterbacks, great pitchers, even great hitters stay around a long time because they use their legs, but I know that my hitting power cannot be measured by leg presses in a weight room or by 40-yard-dash times. NFL scouts have never been able to put a finger on it. For me, it's almost entirely emotional.

In martial arts, you shout words like *hi-ya* or *kee-yup*, before exploding into your most powerful kick or your hardest hit. At the point of impact, my mind is in an attack mode. It's almost as if my inner voice says "GET IT!" Although in actuality, there's no time to say or think anything.

I've never had a word to describe my big hits, but I do call my take-no-prisoners style of football "kamikaze." Ray Rhodes, the 49er defensive backs coach, coined my hard hits "woo licks" because when we watched them in Monday's film study, it never failed that one of the guys in the defensive meeting room screamed, "Woooooo!" Then, someone else shouted, "Ah, coach, could we see that again?" And this went on for several minutes. Rhodes ran the hit back and forth, over and over, and we all got charged up from it. *Woooooo.* It sounds rather bloodthirsty, doesn't it?

The biggest woos in the 49er defensive meeting room always went to predatory hits, those runaway freight train massacres where I plowed through some poor sucker who didn't see me coming. Predatory hits have always been the most fun. The running back is five yards away. I'll focus on him and see the play begin to unfold in slow motion right in front of me. I can anticipate that he's going to make a cut to fake out the line-backer. And with all the bodies in front of him, he won't have a clue that I'm watching him. Playing predator reminds me of those old war movies where the submarine's under the ocean, anchored and waiting for that battleship to cross over it. The sub captain just lines up his target and fires. Another example is the Tom Cruise movie *Top Gun.* The jet flown by Maverick (Cruise) weaves through the sky, dodging other planes, darting in and out of the mountains, then out of the blue, one of the best instructors locks him in his sights and blows Maverick away. On predatory hits, I say to myself, "Yep. That MiG is coming right to me. Got to come. He's coming here, baby."

I don't have a word to describe the moment of vicious, violent, total impact. Whatever it is, my body feels it, and even after ten seasons it never quite gets conditioned to it. I know instantly if I've made a good hit. It's like Jack Nicklaus on the driving range whacking golf balls 400 yards. He can tell you which ball he hit right on. Or Magic Johnson sinking fifty straight free throws. He knows which ones dropped right through the middle of the basket.

To the fans in the stands, a big hit sounds like shoulder pads and helmets colliding. Leather against leather. Plastic against plastic. But when I make a big hit and release every molecule of

Dad taught me to respect my uniform.

My first sports hero, Roy D. Lott, in a basketball game at the Air Force base.

I have always taken sports seriously. At an early age I had the Bobo Scowl.

When I started playing football I wore number 10. In high school I switched to 42 in tribute to Charley Taylor, the Hall of Fame receiver for the Washington Redskins.

My godparents, Chuck and Eva Young.

John Robinson, my coach at USC. *(USC Sports Information)*

The Three Blind Mice: Dennis Smith (49), Eric Scoggins (15), and me. *(USC Sports Information)*

I played on the USC basketball team as a junior. *(USC Sports Information)*

In 1981, my first year with the 49ers, we started three rookies in the secondary. Me, Eric Wright (21), and Carlton Williamson (27). *(Photograph copyright by Michael Zagaris)*

Relaxing after my interception in our 20–17 victory over the Los Angeles Rams in 1981. *(Photograph copyright by Michael Zagaris)*

We stopped the Cincinnati Bengals in Super Bowl XVI on four consecutive downs in a dramatic goal-line stand. *(Photograph copyright by Michael Zagaris)*

my emotion into the impact, the world around me goes silent. I don't hear a thing. The stadium seems empty. I can be in the biggest game of my life, a Super Bowl in the noisy Louisiana Superdome, or playing in front of 100,000 at the Rose Bowl, and not hear a sound.

At the point of total impact my eyes close, roll back into my head, and begin to tear. Oftentimes snot sprays out my nostrils, covering my mouth and cheeks—and squirting on anybody nearby—and my chin strap lodges under my nose. My ears slowly begin to ring, and my brain goes blank. It's hard to catch my breath. The wind gets knocked out of my lungs and I gasp for air.

As for the well-being of my opponent, well, I can only believe he's worse off than I am. Lord only knows how Cleveland Brown wide receiver Webster Slaughter really felt in 1990 when I ran into him and jammed my forearm into his chest. Slaughter went down with a thud, but he bounced back and ran to the huddle. His body language seemed to be saying, "Hey, Ronnie, that was nothin'." That puzzled me.

Dammit, I thought. I hit this guy pretty hard. I wonder what's going on in his mind?

The Browns called timeout right after the play, so I glanced over to their side of the field. There was Slaughter, fixing one of the pads on the inside of his helmet. And I said, "Now, did I do that? Did I jar something loose in his helmet? Perhaps. But I know there has to be something else loose upstairs."

It has always intrigued me that when I tattoo somebody I never wind up tattooing myself. Jennie Winter, a massage therapist who has treated me once a week since 1988, has never found any bruises on my body from my hard hits. Not a single tattoo. To me that is unbelievable. Mystical. Winter, a rabid 49er fan, always laughs about the way I relish my hard hits. Every week she watches me throw my chest into somebody and secretly expects to lift my shirt on Wednesday night and find massive internal injuries, a couple of broken ribs, or, at the very least, a bunch of bruises.

Winter, a spiritual healer, believed in the astral body, and explained that people were beings of light who inhabited physical forms. We all have the ability to attach our astral bodies to solid places to maintain our balance in space. Winter cited tightrope walkers or gymnasts who focused beams of light on a wall to keep from falling. Analyzing my hard hits from a spiritual, astral body perspective, I believe I have the ability to shoot an energy beam through my opponents. On the field I'm like the black-belt karate master who keenly focuses his energy to split a stack of boards or chop through a bunch of bricks.

After games, I get bombarded with the same questions. Friends who were sitting in the stands will say, "That was a hell of a hit you made. Did you hear that?" And like clockwork they will follow that question with, "Did you know how big a hit that was?" Well, to me, big hits are like earthquakes. You recognize that there was definitely an earthquake, and you know you survived it, but you have no idea what size it was because you were standing right there. You have to wait until you see the reading on the Richter scale, or in the case of big hits, until you see the game films.

Perhaps one way to measure the impact of my hits would be by the number of times I've been knocked out. I've had at least a dozen concussions in my ten years in the NFL, several others while I was at USC, and one at Eisenhower High School in Rialto. And that doesn't count the number of times I have been sent into never-never land.

In the Pro Bowl in February 1990, I put a serious woo lick on Kansas City Chief running back Christian Okoye. He's known as the Nigerian Nightmare, and if I had only stopped to think about his nickname before hand, maybe I wouldn't have been so vicious. My head-to-head collision with 256 pounds of solid muscle knocked some sense into me. Not immediately, mind you, but as soon as the fog cleared.

After we collided, one side of my brain said, "Get back to the huddle." The other said, "Jeez. I've got to go to the sideline." My left eye twitched, and I couldn't get it to stop. I tried to focus, but I couldn't get my eyes to clear. I was in a semiconscious state. I felt like a robot that had been thrown into a malfunctioning mode or a computer that was moving without being programmed. Somebody on the NFC defensive unit yelled at me to get off the field. I was in such a deep, deep fog that it didn't register.

Concussions take you on long, strange trips. You never remember the hit or who tackled you. You seldom remember the score, what quarter it is, what plays you were running. You might forget who you're playing, what stadium you're in, and how you got there. You might not even recognize teammates, friends, or loved ones.

When I have concussions I feel like I am looking through a drawer packed with files, searching for a piece of paper I've misplaced. It's in there somewhere, but I just can't remember what I filed it under. How long it will take to get my bearings, I can never predict. If I'm lucky my memory will come back quickly, and I'll be in tune with everything but the play that did me in.

When 49er tight end Brent Jones suffered a concussion against the Los Angeles Rams in Anaheim Stadium in 1990, he came up to me on the sideline with a glazed look on his face.

"Ronnie, what are you doing in street clothes?" Jones asked. "Why aren't you playing?"

I had to laugh. Just two weeks before, 48 million people had watched our Monday Night Football game against the New York Giants and most of them were aware that I had badly sprained my knees and wouldn't be back on the field until the playoffs. I gave Jones a break. Hey, at least he recognized me without my jersey on.

Concussions can make you dizzy and nauseous. Some guys have severe, nonstop headaches for days afterward. Mine are more like a prolonged buzzing in my ears, like a never-ending dial tone on a telephone. I have one definite rule of thumb. Never be tentative about playing after you've had a concussion. The instinct is to protect your head, but if you do that, you'll probably end up changing the way you tackle. You won't put your head in there as much.

Here's a typical Lott fog scene on the field. I knock the crap out of some guy. Snot's all over my face. My eyes are glassy. I stagger back to the huddle like a boxer, bend over and try to get my wheels back in gear. But I'm not fooling the other defensive backs. They can tell I'm not registering anything because more often than not my chin strap is still pushed up over my mouth.

"Ronnie, Ronnie, come on, let's get out for a second," one of the defensive backs pleads with me. "Get out of the game. Just for one play."

At the same time, another defensive back signals to the sideline to send in a replacement.

"I ain't going out!" I scream. Then I madly curse. Out of the corner of my eye, I can see my backup halfway out onto the field. As he gets closer to the huddle, I yell, "Get the fuck out of here. I'm playing. Go back to the sideline."

I have no idea what defense we're about to run, but it would hurt worse to leave the field. When I get to the sideline after that kind of series, the team doctors always ask if I'm okay, and I always say, "Yeah, I'm all right." But that's far from the truth.

Very far from the truth. I have to lie. Otherwise they'll hide my helmet to keep me on the bench.

In 1984, after I blasted Houston Oiler tight end Jamie Williams in the Astrodome, one of our team doctors, James Klint, grabbed me by the waist and shouted, "Ronnie, you're not going back in."

I was crazed. "What the hell do you mean?"

"Where are you?" Dr. Klint asked.

"Houston."

"Okay, what's the score?"

I paused. Now, that was a tough question.

"See, you don't have any idea what the score is," Klint said. "You can't play."

"Sure I know the score."

I snuck over to ask one of my teammates the score, and then I slipped back to give the numbers to Klint. "No, you're not going back in," Klint reiterated. Time and again I repeated the process, bugging guys for the score and then bugging Klint with the correct answer. After halftime I guess he finally believed me, and I happily—if groggily—raced back onto the field. Through the years my doctors, trainers, teammates, and coaches have tried to suggest that I let up a little, that I start picking and choosing my hard hits to save my body. George Seifert was forever reminding me to protect myself. But I just couldn't do it. I'd lose too much of Ronnie Lott. I wouldn't be the same player—or man—without my strike.

My all-time greatest hit occurred on December 19, 1982, against William Andrews of the Atlanta Falcons at Candlestick Park. That hit didn't hurt me or Andrews, much less put either of us in a fog. In fact, it was rather embarrassing because I have to admit I didn't even bring the guy down.

Andrews had been crushing opponents that season, bowling over one defensive back after another. He was terrifying to watch on film. For me, stopping Andrews represented the ultimate challenge. I had to be the first to smother him. I was driven. There were no open, unprotected areas on his body to get good, solid hits. I calculated that I had to hit him at his strongest points—in the shoulders and legs—to haul him to the ground.

Falcon quarterback Steve Bartkowski called for a screen pass. We were in a defensive coverage that made it look as if I were going to drop back and play deep. Actually, I was going to roll up and play the short flat. Ah, yes. The perfect woo lick position.

The predator mode. I thought, He's got to come. He's coming here, baby. That MiG is coming right to me. I ran up from behind and unloaded everything I had. I clobbered Andrews in the back of his head with my right forearm and smashed him in the face. But I rolled right off him. Slid like butter. Miraculously, Andrews stayed on his feet. Carlton Williamson, our strong safety, tried to hit Andrews around the shins, but he ended up too high, shattering his finger. He needed to have three pins inserted later that season. Finally Eric Wright, our other cornerback, sprinted from the far side of the field, hurled himself on Andrews' back and rode him for ten yards like a bull, wrestling him to the turf. I'm sure that play will always be at the top of William Andrews' highlight film.

Later, Bartkowski completed a long pass on me and a fan behind our bench began yelling, "Hey, Lott! What the fuck kind of All-Pro are you?" I was so frustrated at this point that I lost my temper. I stormed over to the stands and laid into the guy: "What the hell are you talking about?" After cooling off at halftime, I felt embarrassed by my actions. Before the third quarter started, I apologized.

Let me put my perception of hard hits into simpler terms. If you think you want to play in the NFL, and, if you want to find out if you can handle being hit by Ronnie Lott, here's what you do. Grab a football, throw it in the air, and before you can catch it, have your best friend belt you with a baseball bat. No shoulder pads. No helmet. Just you, your best friend and the biggest Louisville slugger you can find.

That's what it feels like to be hit by me.

And that's the feeling I thrive on.

RAGE

Rage is that despicable smell under your nose. It's like stepping in dog doodoo. You wipe it off your shoes, but still the smell lingers. You're angry because you walked in that pile of crap in the first place, and then it follows you everywhere. You're constantly pissed off.

I aim for the level of rage possessed by linebackers Dick Butkus of the Chicago Bears and Ray Nitschke of the Green Bay Packers, who were the meanest and nastiest sons of bitches of all time. The inner force behind their rage must have chanted: You've got to be mean. You've got to be tough. And you've got to be physical.

When I line up in the defensive secondary, I want pulsating through my veins the larger-than-life rage of somebody like Pat (Mouse) Fischer, who played for the St. Louis Cardinals and the Washington Redskins. He stood only 5 feet 10, 170 pounds, but he more than held his own at cornerback in the NFL for seventeen years. In the heat of battle, I hope to perform like another one of my favorite tough guys, former NBA guard Calvin Murphy. Nobody messed with him. Like Fischer, Murphy was small (also 5 feet 10), but when he got into scuffles, he wouldn't back down.

You've got to be mean.
You've got to be tough.
And you've got to be physical.

When I'm on the field, my rage exists beyond my skin. It is an invisible force field that pushes out farther and farther as the game progresses. It's like a huge suit of armor. I reach such a heightened state that I can literally feel the hair stand up on my arms. I describe my rage this way. It's like riding on a twisting, twirling, skyrocketing roller coaster. It's just one loud, long, glorious *SSCCREEEEAAAAMMMMM.*

In a matter of microseconds, my rage transforms me into a human lethal weapon regardless of who the opponent is. Several years ago, the 49ers were playing the New Orleans Saints at Candlestick Park. Their tight end Hoby Brenner was a teammate of mine at USC, and I've known Hoby and his wife Alexis since they were college sweethearts. Alexis had baked a couple dozen cookies and sent them to me the day before the game. In the first half, I knocked the shit out of Brenner. Absolutely cleaned his clock. He had caught a pass over the middle, turned upfield, and hadn't seen me coming. *POW!!* It must have felt as if he had run into a brick wall. I went over to see if he was okay, and he was out cold. I figured he'd eventually regain consciousness and fully recover, but in the meantime I felt guilty. After all, Alexis had baked me some great chocolate chip cookies, and I showed my thanks by coldcocking her husband. On second thought, maybe I should have gotten her recipe. Why?

You've got to be mean.

That wasn't my worst moment as a raving, raging maniac. In my rookie year in 1981, we met the Atlanta Falcons at Candlestick Park in a divisional showdown. The reigning NFC West champions against the 49ers, who were the new kids on the block. In the third quarter, while driving for a touchdown that would put them ahead, Falcon quarterback Steve Bartkowski called a sweep to the right side. Since it wasn't a pass play, all I had to do as the left cornerback was jog next to their veteran receiver Alfred Jackson. For no apparent reason, he threw a forearm to my face, hitting me underneath my chin.

Blood was everywhere. Smeared across the front of my jersey. In huge splotches on my pants. Sticking to my fingers. The blood gushed from my chin. Jesus Christ, what the hell happened? I went to the sideline at the end of the series and asked Eason Ramson, one of our tight ends, to look at my face. Jackson had split my lip wide open.

"Hey man, check out my lip. How does it look?"

Ramson screwed up his nose. "Oooh, God. It's gross."

I sought out our trainer Lindsy McLean. "Hey, Lindsy, what's the deal with my face?"

McLean calmly told me that my front teeth had severely busted my lower lip. He crammed gauze in my mouth and had me hold ice on the cut. By this time I was fuming. And getting hotter under the collar by the second. My jaw tightened. My eyes grew large and puffy. I took a seat on the bench and repeated over and over, "I'm going to kill this motherfucker . . . I'm going to kill this motherfucker . . . I'm going to kill this motherfucker."

A couple of defensive series later, one of my cohorts in the secondary, Saladin Martin, intercepted a Bartkowski pass at the San Francisco 43. I immediately clicked into a blocking mode, and when I turned to cut down some Falcons, guess who was in front of me? Alfred Jackson. Accidentally on purpose, I clubbed him with my right forearm. Sorry, Alfred. The funny thing was he didn't go down, so I just hit him again. And again. And again.

I pummeled him as if I were Mike Tyson. Finally Jackson dropped to the ground. I noticed there wasn't any blood on his chin. So I hit him some more.

The referee penalized me for unsportsmanlike conduct, nullifying Martin's 30-yard interception return, and I was ejected from the game for the first and only time in my career. That didn't calm my rage. On the sideline, I kept smoldering. As I looked at Jackson across the field, I kept muttering, "I'm still going to kill you!" The thought crossed my mind to follow him to the Falcon team bus after the game. But I *did* have more sense than that.

We beat the Falcons, 17–14, and in the locker room our owner, Eddie DeBartolo, Jr., flew into his own rage.

"You almost lost the fucking game for us!" he bellowed.

The coaches weren't happy either. Bill Walsh's face turned red when he bawled me out. "That was stupid, Ronnie! A total lack of discipline! That'll cost you five thousand dollars!"

My rage had conquered me, although I couldn't admit it then. I had worked myself into a wild, volatile state where I couldn't even eat dinner later that night. I was so stubborn about the incident that I was determined to make Walsh, Mr. D, and everybody else on the team understand that there had been a method to my madness.

I found George Seifert, who was our defensive backs coach that season, in his office Monday morning, prior to our meetings.

"George, if somebody hits me in the fucking mouth again, I'll fight! I don't care what it costs. No way am I losing my manhood to anybody. I want these guys to respect me."

"What are you talking about, Ronnie?"

"Check out Jackson in the third quarter."

Later that morning, while we were watching game film in our defensive meeting, Seifert came across Jackson's blatant cheap shot. He later showed the film clip to Walsh, and lo and behold, my fine was forgotten. Well, $4,500 of it.

People will always test your will and strength in certain situations on the football field. It makes no difference if you're winning or losing. Never let them see they can defeat you.

You've got to be tough.

Rage is an inborn trait. It can't be taught. The greatest athletes have the ability to raise their adrenaline level to the outer limits every single game, but still play totally in control.

Many players can only tap into this reservoir of rage once a season, and some poor souls can do it just once in a lifetime. Keeping the rage turned up all the way takes concentration and discipline.

After the Jackson incident in my rookie year, I learned how to stay within rational boundaries when my adrenaline was flowing. Although I hate to mention his name, I have to give some credit to Kellen Winslow, the former San Diego Charger tight end. Winslow was such a bully and a blowhard. He always had something condescending to say. At 6 feet 5, 250 pounds, he was bigger than every defensive back, and he loved to strong-arm us. On game films, you'd see him messing with defensive backs. After you tackled him, he'd toss the ball like he was throwing it in your face. When you covered him, he'd push you.

Real tough, huh? That's intimidation?

Defensive backs have a strong alliance with one another. I can remember watching films of Winslow and saying, "The hell with him. That's bullshit. He's not going to do that to us." It made me so mad that I wanted to destroy him. But I learned to channel that rage.

Just as I remained in control in 1989, when Shawn Collins, then a rookie wide receiver with the Falcons, claimed that I had tried to take his head off. All I did was make two routine tackles. The first was simply a hard hit, and he made the catch. I complimented him afterward, in fact. I encouraged the kid. The other hit, at the end of the game, came after he caught a pass over the middle. Three of our guys tried to tackle him but missed. I grabbed Collins and rode him to the ground. Then I laid on him to kill some time off the clock. Well, he got up and pushed me. Then he threw the ball at me and started talking shit.

When an opponent pushes or throws a ball at me for no apparent reason, it immediately tells me that he has some emotional weaknesses that I can exploit. I'll put that player under the microscope in the film room until I discover every flaw. His actions will bring out a higher level of rage in me. I feel like the pitcher who has allowed a home run and the batter showboats his way around the bases. Next time up, I'm throwing high and tight, and that hitter is going down.

After the game, a reporter came up to me and said, "Shawn Collins is saying in the other locker room that you're a headhunter." Well, that rubbed me the wrong way. Sure I hit hard, and for the most part, I play within the rules. Players don't call me dirty, and I won't tolerate anybody questioning how I play the game. If you cheap-shot me, I'll retaliate.

As I recall, a couple of years ago a wide receiver came by and knocked me down after the play was over. "God, man," 49er linebacker Charles Haley said in the huddle, "that's the hardest you've been hit in a while, ain't it, Cuz?" The next play, I blew right through the guy.

All it takes is one play. I promise I won't forget you.

I suppose Shawn Collins had something to prove that afternoon. He wanted to show everybody how tough he was. But you make your point at the beginning of the game. You don't wait until the game's over and you're in the locker room. You don't push people and go through childish antics. Plain and simple. You just play the game. A tough receiver is one who goes over the middle to make the catch and then keeps his mouth shut.

After I showered and dressed, I sought out Bobby Butler, the Falcons' veteran cornerback. "You tell that little kid that I'm coming after his ass the rest of my career," I said. Don't forget: *You've got to be physical.*

With the fiercest competitors in the NFL, you can see rage permeating through their uniforms. Bear linebacker Mike Singletary has split his college and pro helmets sixteen times. Linebacker Matt Millen regularly yanked the facemask of offensive linemen who held him. "You're going to cut this out right now," Millen would say, eyeball to eyeball with his opponent. "Do you understand? No more."

The most feared defensive player in football, Giant linebacker Lawrence Taylor, wears his rage like a shield. You see it in the way he explodes into a quarterback. Not to be disrespectful to Carl Banks and the other Giant linebackers, but their rage isn't anywhere near that of L.T.'s. Even if one of them slipped on a No. 56 jersey, the difference in emotion would be very obvious.

The public mostly sees the joyous side of Joe Montana's rage when he shoots his arms in the air after throwing a touchdown pass. What the TV cameras don't reveal is Montana's nasty rage. He has stepped in dog doodoo plenty of times. Defensive players took dirty shots at him, he went nuts. He became verbally and physically aggressive—at times, downright mean. The 49er offensive linemen told him, "Joe, shut up! You're getting the guy mad, and we're the ones who have to block him!"

There's a trick to tackling players filled with rage. You have to break their tenacity immediately because they're able to regenerate their force field again and again. Each time, their rage just gets stronger. Some guys you hit, and boom, you stall them. Others just seem to bring up a second surge of adrenaline. Whoever taps into his second jolt of rage the quickest wins the battle. The great Walter Payton brought forth his rage quicker than any running back I've ever played against. If I didn't match his rage, desire, determination, and attitude on the days we played the Bears, there was no way I could bring Payton down. His was a designer rage. Everybody wanted it. Payton's rage radiated so brightly that you could almost feel the fans bouncing off it.

A classic example of his second surge of adrenaline occurred late in a 41–0 rout of the Bears at Candlestick Park in 1987. The Bears had a fourth-and-one on their 40, and Payton carried the ball into the line. Our 325-pound nose tackle, Michael Carter, smacked into Payton, knocking him back a yard. Now he had to cover two yards instead of one for the first down. Payton's feet kept pumping. That wasn't leg strength. It was rage. An inner power. A mystical strength that couldn't be seen on game film. Payton wound up getting the first down, and even though I was on the field trying to stop him, I couldn't help but admire his effort.

It'll probably come as no surprise that off the field I'm not an even-tempered, stable guy. In fact, my moods go way up and way down. Take a look at my daily biorhythm sheet, and you'd say, "Something's weird with this guy." But these mood swings help make me the kind of player I am. To get to the outer reaches of my rage—to get to the top of the mountain—I better have a serious mood swing or I'll get my ass kicked. What's the most dangerous part of my rage? It's hard to turn off after the game. I can turn it down, but I can't actually turn it off. It's like the pilot light on a gas stove. Or the television set in the living room that has just been shut off—you can still see the outline of a picture on the screen. Nights after games, I'll lie in bed and feel my muscles twitch as if I'm still on the field.

I'd like to think the reason I'm a moody person is because my highs have to be so high when I'm on the field, and the only direction my moods can go when I'm off the field is down. In my experience, elite athletes are moody people. Los Angeles Laker Magic Johnson, a friend of mine, is moody. When he's playing basketball he's as high as a kite, with that big, warm, magical smile. But, believe me, there are plenty of hours after a big game when he sits around his house mellow and contemplative. He's a different Magic.

I have never had any problems with my lows, but others certainly do. Teammate Eric Wright has known me for eleven years. Our first four years with the 49ers, we were roommates in training camp and on the road. We've been longtime business partners in Sports City Cafe in Cupertino, California. Yet Wright says he still can't understand or adjust to my mood swings. Some days I'm outrageously happy. Giddy. Childlike. Others, I'm distant and quiet, almost sullen. I put on what was known around the 49ers as the Bobo Stare, a scary, somber scowl. My 49er teammates knew to keep their distance because I could flare up quickly. Luckily, some of them merely laughed at my moods. Montana, for instance, presented me with a photograph of one of his daughters imitating the Bobo Stare. My wife and I got a kick out of that. It's one of Karen's favorite pictures.

I'm sure my teammates will agree that the Bobo Stare is more acceptable than the Bobo Scream. During games, I'm filled with so much of that loud, screaming rage that I drive my teammates on defense crazy. I'm always yelling at them for making mistakes. I expect perfection. My voice reaches a high pitch. My feathers stand up. Whenever a team completes a big pass on us, I blow a fuse. And that includes getting pissed at myself if I'm the culprit.

"Goddamn you! Get your ass in gear!" I'll scold. "You're fucking up!"

Early in my career, my 49er teammates Dwight Hicks and Hacksaw Reynolds had to constantly remind me to chill out. They claimed that all the yelling would eventually distract me. I listened to their reasoning—and kept right on screaming. Why? That's the way I have always motivated myself. It's how I keep my rage turned on. My teammates could be on their last legs, beaten up and exhausted, and I would still be jawing and bitching at them.

"You've got to make the play!" I would shout.

I'm sure most everybody on the defense said, "Screw Ronnie," under their breath at one time or another. Behind closed doors, Wright and linebackers Keena Turner, Mike Walter, and Riki Ellison called me Big Cheese because they thought I demanded too much from them. And word has it that cornerback Darryl Pollard referred to me as the King. When I got too out of control for Millen, however, he just ripped into me and reeled me in with three words: "RON, SHUT UP." The first time he did that, you could see jaws dropping on the players in the huddle. For some reason, most of my 49er teammates were always afraid to tell me to shut up, but believe it or not, that's all it would have taken to turn down my rage a notch.

I came close to blows dozens of times right on the field with 49er teammates who blew coverages or missed tackles. Ask Carlton Williamson, Jeff Fuller, or Haley. Haley loves to tell the story about the time I screamed at everybody in the huddle because our opponent had gained 15 yards on us.

"What the hell are you guys doing?" I bellowed.

"Ronnie, calm down," Haley said, grabbing my arm. "Chill out, man. Just chill."

I quickly forgot about the mistake, and began yelling at Haley for telling me to calm down.

Imagine trying to concentrate with a madman yelling in your ear. Mike Walter knows what that feels like. He took the brunt of most of my rage. When he came to the 49ers as a free agent in 1984, he had been an outside linebacker with the Dallas Cowboys. Seifert moved him to inside linebacker. He became Seifert's project. I always wanted Walter to get the most out of his talent. If Seifert thought Walter was that good, then he should be setting the world on fire. In the beginning, any time there was a run up the middle into the secondary I went looking for Walter.

"Goddammit, Mike! Wrap up! Take on the guards! Stop the run!"

During the course of a game, there wasn't time to stop and remind myself, "Ronnie, you know Mike might not be able to handle your yelling. Speak to him calmly." Even if I could have been tactful, I would be incapable of speaking to anyone in a calm voice during a game. If I tried to nurture teammates on the field, it would take me out of my game, ruin my intensity.

How was I to know Walter couldn't handle the criticism? Unbeknownst to me, Walter constantly complained to Turner about my yelling, and Turner told him the best way to deal with me was to scream right back. Finally, Walter got the hint.

"You're always yelling at me, Ronnie!" Walter screamed one day. "If you would just relax and not yell at me, I'd probably feel more comfortable out there and make fewer mistakes."

So I went out of my way not to yell at Walter anymore. Although I think I slipped every once in a while.

The guys who bore the brunt of my wrath in recent years were linebacker Bill Romanowski and Pollard. I rode Romo a lot. I thought he could be an All-Pro, but he has to go to another level of greatness. He works out all day long, running and lifting weights, but he still doesn't get it. He needs to study the finer points of the game—how he matches up against specific players, the ways an offense will attack him on certain downs and distances, and how to play situations using the game clock. Pollard must learn to concentrate every single play. I regularly challenged him on the field—and again on the sideline. At our 1990 minicamp I gave him an earful when he had to sit out practice with a strained hamstring.

"Don't forget where you came from," I said, getting right up in his face. "You were a free agent from Weber State who got cut five times before you made the team. You ought to be able to practice with an injury like this."

Then I stepped away and disgustedly thought, "Darryl can't just become content. He can't be satisfied with being a starter. He should always try to push himself."

I don't recall Pollard skipping another practice.

There are only two ways to do things on the field. A right way and a wrong way, and there's no in between. A lot of the 49er defensive players didn't believe that. You're going to win games because you execute, and you can't just show up and fake it. True, I'm a perfectionist. But I also know if you screw up, the weakness in a defense could be exposed. Your weaknesses could be exposed. Mine could be exposed. We could all look foolish out there. By yelling, I'm just trying to cover all of our butts.

You should never assume, just because this is professional football, that players are going to do it the right way. If you want to win, you can't tolerate mistakes as a player or coach. If you excuse one wrong decision, somewhere down the line you'll lose when that person makes a similar wrong decision. Then you'll say, "I should have spoken to him. I should have coached him." But it's too late.

Turner told me I was too judgmental, that I was too harsh on players, especially during games. That was where we always clashed. I told Turner, "If I say somebody's not committed to winning, that's my opinion. I'd rather play with a less talented guy who is willing to make sacrifices. I can't live with a guy who's not totally committed to winning."

When I screamed at the 49er players, I wasn't trying to be unfairly critical, or condescending, or do anything that would be detrimental to the team. I wasn't trying to be intimidating or manipulative—although some of my teammates accused me of being both. I wasn't pressing others and not pressing myself. I was yelling because I was mad—I just wanted to win. Any player who didn't understand my motives was insecure with himself. He should have figured out why his buttons were getting lit when I yelled at him, and perhaps he should have taken more responsibility and told me to go bite the big one. I'm a bitch on the field and a bitch to play with. But the bottom line was—and always will be—getting the job done.

FEAR AND FOCUS

What scares the hardest hitter in the NFL?

What makes the hair stand up on my spine?

Horror movies. I've been petrified of them ever since I watched *Wait Until Dark* as a nine-year-old. Audrey Hepburn played a blind woman who is terrorized in her New York City apartment by an evil killer. He is searching for a drug-filled antique doll that Hepburn's husband unwittingly smuggled. The blind woman breaks all of the lights in the apartment but forgets about the one in the refrigerator. When the killer cracks the refrigerator door open, he discovers her hiding in the kitchen. The next thing I remember, a knife seemed to jump right through the movie screen at me. Thinking about the movie still gives me the shakes.

I'm afraid of heights. I've had dreams about falling off bridges, and I always drive in the center lane because I worry that my car may swan-dive into the water. The Golden Gate may be the most picturesque bridge in the world, but I'd rather see it on a postcard than make a trip over it.

Cats drive me crazy, too. I can't be anywhere near them. I'm fearful they're going to jump on me, catch their claws in my clothes, and badly scratch my skin.

The only real fear I have on the field is the fear of failure. That's the fear of all fears. That is what drives the best athletes, actors, musicians, and entertainers. We stand alone in the spotlight, in front of millions of people, our hearts and souls exposed, our mistakes so easily seen. I have found that the most competitive people are highly insecure. Even Joe Montana, the greatest quarterback of all time, fights through his own bouts of insecurity. He has performed such mythological feats throughout his college and pro career, he is afraid he won't be able to live up to his past. Sometimes it makes me feel better to know Joe Montana is mortal.

I can count the number of times that I've actually felt fear in my face during a game—but maybe that's all I am capable of admitting. In a playoff game after the 1985 season, I experienced fear while looking into the mirror in the locker room right before kickoff. The pinkie on my left hand had been crushed the week before, and I knew I would have to tackle with one hand. I had never done that before. I couldn't stop wondering, What if I can't tackle? What if I can't get the job done? Another fearful moment occurred during our two playoff games in January 1991. I had sprained my knees against the New York Giants on December 3 and was afraid that in crucial passing situations against the Washington Redskins and the Giants my knees wouldn't provide me with the speed I needed in coverage. I also feared that a direct blow to the left knee, the more damaged of the two, would result in torn ligaments.

When I am truly honest with myself, I can admit that the older I've gotten, the more I've sensed and explored my fears. That's because in the twilight of my career, I've already seen so many brutal hits and breathtaking injuries that I have to work harder to keep them out of my mind. I've noticed fear creeping into my thoughts in the locker room and on the field, where it wouldn't have when I was younger, idealistic, and invincible. At times during the 1990 season I noticed myself daydreaming, thinking, "Am I losing it?" I became very nervous before games in 1990, something that hadn't happened to me before. I had self-doubts, questioning whether I could still accomplish great feats. It's frustrating to see a play develop and know that five years ago I could have made the tackle, that I would have been two steps closer. That's when it gets scary. And now at the end of my career I find myself worrying about the future. God, I haven't gotten that serious injury yet. When will that strike me down?

My mom has a favorite saying: "The older you get, the dumber you get." As a defensive player, my job is to react instinctively. I can't afford to think too much because, in that split second of overanalysis, I could get badly burned by a receiver, or suffer an injury. A lot of players who have had the reputation of being hard hitters became tentative in their old age—we know it's going to hurt and we have a lot more to risk personally and financially—but I'm going to try not to let that happen to me. I won't fall into the category where the spirit is willing but the flesh is weaker.

In the spring of 1990, I decided to explore the different degrees of fear and expand the depth of my courage. I've always believed that certain people not only want to experience fear and thrive on it, but they have the ability to withstand it. But where does that trait come from? Is it learned? Or is it inborn? I figured one of the best ways to find out was by flying with the Blue Angels, some of the best pilots in the Navy and Marine Corps. People have always said I had the right stuff on the field, so what better way to test that than by being in the company of the men for whom the phrase was coined?

I was invited to ride in the back seat of a F/A-18 jet going 700 mph in a practice drill at the Naval Air Facility in El Centro, California. I was never so afraid in my life. There I was, 7,000 feet in the air, telling myself the same words I do on the football field.

"You can handle it, Ronnie. You can take it."

I pictured the moments of my greatest mental toughness.

"You'll survive this, Ronnie," the voice tried to reassure me.

But I couldn't fool myself. The fear the Blue Angels must conquer is so much greater than any I've ever had to face. There are no little mistakes in aviation. In football I can get hurt but I never stare death in the face.

"You can't hyperventilate," I repeated as I walked out to the jet in my blue flight suit and helmet. "You can't hyperventilate. You can't throw up. You can't throw up. You *can't* throw up!"

Am I tough or what?!

Lt. John Foley, my pilot in the Blue Angel number 7 jet, started our journey into the wild blue yonder with a high-performance climb. Holding the jet at the beginning of the runway, Foley ran the engine to full power and then released the brakes. The force drove me back in my seat. He plugged in the afterburners—32,000 pounds of thrust, which buried me even further—put up the flaps, pulled back the stick, and we climbed at forty-five degrees, although it seemed a lot steeper.

We spent most of the next forty-five minutes at 7,000 feet doing the Blue Angels' version of show-and-tell. Foley began with gentle maneuvers. First some barrel rolls. Then wing overs, in which the jet tips to ninety degrees and travels on the edge of its wing, and then tips upright. I felt as if we were floating. Next he performed vertical loops. He aimed the nose up, and we tumbled backward. The maneuver looks graceful from the ground, but my body responded as if I had been hit by several offensive linemen. The muscles in my face tightened, and the blood began to rush from my head down into my extremities. My vision became cloudy, and I felt as if I were looking into a long gray tunnel. I was experiencing a G-force of four, meaning that with the force of gravity in this maneuver my body was four times heavier than it was on the ground, or close to 800 pounds. To counter the G-forces and keep me from passing out, Foley instructed me to scream "Hook! Hook! Hook!" from the moment we entered the maneuver until we had finished it. He also told me to squeeze my stomach and thigh muscles to push the blood back into my head.

"Hook! Hook! Hook!" I yelled.

Then Foley gave me the sensation of negative G-forces. He flipped the plane over, and we flew upside down at negative one G. Held snugly into the cockpit by eleven straps attached to my ankles, thighs, crotch, lap, chest, and shoulders, I felt as if my insides were about to explode through my skin and splatter on the glass canopy that covered the cockpit.

It's much easier to get a feel for speed in a Blue Angel jet than in a commercial airliner because flying at lower altitudes allows you to pick out points of reference. Nevertheless, I still found this flight somewhat disorienting. Because the McDonnell Douglas Hornet jet has such excellent maneuverability, my body was being pushed and shoved in different directions faster than my ears and eyes could register. My sense of balance told me my body was in a certain position, but my eyes didn't see it that way. I simply didn't know which end was up. To combat against air sickness, Foley kept the air conditioner in the back seat on full blast. Well, I didn't have the nerve to tell him that I needed to suck up every oxygen molecule I could find. Instead of yelling Hook! there were so many times that I wanted to just plain scream!!!!!!!!

As we flew through the Imperial Valley, weaving in and out of the Chocolate Mountains, my moods fluctuated between exhilaration and terror. Foley, thirty, a defensive back at the United States Naval Academy from 1978 to '82, seemed relaxed and in ecstasy. He loved flying. He served aboard the USS *Enterprise* in the West Pacific, Mediterranean, and Persian Gulf from 1986 to

'88. He was in Libya in 1986 and flew combat missions in 1988 during a Persian Gulf crisis. Clearly, Foley had the right stuff.

And so did the rest of the Blue Angels team. Every January, they endure a grueling three-month training camp in the desert at El Centro. They practice maneuvers twice a day, six days a week, and work out at the gym for two hours of intensive weight training, concentrating on the upper torso, in a program designed to increase their tolerance to G-forces. The Blue Angels' air demonstrations are so physically and mentally demanding that Foley has lost more than five pounds during a forty-five-minute flight.

It wasn't until we were headed back to the base that I felt a little embarrassed about only pulling four Gs. Would my guilt override my terror? Former Los Angeles Ram defensive tackle Merlin Olsen, who was a member of the Rams' defensive line known as the Fearsome Foursome, had taken a ride with Foley right ahead of me. And wouldn't you know it? Olsen managed to survive more than seven Gs.

"How many Gs did Merlin really pull?" I asked Foley.

"Seven point two," he replied.

I gulped. "Shit. I'll never hear the end of it. I can't let a Ram beat a 49er in anything."

"I can take care of that, Ronnie," Foley said. "Hold on!"

I had no idea what Foley had in mind but I figured I had to at least be as daring as Olsen, even if it was going to scare the hell out of me. Foley proceeded to simulate an aircraft carrier landing right there in the Imperial Valley. I held on for dear life and shouted "Hook!" He rolled the jet ninety degrees, then pulled the stick back to "spike" the jet, which gave us an instant heavy G-force. He threw the stick over and the plane turned as hard as it could, and we roared onto the runway at the Naval Air Facility in El Centro on a 360-degree turn.

"How did we do?" I asked as my body quivered.

"Seven point two!" Foley answered.

When I stepped out of the jet, I realized I had perspired so heavily that I was drenched from the tip of my butt all the way to the back of my neck. I couldn't speak. My heart flapped against my chest and my blood pumped madly through my veins. I had a tight butthole. I felt as if my body had undergone a chemical change. After such a physical and emotional ordeal, I told Foley that I couldn't have played football later that day. It took me a couple of hours just to get my legs back and quit perspiring.

The flight was a great revelation. I had pushed my body and mind farther than ever before, and I learned that I hadn't yet reached the outer limits of my courage. Football hadn't made me tough. There were other arenas to conquer.

My long list of pregame superstitions and rituals help me channel fear, eliminate doubt, and move me to the perfect focus. Most of the time, I don't even think about my rituals. I just do them. They add up to one singular purpose: to get me inside my tunnel; to take my mind to another level. Some of the rituals I followed throughout my 49er career were childish. Others were ridiculous. For instance, parking my car at the San Francisco International Airport to catch the team plane for road trips, I made sure to take the same spot in the ramp that I had for the preceding road trip, provided we won that game. If I couldn't get the exact space, I parked as close to it as possible. (In the off season, I actually caught myself doing this, too.)

I started putting on my game face the afternoon before our game, kicking back in my den and watching some college football. Seldom did I make personal appearances on Saturday afternoons. I thought it was better to stay off my feet, give my legs a rest. Occasionally I left the house for a chiropractic adjustment or to eat some lucky meals. A few years ago I had to have fried catfish for lunch on Saturdays, and then for dinner I loaded up on two hamburgers, french fries, and a vanilla shake at McDonald's.

For home games, we were required to check into the Marriott Hotel at the airport by 7 P.M. After meetings, we had a few hours to ourselves, and that's when Fred Tedeschi, our assistant trainer, treated me with a microcurrent machine that sent tiny electrical impulses through my muscles. He did it periodically from 1988 to '90, and we won every game after his microcurrent treatment, except for a 1989 loss to the Green Bay Packers. My bedtime snack was a bowl of vanilla ice cream with chocolate syrup and coconut flakes. Not the powdered stuff. Real coconut flakes. Why? Who knew. It just made me feel good. I had eaten it before a game seven or eight years ago, and we won—so I continued to do it. Bill Walsh always wanted us to eat our snack as a team and that didn't sit well with me. I wanted to be alone. I stayed for a little bit, and then walked out and returned to my room. I felt more comfortable there. That was my routine. That was my way of finding myself.

(Speaking of bedtime, you know the old wives' tale that boxers will be meaner and nastier if they abstain from sex for several weeks prior to their big bout? Well, that's true of hard hitters, too. The day and night before games, nothing—and nobody—messed with my focus. Anything that took my mind off the game was forbidden. I will tell you that I slept in the same pair of gray gym shorts. But if you were hoping for a chapter on sex before games, forget it. The subject could be covered in two words: No Way.)

On game day, I got up at seven o'clock to shower and ate a light breakfast of hot oatmeal or fruit and a croissant. I liked to be at Candlestick Park by 9 A.M., so I never took the team bus from the hotel that left about an hour later. For road games, I caught a cab. The size of the game determined my passenger list. Whenever I rode to games with Montana, we never lost, so when I needed a sure bet I corralled Joe in the hotel lobby. In 1989, for instance, when we were going for back-to-back world championships, I made sure we rode together the last three games—the two playoffs and Super Bowl XXIV.

I always listened to the same music during every ride. James Brown. Michael Jackson. M. C. Hammer. L. L. Cool J. And the volume had to be turned way up. LOUD. When Montana rode with me, though, I kept the noise level down. No need to get Joe too revved up.

I was just as fanatical about my equipment. I had to have tight-fitting pants. When the 49ers changed uniforms a few years ago, I refused to turn in my pants because they were made of a nice, heavy material. If you looked closely, my pants were a duller shade of gold than those of my teammates. Tedeschi always taped me, and Tommy Hart, a former 49er All-Pro defensive end who was a defensive assistant, helped me put on my jersey. My socks had to be perfect. During the preseason, my mission was to find the perfect pair. The equipment guys brought in big bags of socks, and I tried on a zillion until I found several pair that felt comfortable. I wrote my number 42 on them with a black magic marker, and I tried not to lose them. If the socks disappeared on game day, you would find me frantically digging through the sock bag to find the right ones. Each game, I wore two pair of socks pulled up tight to my knees. They couldn't hang, and I didn't like too many red stripes showing. The tighter they were the faster I felt.

For some games, I wore old shoes. For others, I used a brand-new pair from right out of the box. It depended which ones made my toes feel good. I had this weird reaction on game day. My toes numbed up right before kickoff. I experimented with different kinds of shoes, but nothing changed the numbness. (Maybe it was just nerves.) I finally decided to wear the most comfortable pair even if the shoes looked as though I had walked thousands of miles in them.

Forty-five minutes before kickoff, I walked up the steps in the dugout at Candlestick Park, with the last handful of 49ers, to take the field for warm-ups. I ran along the sideline to the opposite end zone, touched the pylon in the back corner, and proceeded to stretch out by myself. A few minutes later assistant coach Ray Rhodes rallied the defensive backs, and I waited until everyone gathered around him before running over. I liked to be the last in the circle. Then we ran through our defensive secondary drills, and I led the pack.

We backpedaled on the 50-yard line, first straight back and then with quick cuts to the left and right. Next, we doubled up, one defensive back playing the role of a receiver, and worked on batting down passes. Then it was onto George Seifert's infamous tackling drill. The defensive backs dreaded it. Seifert created the drill in my rookie year, when we were forcing turnovers in bunches. It's something you would do in junior high school, and if you're not ready to tackle, it's an easy way to get hurt. One defensive back held the ball on his hip, while another ran toward him, slamming his helmet into the ball, knocking it into the air, and tackling the guy at the same time. Guys fell on their wrists, and they got major bruises all over the place. We fought with one another. I'll admit, though, this drill did get my intensity up. At this point I began speaking to myself:

Got to play 110 percent.
No mistakes.
Got to be 110 percent.
No mistakes.
Got to give it up.
Got to give it up.
Got to leave something on the field.
Got to leave something on the field.

We then shifted to the far end zone for drills, matching the offense against the defense. From time to time I took a break, walked to the 40-yard line, and stretched. I peeked at the plays the opposing offense was running. I studied the flight of the quarterback's passes. Did he have any zip on the ball? How long did it hang in the air? I checked out the demeanor of the quarterback and receivers. How were they feeling? Was there bounce in their stride? Did they seem frustrated? I clicked through a checklist of reminders of how their offense would play me and what I had to be ready for. For example, while watching the Los Angeles Rams warm up, I pumped myself up for trick plays:

Nickel-and dime-team.

Look out for tricks.

I know they're coming.

Got to be ready.

Got to tackle.

Got to play hard.

Going to be a tough game.

They think they can get to you.

Got to bring something to the table, bring it from deep down inside.

If you don't bring it to the table, Ronnie, you're not going to be fed.

This is the stage when my adrenaline began to rise. If somebody pinched me right then, I wouldn't know it. My focus was very intense. My Bobo Scowl so deep. My words hypnotic. There were pregame warm-ups where I got myself too intense, and I hyperventilated. I never worked my nerves into a state of nausea, though. I was once so high before kickoff, however, that I asked one of the 49er trainers for some muscle relaxers to calm me down. He gave them to me, and I played wonderfully.

After warm-ups, when I got back to our locker room I went straight to the bathroom and threw cold water on my face. The 49er coaches and players gathered in the center of the locker room and recited the Lord's Prayer. Afterward, if I didn't feel the team was in the right mood, I then launched into one of my emotional pep talks. As I walked through the tunnel to the field at Candlestick Park, my mind started to roll:

Got to be 110 percent. No mistakes. Got to tackle. Got to play hard.

Then, I heard the ring announcer at Caesars Palace in Las Vegas starting the heavyweight championship bout. "Gentlemen," he said, "it's time to rumble." And a bell rang in the back of my head.

COPING WITH PAIN AND INJURY

The collision occurred about 10 yards in front of me on October 22, 1989. The horrifying crack of helmet on helmet sounded like two large cement blocks banging together. Jeff Fuller, who was fill-ing in for me at free safety, had slammed head-first into John Stephens, a running back for the New England Patriots. Fuller's neck snapped from right to left. He and Stephens crumpled to the ground.

At the moment of total impact, I could feel myself beginning to twitch. Eric Wright, who was standing next to me on the sideline, asked me if I thought Fuller would be okay.

"No, E., I don't think he'll be all right on this one," I replied.

Neither Fuller nor Stephens moved.

"Get up, Jeff," I said. "Get up."

Something was very wrong.

Cornerback Darryl Pollard fell to one knee, closed his eyes and prayed: "Lord, give him the strength. Let him get up and walk." Pollard crossed himself and walked back to the huddle. Fullback Tom Rathman wondered if prayers were the answer. Before every game, he asked the Lord to help everybody survive without serious injury.

It was difficult for me to understand God's will, His ways, and His plans at that moment. Five days before—October 17 at 5:04 P.M.—the Bay area had been devastated by an earthquake. The game had been moved 30 miles away to Stanford Stadium in Palo Alto for safety reasons because Candlestick Park was still being checked by city engineers to see if it was structurally sound. Collection booths for food, clothing, blankets, and cash donations were set up outside Stanford Stadium. There was a moment of silence for the earthquake victims before the kickoff. Our game was supposed to have been a much-needed diversion from the tragedy around us. But two plays after the opening kickoff, reality struck again with Fuller's collision. Why was He doing this?

Stephens got up. I prayed that Fuller would get up, too, but he didn't move at all. Why wasn't he moving? What was wrong? I was in a state of shock. Though we weren't close friends, we were close as teammates, having practiced together every day since 1984. I always felt Fuller could be an All-Pro safety.

Our orthopedic surgeon, Michael Dillingham, pried Fuller's tongue from deep inside his throat. Soon the rest of the team's medical staff gathered next to Fuller, until twelve people in civilian clothes formed a ring around him on the Patriots' 28-yard line. Fuller was hooked up to a small oxygen tank. Gradually, Fuller moved his legs and bent his knees. Dr. Dillingham motioned for a stretcher.

At the edge of every NFL field there's an ambulance. I notice it when I walk out of the locker room on game day. At no other major sporting event except auto racing are the fans and participants as conscious of seeing an ambulance. You won't find one parked in the outfield or underneath a backboard. Still, I never walk by and wonder, "So, are these guys going to work today?"

The paramedics carefully lifted Fuller onto the stretcher and wheeled him to the ambulance. George Seifert, who looked as if he were in a trance, walked over to the vehicle and waited with Fuller for several minutes until the ambulance left for the hospital. When Dr. James Klint returned to the sideline, I asked him about Fuller's condition. "He's not in great shape," Dr. Klint said.

The risk we take on the football field is far greater than we'll ever admit. Injuries are something we take for granted, something we lose touch with. I remember the times my teammates Keena Turner and Mike Wilson suffered neck injuries and lay on the field partially paralyzed. It scared me to death. I'll never forget the look in their eyes. At their point of total impact, I said, "That's it. He's gone. He's out." I was referring to a concussion, not paralysis. We keep the thought of paralysis locked in the dungeons of our soul.

After the Patriots game, Dillingham gathered the team in the locker room to explain Fuller's condition and prognosis. Fuller had severed nerves on the right side of his neck. We were told he might never regain full use of his right arm. Seifert could barely speak about Fuller to reporters. Jesse Sapolu, one of our strongest offensive linemen, cried in front of his locker. "I was just thinking about what was important and what's not," Sapolu told the media. "The public puts our occupation on a high pedestal. Sometimes we all forget the most important thing is people's lives."

Wright, Turner, and I went directly to the intensive care unit at Stanford Hospital. The 49er doctors wouldn't allow us to see Fuller for at least an hour. When they finally escorted us to his room, Fuller was immobilized. He was heavily sedated but conscious enough to speak. His neck was so swollen on the right side that it looked as if it were on his shoulder. Fuller said he was partially paralyzed.

"I'm in a lot of pain," he said softly.

Fuller described the sensation of paralysis in two ways. As a jolt of electricity traveling through his body and as a constant tingling, as if he had hit his funny bone. The doctors asked us not to stay longer than five minutes, but I had a hard time leaving Fuller alone in his room. There wasn't much I could say, except that we loved him and were praying for him. I knew by looking in his face that my eyes weren't hiding my concern, fear, and hurt. God, I felt so helpless and frightened. In my mind I kept saying, "This guy was one of the strongest, most gifted athletes I've ever known. How could something like this have happened?"

As I drove home that night, I didn't think about the game. I had forgotten that we had beaten the Patriots, 37–20, and taken a one-game lead in the NFC West division. I just kept praying that Fuller would be okay.

For me, being in pain and coping with injuries is the loneliest part of professional football. Pain is personal. I've conditioned myself not to need anybody to help me cope with it. Wives, mothers, and female friends can comfort players, but that's all. My father and my male non-football-playing friends try to be compassionate, but they can't experience the depth of my pain. My attorney, for example, once sprained his ankle and had to have it placed in a cast. I've had to play football games with ankles in worse shape. Game after game after game.

Injuries are isolating and embarrassing. In the blink of an eye, a player is transformed from a strong, vital, functioning member of the team to a scared, crippled outsider. It's funny—and chilling—how coaches, players, even front office officials do their best to tune you out, avoid you in the halls, discount your presence. They don't want to look reality in the face or recognize their own demise.

A friend of mine, John Frank, played tight end for the 49ers from 1984 to '88. One of the most tenacious blockers and gutsiest players the team ever had, Frank retired from football prior to the 1989 season at age twenty-seven. He walked away from a bright NFL career and an annual salary of $357,500 to attend Ohio State University Medical School. Upon retirement, he said he could no longer desensitize himself from pain and injury. In the end, he found the macho football mentality inhumane.

"If someone dislocates his shoulder on the practice field, the coaches just move the drill," Frank explained after he retired. "If your good friend goes down, you can't go over, pat him on the head, and hand him a cup of water."

Football players learn at a young age to get accustomed to their own physical pain, to bring themselves to the point of not noticing it, separating it from their body. I like to use the analogy of pounding your hand into a brick wall. After awhile, the hand's going to get accustomed to it. It will scar and calluses will form. Your mind will become conditioned to the brutality. At some point you'll be able to say, "I can do this." Dealing with my own pain, I believe, is like dealing with life in solitary confinement. Eventually your mind shuts off to certain hurts and emotions. However, you still routinely have to recondition yourself.

The past few summers in training camp I've subjected myself to a psychological drill developed by Bob Zeman, the 49er linebackers coach. I beat the inside of my forearms around a large leather tackling bag. I beat the bag until my arms became numb and bruised. The other 49er defensive backs called this an act of masochism. I am sure safety Dave Waymer, with eleven years in the NFL, still wonders about the drill. But I think conditioning my body to pain goes with my job. As a defensive back, my arms and hands endure most of the contact, so this exercise got me used to hitting. At the beginning of training camp, my arms stung, but by the end, I could beat them against the bag over and over and almost not feel it. The sensation was like this: if I slapped somebody in the face ten times, the first slap would sting, the next two or three would hurt a little bit, and the last few would be barely noticeable. That's the conditioning I want to subject my body to.

There's a mental process involved in blocking out pain. I believe that if I admit it, it will kill me. I find something to identify with like wounded soldiers who suffered for days, stranded deep in the jungle. They came home alive. I remind myself it could be worse.

Lindsy McLean, the 49er trainer, had a knack for knowing exactly when I was badly hurt. On the sideline he would ask me how I was and I would just stare straight ahead. I refused to look at him. I said two words—I'm okay—and that was it. Hey, but that was more than I told my 49er teammates. I hid my injuries from the 49er defensive players. If I admitted to being hurt, I felt I would relive the experience and reinforce the pain.

Engaged in action during a game I'm lucky, in a sense, because my body will help me deal with pain. My neurological system works on overdrive, secreting hormones to enable my body not only to repair itself but to speed up the healing process. I'm in a survival mode that I call fight or flight. It's my theory that injuries sustained in the early stages of the game hurt more than those that happen after halftime. In the first quarter, there's not as much adrenaline flowing through the blood stream. This fight or flight survival instinct allowed me to forge on while in pain against the Green Bay Packers in 1986. Packer wide receiver Phillip Epps ran a slant pattern, and just as I went to hit him, Epps tripped and fell in front of me. I couldn't get my leg out of the way, and his helmet glanced my knee. The fibula, the smaller, non-weight-bearing bone in the leg, was broken, but I still played the last three and a half quarters. When the adrenaline stopped flowing—after the game—the pain became excruciating. Thank God for Tylenol with codeine.

Several years ago I played with a badly dislocated finger. It was typical Lott. No pain no gain.

"Pull it back!" I shouted at Tom Holmoe, a 49er safety.

He winced.

"Ronnie, go get the trainer to fix it," Holmoe said. "I don't want to have anything to do with it."

"No!" I pleaded. "Pull it back!"

And then I demanded that somebody else—anybody else—in the huddle put the finger back in its socket. Immediately! Someone finally did, but I was in too much pain to remember who helped me.

You know the old saying that most accidents happen in the home? Well, when I've sliced my finger working in the kitchen, I'm the first to shriek, "*Owwwww!* God. That really hurts!" Yet I can be deeply engrossed in a football game, get scratched on my hands or skin my elbows on the turf, and not know it until the blood shows up somewhere else. I can't count the number of times I've said, "Man, where's this blood coming from?" Again, that's the fight or flight mode.

Playing with pain is a big part of my game. It's the most important quality I want people to remember about me. I strive for mind over matter. Sometimes I have surreal experiences on the field. Part of my brain knows I'm hurt. The other knows I'm deficient. I don't slow down unless the play is away from me. If the play is coming toward me, rarely will you know I'm injured. To concentrate on blocking out the pain, and then to be able to concentrate on performing takes a unique individual because in the end it's easier to shut out pain than doubt. Doubt always taps you on the shoulder, leaving you a step behind. That's why I admire running back Roger Craig. He might have endured more pain than anybody else on the 49ers. His high-knee running style made it difficult to bring him down. Oftentimes he got hit in the chest and back by three or four defenders on each play. After a game Craig sometimes looked as if he had been whipped with a thick rope across his torso, with gashes, scratches, and gouges on the sides of his body.

My body carries a reminder of every major collision and injury that I've ever had. My left hamstring area looks like a relief map of the Rocky Mountains. Nubby, knotted, and full of divots. To the touch, it's real mushy. I tore it the first time in a preseason game against the Denver Broncos in 1988, chasing quarterback John Elway. When it happened, it felt like a big cramp that wouldn't release. There are now four or five golf-ball-sized lumps of muscle fiber scattered within my hamstring from subsequent tears. There was the time in 1984 my right shoulder looked as if it were attached to the front of my chest. I dislocated it out the front of the shoulder socket—a rare dislocation, according to the doctors—when I tackled Tampa Bay Buccaneer running back James Wilder. Because I had stretched the nerves in the area, I felt tingling in my wrist and hand. For four months I had little strength on my right side, though I kept right on playing, and it took almost a year until I was back to normal. Instinctively, I began tackling with my other shoulder—I wasn't cognizant of that until I saw myself on game films—and it is something I continue to do today.

The first time it really occurred to me that playing in pain was a part of professional sports came while watching center Willis Reed lead the New York Knicks to the NBA Championship in 1969–70. I was only eleven. That season he was named the Most Valuable Player in the regular season, the playoffs, and in the All-Star game. What really caught my attention was how Reed played with a painful hip injury in the seventh game of the championship series against the Los Angeles Lakers, limping down the floor and boxing out Wilt Chamberlain, trying to keep the Dipper away from the basket.

A few off seasons ago, Lawrence Taylor and I were having a conversation about all the new, young players the media referred to as "the next Lawrence Taylor" or "the next Ronnie Lott." And L.T. said, "Those guys don't understand what it is to play hurt. They can't be like us if they don't play hurt." Forty-niner linebacker Charles Haley always asked me "Ronnie, where are all the raw dogs?" That's how Haley characterized players who weren't afraid to make sacrifices for the game. The tough, the hungry, and the fearless. Very few players entering the NFL these days say, "I'm ready to throw my body around and knock the shit out of anybody." Instead, the new puppies are thinking, "I'll knock the shit out of anybody—as soon as I get my next paycheck. I've got to be careful." Why are there no more raw dogs? Because players are making too much money. There's too much to lose.

In many ways, I can better block out my own pain than that of others. My first instinct is to walk over to an injured player. I can feel the agony of a man sprawled on the field. I want to be the first player at his side to comfort him. I sprinted over to the spot where linebacker Mike Walter lay motionless after making a tackle with his head on a Green Bay Packer running back in 1990. It was an inspiring, hellacious hit, but it made me nervous and scared. Walter couldn't move his right arm. He told me later that the pain felt as if someone were running a blowtorch up and down his back and neck.

Walter had just returned from four weeks on injured reserve.

"I'm sorry," Walter apologized. "I'm letting you guys down. I didn't mean to do this to you."

Often the thoughts that go through a player's mind at the time of injury have little to do with pain, so Walter wasn't saying anything out of the ordinary. I've spoken to badly injured players whose first words were "Did I stop the play?" or "Did I make the tackle?" It relieves the tension and—believe it or not—makes everybody laugh a little.

Few players feel the urge to tend to their injured teammates. Coaches shy away even more. John Robinson of the Los Angeles Rams is one of the few NFL coaches who always tends to his players on the field when they go down. That's impressive, the way it should always be, the humane approach to football.

Teammates don't talk about their injuries or share their pain. Forget intimacy. Talking about pain makes you seem vulnerable. Players don't discuss pain of any kind—physical or emotional—because vulnerability doesn't breed winning. The

Catch-22 in this approach is that it's hard to describe your pain to others anyway. Each person has his own threshold of pain that is drawn from his unique personal experiences. Even two raw dogs don't comprehend pain in the same way. One night in 1990, Jennie Winter came to my house to give both Haley and me massage treatments. After she finished with Haley, he slowly lifted himself to his feet. Agony was written all over his face.

"Ronnie, does she hurt you like that?" Haley asked, grimacing.

"No, man," I replied matter-of-factly. "It feels good."

Winter laughed.

"Haley," she said, "Ronnie just takes it better."

LEAVING SOMETHING BEHIND

I can hear Dr. Vincent Pellegrini's words as though it were yesterday: "Why don't we amputate? You'll still have all the joints in your finger. You'll still be able to function on the football field. The feeling at the tip will be close to normal. But you'll be able to use it normally. You'll be able to grab jerseys. Ronnie, it's just the tip of your little finger."

Just the tip? Yeah, only one centimeter. In medical terminology, it was a fracture fragment. Ronnie, let's excise your fracture fragment. The word "amputate" scared the hell out of me. It smacked me between the eyes.

But I'm getting ahead of myself. Let me start from the beginning.

I left the tip of my left pinkie somewhere near the 30-yard line at Candlestick Park on December 22, 1985. We were playing the Dallas Cowboys, historically a tough opponent for the 49ers, and with a 31–16 victory we earned a wild-card berth in the playoffs.

Late in the fourth quarter, running back Timmy Newsome was charging my way under a full head of steam. He was a powerful runner I always found difficult to tackle. This time I planted myself in front of him and squared up on his chest. If he ran me over I could always grab his jersey and horsecollar him to the ground. As I extended my arms to grab him, somehow I caught my left hand in front of my chest, and before I could set it free, Newsome's helmet barreled into it. The nail caught on an edge of the helmet and ripped off, pulling a chunk of skin from the top half of the finger with it. My chest acted like an anvil upon impact, and my pinkie splattered onto my jersey. All I saw was blood and a mashed finger.

The finger was throbbing. As we huddled before the next play, I couldn't focus on anything but the excruciating pain. I held my hand and rocked back and forth, hoping to push the pain out of my system. Blood oozed through my hands and dripped onto my pants.

"Are you okay?" strong safety Carlton Williamson asked.

I didn't answer.

"Ronnie?"

Still no response.

"Get out of the game, Ronnie!"

"I'm all right," I mumbled. "I'm all right."

I tore off my helmet and raced to the sideline. For the first time, I looked down at my pinkie and discovered that most of the nail was destroyed. The tip was kind of hanging there, flopping over. Oh, shit. Oh, shit. Oh, shit.

Although the pain was intense, it wasn't the most important thing on my mind at that moment. I was concerned about being ready for our playoff game against the New York Giants the following Sunday. I ordered the trainers to wrap the finger, but after taking one look at my hand, our team doctors suggested going to a nearby hospital to get the finger sewn up and X-rayed for broken bones.

In the locker room, the trainers wrapped gauze around the pinkie to reduce the bleeding. They were careful not to touch the mangled skin in case any part of the tip could be saved. The trainers slipped a plastic bag over my hand. I showered and dressed. My attorney, Leonard Armato, drove me to the hospital. Later I was told a chunk of my skin had stuck to the facemask of my helmet.

That night, while waiting in the emergency room, I just wanted to grab some sushi, drown myself in sake, pop a couple of Tylenols with codeine, and climb into bed. Three cortisone shots were needed to completely numb the finger, and with each poke of the syringe I bit the bullet, pretending I was Clint Eastwood. You know, bite some wood, suck it up. That's how the tough guys in the movies always do it.

Somehow, I slept for a few hours, but when I woke up on

Monday morning the pain was so brutal that I wanted to chop my hand off at the wrist. Dr. Pellegrini, a hand specialist at Stanford Hospital, told me I had lost a piece of bone on the front of my pinkie. The tip of the bone was still there, as was the other end that connected at the joint. Missing was a minuscule piece in between. The nail bed—the area at the bottom of the nail—had been gouged out. I was encouraged when Dr. Pellegrini told me I had a chance to play against the Giants if I wore a protective brace over the finger. That was great news.

Dr. Pellegrini numbed my hand with Novocaine between the pinkie and ring finger, opened up the gash, cleaned it out, removed the nail, and sewed the bloody red mess back together. Then he placed it in a splint. Dr. Pellegrini mentioned that I might need more surgery after the season, but that comment floated in one ear and out the other. I was already so focused on the Giants that I couldn't think beyond Sunday.

The trainers concocted a special protective device made from moldable thermal plastic, which fit over my outer two fingers. Before the Giants game, the pinkie was numbed with a cortisone shot. One part of my brain had to block out the pain, and another part had to concentrate even more because of the injury. In the warm-ups, I was able to catch the ball, and the hand didn't feel too bad.

Early in the third quarter, my mind shifted from blocking out pain to a zone that I'd never been in before or since. Attempting a routine tackle on running back Joe Morris, my mind told me not to wrap him with my left arm or hand. Morris ran right through me for a portion of his game-high 141 yards. It was the only time in my career that I wasn't able to conquer mind over matter. The Giants beat us 17–3, and the season was over.

The next three months were the most frustrating, depressing and soul-searching of my life. In the beginning, Dr. Pellegrini would remove the dressing every couple of weeks while we waited for the skin to heal. As soon as that had occurred, he would X-ray the pinkie periodically to check on how well the fractured bone was mending. Every time Dr. Pellegrini read the X-rays, my heart sank. The pinkie refused to heal. The bone at the tip of the finger and the bone at the first joint would not fuse in the area of the nail bed. The tip was also very painful, which Dr. Pellegrini said was unusual. Whenever I bumped it, pain shot through my hand. He figured two nerves might be pinched between the two bones that wouldn't heal. Clearly, I couldn't play football with my pinkie in this shape.

In May I asked the doctor what the next step might be, and he gave me the bad news.

"We can take some bone from your wrist, graft it to your finger, and put a pin in there," he explained. "You'll have the length of your finger, but you'll never have the front of your nail. However, if the finger gets hit, you could break it again. If we do it this way, the finger might not heal until late June—if it heals at all.

Then Dr. Pellegrini looked me squarely in the eyes and said, "Ronnie, we can also shorten the finger—amputate to where it's broken—and remove the fracture fragment."

Amputate?

"If it were my hand—even as a surgeon—that's what I would do," Pellegrini said. "The only difference is cosmetic."

I deliberated for a few days, asking only my father for advice. As a career Air Force man, he gave me the old military spiel. He told me about soldiers in combat who had lost ears, eyes, toes, and limbs. No matter how minor my amputation seemed, my father said, I'd go into shock, I'd never be very comfortable with my hand, and I'd wish I'd never done it. I got so tired of looking at my ugly pinkie that I was embarrassed to show my hand in public. I was so self-conscious that I had a friend make a fake nail to paste over the finger the night I went to the Bay Area Music Awards. My decision seemed so cut-and-dried. Practically speaking, amputation was the only way I could be sure of playing in the 1986 season, and every season after that, without the finger bothering me.

The morning of the surgery, I drove by myself to Stanford Hospital. My mother had asked if I wanted her to come up from Rialto, but I said no. She's too emotional. She gets nauseous just watching me play football. I suspected her stomach became queasy with my decision, and I didn't want to worry about her further agonizing in the waiting room. As I was wheeled into surgery, I tried to psyche myself up as if I were getting ready to play a game. I kept on repeating, "This is going to be great. This is going to be great."

I was given a local anesthetic to numb my hand and Valium to sedate me. I was able to talk to Dr. Pellegrini and the nurses throughout the hour-long procedure. I don't remember much else other than one time blurting out, "How am I doing?" The answer came back, "Everything's great, Ronnie."

Later that day, after the numbness and sedative wore off, I returned to my condominium in Santa Clara with my hand in a big cast that stayed on for two weeks. After a few days the pain became unbearable. It was a terrible stinging sensation, as if somebody had placed a million pins in my hand. It seemed an eternity before the pain fully subsided. When it did, I began moving my hand gently in the cast and squeezing my fingers several times a day so as not to lose my dexterity. I became more and more optimistic.

The moment of truth came in early June, the day the cast came off. Arriving at the doctor's office that morning, I had great expectations, figuring the finger would be as good as new.

"Are you ready, Ronnie?" Dr. Pellegrini asked. "Would you like to see it?"

"Yeah. Let me see it!" I said filled with excitement and optimism.

He unwrapped the bandages and smiled. "It looks great," he said.

"Have a look."

I did. I couldn't believe my eyes. The pinkie didn't seem real. It didn't look like a finger. "Oh my God," I said. "Oh my God." The pinkie resembled a carpenter's lead nail. It seemed as if somebody had taken the air out of the tip and flattened it with a hammer. The skin was folded over and held together by black thread. And if all that weren't weird enough, I was experiencing phantom pains. I was convinced I could feel the part of the pinkie that had been amputated. I could feel my fingernail. I felt as if I were going to pass out.

"Are you all right?" Dr. Pellegrini asked putting his hand on my shoulder.

"Yeah," I responded, feeling a bit strange.

"It looks great," he said sincerely.

"Sure."

But I was lying. I was devastated. Shocked. Confused. Sick to my stomach. A million different emotions rushed through my mind. The examining room started to spin. I felt so dizzy. I was terrified and close to tears. Dr. Pellegrini helped me out of the chair and made me lie down on the examining table.

"I can't believe what this game is doing to me," I said, shaking my head. "My God. It's starting to eat away at parts of my body."

The doctor tried to comfort me. "It's perfectly normal to react this way," Pellegrini said. "But Ronnie, it's going to be all right."

How could I be sure of that? The look in Pellegrini's eyes told me he was surprised by my reaction. I'm sure he figured that away from the football field I was the same brute who could bang his head against three other guys and think nothing of it.

When I got home, all I could think about was nine and two-thirds fingers. Now I only had nine and two-thirds fingers. I stared at my left hand. I held my pinkies side by side. The left was obviously shorter. It just blew me away.

Over and over I kept asking myself, "What the hell have you done, Ronnie?" At first I wondered if I had gone too far for football, and as the hours wore on I worried that I'd gone too far for *myself*. Screw football. What had I done to myself?

For weeks I underwent hand therapy, strengthening the finger by gripping balls of putty. But away from therapy sessions I wouldn't use the finger. Then one day a pair of scissors started to slide into a desk drawer and I reached for them, with the left pinkie slipping through one of the loops. I held the scissors in the air and said out loud, "God, I finally used it."

Accepting the sight of the pinkie took some time. In public, around strangers, friends, and family I hid my hand. Either I kept it under a table or made a fist on my lap. For the longest time I refused to wear my Super Bowl rings because I always felt people would look at the left pinkie and not the rings. Visiting my parents for the first time after the surgery, my dad didn't talk about the finger until I brought up the subject. At that point I said, "You know, Dad, I think maybe you were right. I think if I had to do it all over again I wouldn't."

His answer surprised me. "In anything in life there are only two decisions," he said. "Yes or no. You be strong and smart, and you make your choices and never look back."

The Bay area media sensationalized my surgery, turning me into a courageous person. From the tone of some of the stories, you would have thought I cut off my whole finger or my entire hand. Because they had read and heard so much about it, a couple of my teammates asked to see the pinkie. Kids came up to me in shopping malls and—without even saying hello first— said, "Hey, I heard you cut your finger off. Let me see it." At times I worried that people thought I was a freak, and that at any moment a story on my finger would appear in the *National Enquirer* next to tales of three-headed women and 300-pound babies. Not only was I convinced I was indeed a freak, but all the attention kept me feeling sorry for myself. It took a letter to the editor to one of the local newspapers to put my amputation into perspective for me. A woman wrote: "Why is Ronnie Lott feeling sorry for himself? Think of all the women who have had mastectomies." I felt bad. I had been too self-absorbed.

My closest friends on the 49ers—Keena Turner, Eric Wright, Joe Montana, and Charles Haley—never asked to see the pinkie. They never even discussed the decision to amputate. I'm confident they knew what an emotional experience it was and they probably couldn't have made the same choice.

I never intended to leave part of a pinkie on the field at Candlestick Park. All I strived for was to leave a part of my heart and soul. Maybe if I had scoured the field that Sunday afternoon in 1985 for my nail, skin, and that tiny piece of bone, the doctors could have reattached it and the fragment would not have required amputation. Maybe if I had been wearing gloves in games, as I do now, the pinkie wouldn't have been so badly damaged.

When I finally stopped the second-guessing and came to terms with my finger a year or so after surgery, I dubbed it my E.T. pinkie. I think it looks like E.T.'s head, all plump and puffy. *Ronnie Lott phone home.* But it took a lot of soul-searching to reach that frame of mind. That tip will always be more sensitive and tender than my other fingers. Some days, I swear, I still feel as if the finger is all there.

LEADERSHIP

The sheets of paper flew out of my hands so fast I resembled a Las Vegas blackjack dealer gone mad.

"Sit down! Take your seats! This meeting isn't over yet!" I yelled. "I want you to write down why you play football! Now! Do it now!"

The 49er defense had no idea what was happening. I stalked around the meeting room. My cheeks were red with anger. My heart pounded. My mind raced. It was the morning after our final preseason game in 1987, and we had just bungled our way through a 34–10 loss to the Seattle Seahawks. We had played worse than lousy, in a fitting end to a mediocre and uninspired preseason.

On the plane trip home from Seattle, I sat next to linebacker

Mike Walter, and we spent the better part of three hours discussing the sorry state of affairs and searching for a solution. I was pretty frustrated, and as we flew through the darkness Walter tried to ease my mind. "At least it's the preseason," he said.

At least it's the preseason? That weak excuse for a loss stuck in my head all night. Why would winning in the preseason be any different from winning during the season?

Now, blank pieces of paper were scattered across every desk in our defensive meeting room.

"Come on, come on," I hollered. "It shouldn't take you that long. The reason you play the game."

Most of my teammates were startled by my outburst. I caught a few of them rolling their eyes, as if to say, "Here we go again. Ronnie's on another one of his rampages." A couple of players seemed angry and irritated, resentful that I would pose such a question.

"Should we put our names on it?" a voice called out from the back of the room.

"Excuse me? You're afraid to put your name on it?" I asked. "I can't believe what I'm hearing." Could there be a coward among us?

Then, to make matters worse, I noticed several players folding their papers before passing them to the front of the room.

"What's this? You don't want other people to see your answers?" I asked, laughing. "Well, why don't I just go ahead and read them to you."

I opened up the slip of paper on top of the pile and printed were the words TO WIN.

"That's bullshit," I said. I crushed the paper into a little ball and pitched it across the room.

I went on to the next one. TO FEED MY FAMILY.

"That's bullshit," I said. I tore the response into little pieces and threw it in the air.

I tried another. BECAUSE I ENJOY THE COMPETITION.

I shook my head, took a deep breath, and counted to ten.

"Jeff Fuller!" I shrieked. "What should be the goal of this team?"

"To win," Fuller said.

"That's bullshit," I said. "TO GET RESPECT. RESPECT! That's the bottom line."

"Keena Turner!" I shouted. "What should be the goal of this team?"

"I'm sorry, Ronnie, I have to agree with Jeff," he said. "To win. I play football because I like to win championships."

I heard snickers throughout the room. Turner smiled. He felt as if he wanted to nudge me a little bit. That was okay. Maybe I was offending some of the players by acting like a tyrant. Maybe my tactic of passing out pieces of paper reminded them of an old schoolteacher they didn't like. But the 1987 regular season was upon us, and we needed to come together and turn our performances around. To get us on the right track, I had to cut straight to the heart, make people search their souls and question themselves. It was time for self-examination. How did my teammates want this season to go? For themselves and as a team.

"Look, you guys, I talked to Mike Walter last night, and he said it didn't matter that we lost to Seattle because it was only a preseason game," I said. "You guys are talking about making money and winning championships, but you're missing the point. The most gratifying aspect of pro football is *respect*.

"You go out there and play your hardest. Do that, and you'll get respect from your opponent. You'll stand back and say, 'Yeah, that's what it's all about.' At the end of your life, will people come to your funeral because you won Super Bowls? No! Will they come to your funeral because you made a lot of money? No! They will come to 'pay their respects.' They will come because they respected you as a person."

I joined the 49ers in late July of 1981 full of excitement and energy, and I achieved something most players never get a chance to do in their first NFL season. I was a No. 1 draft pick; I was voted to the Pro Bowl, and I played on a Super Bowl championship team. All in my rookie season. These achievements put me in the spotlight and helped vault me into a position of leadership.

For most of 1981, I observed and listened. The leaders on the 49ers were already in place. Charle Young, Archie Reese, Hacksaw Reynolds, and Fred Dean were all experienced, war-hardened veterans. They carried us physically with their play and mentally with their knowledge of the game, while motivating and inspiring a team consisting of misfits, losers, and wide-eyed rookies to a 26–21 victory over the Cincinnati Bengals in Super Bowl XVI.

Young, a 49er tight end from 1980 to '82, was the most inspirational man I ever played with. He had a marvelous command of the English language and spoke in resonant tones. His words rang with truth, wisdom, and strength. I was fascinated by the manner in which he talked to our team. He transformed players who had accepted losing into men who believed they could work miracles. He constantly put his neck on the chopping block in battles with management, and I sensed that there were many moments when he bit his tongue and saved the criticism for behind closed doors.

Young taught me that leaders sometimes have to make personal sacrifices for the betterment of the team. When those sacrifices are detrimental to the leader, then he either gives in to the higher-ups or leaves. When a leader succumbs, he's in a very compromising position. He compromises once, twice, three times . . . and if he continues to compromise he will lose his effectiveness. Whatever the outcome, he will realize that, in the end, being true to himself and his teammates is the most important part of his job as a team leader.

Being a leader on an NFL team isn't like being a leader at any other level of football. The NFL isn't a game. It's a cutthroat corporate business. Very few pro football players will ever stand up and speak their minds because they know it will eventually mean losing their jobs. Management and coaches don't like to be challenged. They like well-behaved soldiers.

I'm not afraid to be outspoken. I don't speak just to hear myself talk, and I have tried not to speak out of turn. Most players will carefully analyze their words before they let loose. They'll ask themselves, "How will this come off?" But I have never thought twice about what I want to say. I'll say it off the top of my head because I know it's straight from the heart. I never deceive anybody. I don't bullshit. I try to speak the truth. All I want to do is set the facts straight.

One of the messages in the movie *Dead Poets Society* is: Don't be afraid to speak out. That's not showing somebody up. It's giving them another perspective, letting them know what the other faction is thinking but can't verbalize. By being an outspoken team leader that's all I'm trying to do—show my coaches and teammates another side of how people think or feel. In my mind, that's not taking a chance. That's not taking a huge risk. That's saying something that people must hear. They might not want to hear it; often the truth hurts, but it needs to be said.

There were countless team meetings during my 49er career

when Bill Walsh or George Seifert, after their opening remarks, would say, "Okay, break up into your individual position meetings." I would jump to my feet and say, "Wait a minute. There's something we have to discuss. And I want the coaches to hear this, too." Then, I let loose.

I cussed people for not being motivated. I questioned their concentration, toughness, and heart. Sometimes I got so emotional that I blurted out my remarks haphazardly. I'm sure I sounded incoherent, bizarre, and blurry. But I figured that kept people on their toes wondering to themselves, What the hell is Ronnie trying to say?

My 49er rampages weren't confined to meeting rooms. The practice field was just as effective. In a minicamp practice session prior to the 1990 season, rookie running back Dexter Carter, the team's No. 1 draft choice, ran through the line, and I ran up and purposely yanked the ball from his hands.

"Hold on to the damn ball!" I scolded, walking back to the defensive huddle. "You'd better get your butt to work, Dexter, because that's what we expect around here."

I shocked Carter, but someone had to let him know that the 49ers didn't accept mistakes in practice as well as games. Running back Roger Craig pitched in with some advice of his own. "Every time you touch the ball in practice, Dexter, you run 40 yards," he told Carter.

Several years ago, I lashed out at strong safety Jeff Fuller when I discovered him lounging on the field before the start of practice instead of working on his backpedaling technique with the rest of the defensive backs.

"What's wrong with you?" I asked, incredulously.

"Tight hamstring," Fuller replied.

"You've got to get up and do what everyone else is doing," I yelled. "Get off your ass."

"Hey, I'm not about to pull my hamstring," Fuller said.

I recalled an incident earlier in the day, when I had bet Fuller $1,000 he wouldn't make weight and I had had to dip into my checking account to pay up. "We can't get you to do anything unless we bet you, huh, Fuller?" I asked, a touch of sarcasm in my voice.

One of my most eye-opening blowups in practice occurred during one stretch in 1988. The 49ers were on the verge of collapsing and Walsh was close to coming unglued. His relationship with owner Eddie DeBartolo, Jr., was obviously strained. We had just gotten our butts kicked in consecutive weeks by the

Phoenix Cardinals and the Los Angeles Raiders. Our record was 6–5. Against the Cardinals, we had led 23–0 in the third quarter, but wound up losing 24–23, the game-winning touchdown coming in the final three seconds. All three Phoenix touchdowns came on passes.

When I walked into the locker room after the game, I found DeBartolo slumped in a chair with his head down. The only sounds were helmets and shoulder pads bouncing on the floor and into duffel bags, and tape being ripped from ankles, wrists, and hands.

Walsh walked in and began yelling. He never, ever, lost it, but this Sunday he screamed so loud and hard that spit flew from his mouth. He didn't yell at anyone in particular. He just rambled on and on and on. Then he stormed into his office and slammed the door behind him. The door popped open and I saw Walsh with his head in his hands, looking devastated and distraught.

As we walked onto the tarmac to board our flight back to San Francisco, Walsh dropped to his knees. The 90-degree temperatures had sapped his strength, and he had cracked two ribs after two players ran into him on the sideline. On the plane, Walsh looked ashen and appeared to be in great discomfort. The pilot radioed ahead to have an ambulance standing by. In the back of the plane, someone told a joke, causing several players to break out laughing. To Walsh, the laughter was uncalled for. So he instructed Jerry Walker, our public relations director, to walk through the plane and tell everybody to shut up. In quieting players down, Walker indicated that Walsh had threatened to terminate him if there was any more laughter. It was a scene out of the movie *The Caine Mutiny*. Walsh was our Captain Queeg, the captain of the peacetime destroyer who panics during a typhoon, becomes slightly unhinged, and then is relieved of his post after the mutiny of his first officer and crew. I figured if I listened closely I'd hear marbles rolling in Queeg's—er, Walsh's—hands in the first-class cabin.

When we faced the Raiders the following Sunday at Candlestick Park, the team was still floundering. The offense only managed to grind out 219 total yards and in our 9–3 loss we failed to score a touchdown, one of the few times that had ever happened to a Walsh team. An enraged DeBartolo reportedly broke a glass refrigerator door in one of his private boxes in the stadium, and someone smashed a cooler in our locker room. Although DeBartolo had been among the first in the locker room after the debacle, he denied that he had anything to do with the damage.

The wear and tear of the season—and the staggering loss to the Raiders—left Walsh drained and subdued. But instead of falling apart in the locker room as he had in Phoenix, he kept his anger and disappointment locked inside. I knew that wouldn't last long because, unlike other years, Walsh didn't seem to be able to keep his emotions in check. During this dreary stretch in 1988, his feelings had hovered under the surface of his skin. And sure enough, about an hour after the Raiders game, while he was walking through the stadium to join his family, two loud-mouthed 49er fans chastised him. If security guards hadn't been on the scene, Walsh probably would have gotten into a physical altercation.

Obviously something had to be done to turn the team around, but Walsh was too emotionally wrung out to take the first step. So on the practice field the next day I lost my temper.

"What the hell is going on?" I screamed to everybody in sight, while running across the field. I was shocked by the lack of enthusiasm of my coaches and teammates. They were strolling in slow-motion from drill to drill.

"I can't believe your fucking attitudes," I shouted. "You're walking around like you don't give a damn. We've been getting our asses kicked! Look, this is ridiculous! If we're going to lose, then let's go down kicking somebody's ass."

Players stopped dead in their tracks. All eyes were on me.

"We've got to play up to our standard of football," I continued shouting. "If we play up to our standard and we lose, so what? But our standard isn't lethargic football. We don't stroll around the field. We don't act like we don't care."

The next thing I knew Walsh hammered his assistants. "You coaches better kick some asses this week or you're going to be looking for other jobs," he hollered.

The tempo picked up from there. Later in the week, Randy Cross and Keith Fahnhorst, our veteran offensive linemen, each gave emotional speeches. Sunday night, following a workout at Candlestick Park in preparation for our game against the Washington Redskins on Monday Night Football, the entire team clustered together at the edge of the field. We raised our hands in unison and touched fingers.

"Okay, what we're going to do is play up to our standard," I told the guys. "If we play up to our standard each week, who cares if we lose? At least we can be proud that we kicked some butt."

That was our first sign of solidarity in 1988, and we crushed the Redskins, 37–21. We gathered together and raised our hands every week after that. We were ready to rumble—as a team.

The word *team* is so sacred to me that I'll go toe to toe with anybody just to let them know that's all that matters on Sunday. If I have a conviction that I believe is in the best interest of the team, I'm not the kind of guy who talks big behind closed doors, then comes down with a serious case of lockjaw in front of coaches and management. I have never cared about the consequences. Haley has always kidded, "Ronnie, your balls are dragging." Haley said it takes big balls to speak your mind in the NFL. And he was right. But I don't think my balls ever really dragged on the floor in my career with the 49ers because I wasn't trying to challenge authority. I played Robin Hood—fighting for justice for my teammates. I was—and always will be—more concerned with protecting the integrity of the team than protecting my own ass.

Walsh didn't always appreciate my challenging him in front of the team. He seldom understood why I spoke up. I think he sometimes viewed my outspokenness as a vendetta. Walsh liked to be in control of every single situation. If only he knew the number of times I held back because I realized he'd get angry and perhaps feel a bit threatened.

I'll never forget when Walsh suggested we submit to voluntary drug testing. The scene took place in 1986 at our training camp in Rocklin, California, after the cocaine-related deaths of Len Bias, the Boston Celtics' No. 1 draft pick, and Don Rogers, the Cleveland Browns' defensive back.

"See this big pickle jar?," Walsh said, holding up an enormous bottle. "It's the kind of jar an elephant pees in. Tomorrow after practice, I want everybody to fill 'er up."

We all thought he was joking, but sure enough, the next morning before practice Walsh pulled out the jar. Cross got angry.

"We don't have to take a drug test!" Cross told Walsh. "It's against our civil rights."

Fahnhorst concurred. "Bill, we're not going to test."

Several players nodded their heads in agreement with Cross and Fahnhorst. In training camp, we normally submitted to a drug test as part of our physical exams, but now I wondered if the deaths of Bias and Rogers would lead to random testing. I was all for testing if it helped save lives, but since the majority of the players on the team complained about its being a violation of their civil rights, I had to side with them.

Walsh got upset. "Goddammit," he said. "This is important. I can't believe you guys aren't going to test. This is serious. This could prevent needless deaths."

I stepped forward and spoke from my heart. "Bill, if it's so serious, then why did you joke about it last night?" I asked. "You kidded about everybody peeing in one big bottle, and two pro athletes have died. Now you want us to get serious and take a test?"

If he really believed in random drug testing, why had he made fun of it? Come at us straight on this issue.

"Look, Bill, these guys don't want to take the test," I told him. "We're not going to do it."

Walsh tried to explain himself. "Well, I was just trying to make light of the test so you guys wouldn't be paranoid about it," he said.

The room was silent.

"I think we should take the test," Dwight Clark suddenly said. Joe Montana agreed. "Yeah, Dwight, you're right. I think everyone should take the test."

The reaction from the rest of the players puzzled me. One minute they were adamant about not taking the test, and then after Clark and Montana spoke up, nobody said anything. Everybody had been vehemently against it. Now they were stone silent. The debating had stopped. Maybe they were too intimidated.

Many times throughout my career I felt like a lone voice crying out in the wilderness, but I risked opening my mouth knowing someone needed to speak up for the team. Some of my teammates thanked me for putting my neck on the chopping block. Few ever told me to sit down and shut up. I wanted their support, but if I didn't get it, that was fine too. Certain things had to be said, and I always felt I was going to have to be the one to say them. Who on the 49ers would have been outspoken if I hadn't been? Maybe no one.

As for the drug test Walsh wanted us to take? We took it.

My role as one of the 49ers' leaders took me through every emotion, and at times it drove me to tears. My most emotional moment occurred in 1987 during the NFL players' strike. From the outset we had problems with team unity. Some players wanted to cross the picket line. Others didn't. Fahnhorst and Keena Turner, the union representatives, encouraged open discussion of the strike issues, in an effort to forestall any hard feelings among teammates. The national media focused on the 49ers because more than any other team our marquee players were among the highest paid in the NFL, and we were looked upon as pro-management because of our friendly relationship with DeBartolo. The NFL Management Council and all of the twenty-eight team owners hoped we would break the strike and pick up our paychecks. However, for the good of the team, we voted to stay out on strike. The strike would be a team effort, but that sentiment didn't last very long.

Fullback Harry Sydney was one of the first to cross the picket line. He explained his decision to the strikers, saying he needed the money, which was understandable. Sydney had signed with the 49ers as a free agent during the off-season after playing three years in the USFL.

On Day 11 of the strike, Montana, Clark, Craig, tight end Russ Francis, and eight others announced they were planning to report.

Montana had lost a lot of money during the fifty-seven-day strike in 1982, and he told us he didn't feel he could afford to lose any more. Clark explained that he needed the paychecks because three off-season knee operations would probably send him into retirement after the 1987 season. Francis, thirty-four, was nearing the end of his career, too, having been placed on injured reserve a few weeks before the strike with a strained Achilles tendon.

"We aren't like steelworkers, who can make up lost wages over a thirty-year career," Montana explained. "Most of us have about four years to make money. Why would anyone try to take that away?"

Those who planned to cross the picket line had spent hours searching their souls, wondering if they were making the right decision. Montana said he had had a hard time sleeping, wrestling with what he wanted to do and what he knew he had to do. Craig admitted that he could be driving a wedge between himself and his teammates. For days Turner had suffered headaches, knowing that his best friend, cornerback Eric Wright, would ultimately cross the picket line and return to work.

Then something strange happened. Montana, Clark, and the

rest of the group reported for work, but suddenly changed their minds and left the 49er facility. Rumors swirled that Walsh had secretly met with them and counseled them to stay out. They had told us they were going back in for personal reasons, but now they claimed they were staying out for the rest of us who hadn't crossed the picket line? Five days later, they inexplicably returned. It didn't make sense.

Of course, very little had made sense during the four weeks we were on strike. Fahnhorst, bless his heart, remained calm throughout the storm. He experienced emotions he hadn't felt at any other time in his fourteen-year career. Listening to us scream at each other in union meetings and having to organize pickets to try to keep teammates from abandoning the strike saddened him. He lost twelve pounds during the ordeal and for a time had to be hospitalized for exhaustion. Two days before the strike ended, Fahny came unglued during a conference call, as members of the NFL Players Association's Executive Committee pleaded with the player reps to keep their teammates from defecting en masse. Reps yelled at each other from one end of the country to the other, until finally Chicago Bear linebacker Mike Singletary offered to lead a prayer. Realizing the solidarity was crumbling and the players were doomed, Fahnhorst hung up the phone, went into the bathroom, and cried.

After all that, Fahnhorst had to brace himself to deliver some bad news to us. He called a meeting of the striking players shortly before we reported back for work. "I think you guys should know this," Fahnhorst began. He said that he had confirmed the newspaper reports that Walsh had met with the strikers, and he told us that not only had Walsh asked them to stay out, but he had also promised that the 49ers would loan them five days salary, thus paying them as if they had reported for work. By telling the guys to stay out and promising to pay them, Walsh thought he was keeping the team together. But he was breaking us apart. What had happened to respect and trust? The revelation shattered us.

"This is a team," I said in anger to the group that day. "I thought we were supposed to be a team, that we'd always stick together."

The first day back at practice, on October 15, there was a lot of bitterness in the locker room as well as on the field. We weren't really talking to each other. I overheard players issuing threats. "I'm going to get that guy," referring to teammates who had crossed the picket line. How in the hell could we win even one game if teammates wanted to injure each other?

It was the first time I ever heard such backbiting and bitter animosity. The closeness among the players had made the 49ers the greatest organization of the 1980s. We were no longer a family. Our strike team had compiled a 3–0 record to keep us in the NFC West race, but with the hostile feelings we were experiencing, I felt the 49ers were in danger of disintegrating.

After practice, Walsh gathered us together in a semicircle on the field. "I know there are hard feelings," Walsh said. "There have been many unkind words said. But we should let things go and they'll take care of themselves. We'll air our differences out during the course of the week. We'll get back on track."

I had one question. "Why did those guys get paid?"

Nobody said a word. Most of the players buried their heads.

"I've got to play with these guys," I continued. "I've got to play in the same backfield with Jeff Fuller. How do I know I can depend on them when the going gets tough? They owe us an apology. They misled us. They told us they were going back in for the paychecks, and then they didn't go in because they all of a sudden decided to support us? Come on. It hurt a lot of players on this team. We deserve an apology."

That was all I was asking for. But the discussion got ugly. Fast.

Francis piped up. "We don't need to apologize to you," he said.

"What do you mean?" I shouted.

"We don't need to apologize to you," Francis shot back. "Who the hell do you think you are?"

Fuller lashed out, too. "Fuck you," Fuller said. "I needed the money. Who are you to tell me how to live my life?"

Walsh squirmed nervously. Just out of earshot stood members of the Bay area media. He worried that our words would show up on the evening news or in the morning papers. He turned to Fahnhorst who was kneeling beside him.

"What do you think, Keith?" Walsh asked, with a confused look on his face.

As always, Fahnhorst remained outwardly composed. "Whatever these guys did, they didn't do it to hurt the others," he said to us. "They had legitimate reasons. Regardless of whether they were selfish or not, they weren't doing it to hurt their teammates. Let's at least try to remember that."

"Fuck that!" I said. "This is crazy, man. You guys want to be a team? This ain't no fucking team."

George Seifert, who was kneeling behind me, tried to put his arm on my shoulder to calm me down but then decided otherwise. I was so wound up. I think Seifert worried I might turn around and deck him.

"We're supposed to be a team," I said. "We answer to each other."

Walsh blew up. "This is my team, and I'm going to do things my way," he said.

I could feel the 49ers unraveling. Francis, Walsh, and I argued loudly for several minutes. At one point I exploded and lunged toward Walsh. I don't remember who grabbed me to hold me back, or who tried to calm me down. That's how angry I was.

"Bill, this is no damn team!" I screamed. "We can't be a team if we have a bunch of cliques. We have to believe in the common cause. That's how we've had success here. The common cause. That's the bottom line. We've been taught to do it the 49er way ever since Day One. Not your way or my way. The 49er way."

Walsh walked back to a bench outside the locker room and sat next to Dr. Harry Edwards, the 49er team adviser.

"I handled that badly," Walsh told Edwards.

"You've got to lance the boil, and Ronnie's the guy to do it," Edwards said.

I was disgusted and I had had enough. Heading to the locker room, I walked past Walsh and our eyes met. "I hope you understand," I said to Walsh. "I had to do it." Walsh didn't respond. He just nodded his head.

Later that day, Dr. Edwards found me at my locker and reassured me that something positive would come from this incident. "You guys needed that," Dr. Edwards said. "It is better to burst the boil then let it fester and get red and sore."

Our screaming match had to happen at that precise time. It released a lot of pent-up hostility that would have been disruptive if it had not been vented. Guys would have kept on pouting. They would have taken cheap shots at each other, concentrating on aspects other than football.

The next day, I met with Clark and Turner for beers, two of my partners in Sports City Cafe, to smooth over hard feelings. The strike had turned us into people we weren't. "I can't believe we were so pissed off at each other," I said to Clark. "Why did we act that way?" We had lost together and we had won together. When my football career is over, I'll care more about my teammates than the games themselves.

Before my outburst that day, I didn't know if what I had to say would be enough. Nobody knew. I still don't know for sure. What I do know is whatever transpired that day allowed us to go forward and concentrate on football. We finished the 1987 season with a 13–3 record, including a 36–24 loss to Minnesota in an NFC playoff game. My outburst was enough to allow me to be friends with my teammates, and above all else, to begin to respect them again.

4 | THE ZEN WARRIOR IN ME

PREPARING FOR WAR

"I teach a Korean art, and I'm half Japanese. I speak a little bit of Japanese, not a lot. One day, when Ronnie and I bowed out after a workout, I said thank you, '*Arigato Lottsan.*' And he responded, '*Hai, arigato, gozaimasu*'—thank you very much. I don't even think Ronnie realized he said it. He just spit it out. I looked at him and said, 'Geez, where did that come from?' "
—George Chung, five-time world karate champion

A good football player is somebody who is technically sound. He has perfected all of the right moves. The proper way to wrap his arms in tackling someone who is heavier. How to cut down onrushing linemen. How to handle a football during the last seconds of a game. If I were only concerned with technique, however, I would still be kicking tumbleweeds in Rialto.

On the football field, technique is not enough for me. I have to be a fighter, a man with the ability and desire to say it's time to go for the kill. A true fighter is not the kind of person who lets you get back up once you've fallen down. He finishes you off and kicks you right in the face. It's not a matter of honor. It's a matter of ending the fight. I've been taught if you lose, you die. There's no middle ground. In sports and war, you win or you lose. You have to be mentally, physically, and spiritually prepared for battle. A warrior could have been successful in a hundred other battles, but if he slumps today he's dead.

I have been schooled in the art of war. I have the eyes and heart of a fighter. I possess the killer instinct. Since 1986, I have studied with George Chung at his America's Best Karate Masters Studios in Los Gatos, California. We met at a charity fashion show at the San Jose Fairgrounds in 1986. My hand was in a cast that day because I had just had part of my pinkie amputated, and Chung could sense how physically, mentally, and emotionally beat up I was. I had contemplated adding martial arts to my off-season program after seeing how the training had improved the stamina, speed, and toughness of running back Marcus Allen.

From the beginning, Chung treated me like an Asian warrior, training me as though I were a prized knight in sixteenth-century Japan, molding my mind into that of a general while giving me the body and heart of a soldier. Our workouts are a combination of Tae Kwon Do, which is a Korean form of karate, kick boxing, and his own program of gut-wrenching exercises. He demands that I live by a warrior's code of morals, that I come to workouts sober and focused. His goal is to keep me mentally tough and in top-notch physical condition. He wants me to be able to make quick but rational decisions, and to strike at a moment's notice. Chung calls this Zen and the Art of Football.

Chung claims that athletes like me, who are naturally somber off the field, make the most dangerous fighters. Overly aggressive, uncontrolled athletes release their energy before they have delivered a blow. In an emergency they panic. Their mind, body, and spirit explode in different directions. But quiet, solemn athletes let their emotions brew and storm, and when they hit you, they'll hurt you.

Let me take you through one of my typical, hour-long workouts with Chung as I train like a black-belt fighter. My routine includes more than 1,000 kicks, at least 1,000 sit-ups and 500 punches, 1,000 push-ups and 100 squats. Between each drill I get no rest. That's when Chung has me do the push-ups and sit-ups. The first time I tried Chung's rigorous workouts, my stomach cramped and my lungs burned. I had to bend over to catch my breath. "Get up!" Chung ordered. "Keep your composure! You look defeated! Don't you ever bend over again!"

There were many days I wanted to scream because I felt the need to bend over so many times. But Chung wouldn't let me quit. The pain was torturous. "Deep breaths!" Chung instructed. "Take the air all the way in. Fill up your lungs. Blow it all out. Imagine a fog rolling through your body. It goes in your nose, down to your toes, then back out, cleansing you." My mind kept fighting my body. I can't do this, a voice inside me would say. Then another voice, from somewhere deep in my heart, would force me to take another step when I didn't think I could. I would not allow Chung to break me.

For my workouts, I am barefoot and dressed in sweatpants and a T-shirt. I wear shin pads, adhesive tape around my palms, and padded gloves over my hands. Chung blasts Top-40 hits and lots of Motown tunes, ranging from Janet Jackson to the Temptations. Although music is frowned upon by most martial arts instructors, Chung believes the songs allow his students to ride the momentum in the air. The louder the music, the more I must focus on the exercise and the less likely I am to hear my own breathing. Thus I won't even know when I am tired.

"This is like a $2.99 buffet," Chung, who is twenty-nine, likes to say as he tightens his black belt. "It's all you can eat, baby."

To start the workout I bow to Chung, who ceases to be my friend, peer, and fellow athlete. Instead, he becomes my *sensei*, which is Japanese for teacher. In his instruction, Chung will do a lot of touching to connect with my emotions. Through his fingertips, he says he can sense if I am nervous, fragile, tired, tight, or frightened.

We usually start with leg kicks. There are fifty different leg kicks to choose from. In this workout, for the first exercise I step up on an ordinary desk chair with one leg and do a front-snap kick with the other. Ten to twenty times on each leg. In the next set, instead of kicking out I lift my leg over Chung in an arcing motion. That's called a roundhouse kick. Do it ten to twenty times on each leg. The third set, I step up and do side-thrust kicks. Again, ten to twenty times. Stepping up on a chair works the knees, quadriceps, and hamstrings, developing strength and building flexibility. Right away, I mastered the art of kicking, something that might get me ejected if I tried it in a football game. Chung's patented machine-gun kicks—lifting the leg and extending it as many as 100 times without putting it back on the floor—came easily to me. I excelled at jump kicks, too. Chung says I'm ambidextrous with my legs, which is very unusual. Most athletes favor one side.

Next on the agenda is push-ups. Face down, I straddle two chairs. As I push myself up, Chung forces my neck back down. Each push-up is arduous, but to survive a vicious hit in the NFL you need a strong neck. If the neck flies back on impact, the violent whipping action could knock me out.

Another kind of "push-up" I perform is the squat push-up, which is designed to strengthen my hamstrings. Standing sideways with one foot on the end of a bench, and clutching a pair of 35-pound dumbbells tightly to my chest, I squat up and down. At least twenty times, each side. We then take a break, and I knock off 200 half sit-ups. In 1986, my abdominal muscles were abominable. I dreaded these so-called rest segments, which Chung intersperses throughout the workouts. Because I had always been an instinctive athlete, I never realized how important my stomach muscles were in delivering hard hits. It never occurred to me that strong abdominals translated into a better center of balance on tackles and better posture while running. It helped my breathing and reduced the risk of suffering a lower back injury.

However, no amount of ordinary sit-ups compare to Chung's fan-belt abdominal strengtheners. I lie on the floor and stretch out my legs, with my toes pointing up. Chung threads a 6-foot industrial fan belt over the tops of my feet. A workout partner straddles me at my neck, and I hold onto his calves to brace myself. I rock my body and whip my legs from side to side, while Chung tries to resist my movement. If I fight him, I can tear my hip flexor or abdominal muscles. If I'm relaxed, I will develop a strong lower stomach. Chung recently dreamed up two crazy variations of this killer drill. In one, a 120-pound woman stands on my stomach. In the other, two karate students wearing pads on their hands slap my stomach as I lower my legs to the ground. This forces me to exhale and teaches me to be calm when I get hit.

The next phase of the workout requires a combination of focus, hand-eye coordination, strength, and endurance. I play cat-and-mouse with Chung, chasing him in circles around the studio. The object is to deliver a punch or kick to Chung's hand pads, which to me symbolize a running back or tight end. His hands move faster and in more directions than any opponent ever will, so if I can follow this target I should perform better under game conditions. Chung races around the studio, weaving and bobbing. As he dodges my blows, he also tries to strike my head with the mitts, or kick me in the torso, to test my temperament. How will I react to a sudden blow? In this frenzied activity, it would be so easy for me to say forget it! There's just too much going on. But I have disciplined myself to follow him. The main purpose of this drill, Chung says, is to get me to think both offensively and defensively. He wants me to be a total football player at all times. At first I had a tendency to watch his eyes to keep from getting hit. On the field, I have the same bad habit when I spend too much time looking at the quarterback's eyes instead of taking care of my own business. "Follow my chest," Chung advises. "It's big. I can't move it that fast." Using my peripheral vision I can then see the punch or kick coming.

Chung has devised another neck-strengthening drill for me. I hold 20-pound dumbbells at my sides while Chung, facing me, interlocks his fingers behind my neck. He then darts around the room for ten minutes, and I am supposed to keep pace with him, pulling my head up to see the direction in which we're moving while he pushes against me. This "dynamic tension" exercise is dangerous, and I would not advise anyone to try this one—or any of the others—without Chung's supervision. The wrong move, and you could suffer whiplash or break your neck.

The third phase of Chung's workout takes place on a thick crash mat that high jumpers use for a landing pad. It simulates running on the beach, which makes your legs weary awfully fast. Scurrying after Chung from one end of this awkward, mushy pad to the other, trying to deliver punches and kicks without falling, will allow me to run faster on a football field and develop my balance in traffic. This frustrating drill also tests my patience.

Our final segment consists of fifteen minutes of sparring with gloves on. It's our own demented form of kick boxing. Chung tries to kick me in the head, and I go after him with everything. Hands, feet, elbows, and knees. That's when I truly appreciate his quickness. He can throw a kick to my midriff, and by the time I make a move to block it his foot is flying toward my teeth at the clocked speed of 80 mph. That's the only time Chung ever sees fear in my eyes. Under my breath I say, "Thank God he didn't hit me."

In one respect, Chung seems to have the advantage in our sparring sessions. At 5 feet 11, 200 pounds, he's a tad lighter and smaller than I am, and of course after eighteen years of training, his fighting skills are much more refined. But I look at it from another perspective. Chung could kick me in the head all day long, but if he angers me to the point where I abandon the concept of the cool-headed Zen warrior, I'll forget where I am and tackle him. Chung knows there's always that possibility.

THE HUMAN TOUCH

"In many ways, Ronnie reminds me of an old-style warrior. He is as concerned with his wounds as the ancient Asian warriors, many of whom were monks who healed themselves through acupuncture, deep massage, and herbs. Ronnie readies himself for battle like the Indians who did their war dances to get themselves psyched and focused, fine-tuning their energy in the direction they thought it should go."
—Bo Elliott, Acupuncturist/Chiropractor

To stimulate my endorphins, the proteins produced by the brain that act as painkillers and tranquilizers, I wear a tiny gold ball inside the upper part of both ears. A machine spewing out an electrical current locates the exact acupuncture points in each ear, and that's where a gold ball is placed. By pressing the balls into the skin every so often, I can stimulate my endorphins, which I believe make me quicker, faster, and stronger.

To soothe my aching muscles, after practice as well as before games, I use a warm Chinese ointment that reminds me of Ben-Gay. Fred Tedeschi, the 49er assistant trainer, always used to fuss about this potent ointment. To protect his hands, Tedeschi wore rubber gloves when he massaged the ointment into my muscles.

To speed up healing in my muscles, I drink a bitter herbal tea concocted from ginseng and the twigs and roots of fifteen different Chinese plants. It promotes circulation of the blood and breaks up clots. One Saturday morning in 1990, when I was suffering from a pulled hamstring, I boiled the tea in the second-floor lounge at the 49er facility in Santa Clara. A number of 49er employees were forced to leave that area of the building because of the strong stench from the tea. "Are you a witch doctor?" asked guard Guy McIntyre as I sipped the brew in the locker room before practice. None of my teammates dared to drink the tea, which was probably a wise decision, because it tasted worse than it smelled. The first time I drank it, I gagged.

To reduce swelling and pain from bruises, sprains, and muscle tears, I burn a dark gray moxa stick. When I was introduced to moxibustion in 1984 by an acupuncturist, I was told a story about ancient Chinese soldiers who ran thousands of miles without injury because they burned moxa over their legs before and after journeys. I light the moxa stick on one tip—it smells like dope—and hold it a few inches from my skin at specific points. The combination of the warmth and odorous fumes increases my white blood cell count and opens the blockage. That elevates my energy level and promotes healing.

My private team of healers includes acupuncturists, herbalists, massage therapists, and chiropractors. My home is equipped with four different physical therapy gadgets: two electronic stimulator units that transmit current through the injured area via electrode pads, a device that sends microcurrents through muscle tissue while I sleep, and a portable rehabilitation machine to treat my knees. The total cost for this equipment is $7,500. There are other rehab items such as cold packs, bags of ginseng tea, vitamins, herbs, hit pills, linaments, and moxa sticks.

On some days, when I received treatment in the 49er training room, it was comforting to hear the jokes and smart-ass remarks of Charles Haley or Joe Montana. But more often than not I preferred to be treated in the quiet office of my chiropractor or, better yet, in the privacy of my living room.

Wednesday nights were reserved for my spiritual guru, Jennie Winter, the massage therapist from Foster City, California, who has worked miracles on my body the past three years. The Friday before a road trip or Saturday afternoon before a home game, I visited Bo Elliott, a chiropractor who combined massage and acupuncture. Depending on how physically beat up I was, I also saw Elliott the day after games or in the middle of the week. Elliott balanced my muscular, skeletal, neurological, and bioenergetic systems. In simpler terms, he aligned my skeleton and freed my joints, paying particular attention to the kinks in my pelvic and hip areas, legs, back, shoulders, and neck. He massaged me from my feet to my scalp, removing the hard hits as well as the pressures, tension, and stress I encountered both on and off the field. After games, rubbing the scalp, according to Elliott, helped to get rid of the frowns, meanness, and negative vibes that I built up playing football. Elliott, who wears a beard and pulls his hair back in a small ponytail, liked to describe himself as a "consultator" or "go-between" who opened up energy pathways in my body so it could heal itself.

At the end of each treatment, he performed auricular therapy. He stuck a gold ball at specific points inside the top of my ears to direct neural inputs to my brain. These tiny balls stimulated endorphins that made me relax or relieved my pain. He also put the balls in spots that directed energy to or from particular injuries.

My Bay area healing team also included a marvelous acupuncturist/herbal expert from Berkeley, California, named John Steinke, who developed a sports medicine program using Chinese techniques. He studied for four years with a master acupuncturist who treated several members of the Golden State Warriors basketball team. Steinke told me that my resting heart rate was so slow—42 beats per minute, which is similar to a long-distance runner—and my circulation was so strong that he could treat many parts of my body with just a few needles.

Most of my 49er teammates thought that it was bizarre that I was so involved with ancient Asian medicine. Haley refused to stay in the same room with me when I received acupuncture because he was deathly afraid of needles. I can only imagine what their reactions would have been if they had walked in on Steinke as he was treating the sprained left knee I suffered against the New York Giants in December 1990. He lanced a blood vessel in back of my right shoulder, then placed a glass cup over the cut to suck out the blood. With every injury, Steinke explained, circulation has been disrupted somewhere else in the body, oftentimes in remote unrelated areas. This acupuncture technique of bleeding releases the "congestion." Another time Steinke bled my little toe to give me more range of motion in my hamstring. To treat concussions he bled behind the knee. Weird stuff, huh?

Since 1986 I've had so many different healers and pairs of hands working on my body that I'm willing to explore any new treatment. During the Christmas holidays in 1990 I tried a little old Chinese man I met in a San Jose herbal store. A traditional acupuncturist who spoke no English, he proclaimed through an interpreter that he could cure my sprained knees. What did I have to lose? In his first treatment, he inserted needles into my muscles and at various points on top of my skin that had never been penetrated before. At first I shot off the table. He had stirred up my *chi*, the Chinese word used to describe the life force. Chills rocketed up my spine. My muscles throbbed, and I began to sweat. However, by the end of his treatment I felt invigorated. That is, until the old man's assistant advised me not to have sex. Sex, he explained, weakened the knees and some of the internal organs. I pondered that idea for a few minutes and then decided that I didn't have to be amenable to every piece of advice.

Why do I put myself through all these healing rituals? Because I never want to be accused of not earning my paycheck, and I feel this is necessary to prolong my career, prevent injuries, and quicken recovery time between workouts. Defensive backs are smaller than everybody else on the field, with the exception of a few "smurf" receivers here and there. We hurl ourselves into running backs, tight ends, and wide receivers, and though we get beaten up beyond belief, we are still expected to run like thoroughbreds. By the fifth week of a sixteen-game regular season, our bodies begin to break down. Doctors, chiropractors, and massage therapists have told me that athletes seem to be blessed with the ability to recover more quickly than the average person. In my drive for excellence, through a combination of acupuncture, massage, and Asian herbs, I've discovered ways to stimulate and further accelerate my body's natural healing processes.

Ignorance makes coaches and players skeptical of Asian medicine, even though it's virtually free of side effects that Western treatments may cause, like dimethyl sulfoxide, better known as DMSO. Most amateur and professional athletes call this stinky ointment a wonder drug. DMSO has been used for decades by veterinarians, and it is also used as an industrial solvent and paint thinner. The Food and Drug Administration has approved it for only one human use—the treatment of a specific bladder infection. NFL trainers generally do not prescribe it, but from time to time you'll pick up a whiff of DMSO in the locker room. It smells like garlic, rotten eggs, and turpentine. When a player has used it you can taste the stink in your mouth. In training camp a few years ago, I patted talcum powder on my legs and then applied DMSO to my groin. The DMSO sucked the powder into my body through the skin in my testicle area. I was in agony, and for a couple of days I had a great deal of trouble walking. I was petrified, thinking I had contracted a venereal disease.

That episode was a painful reminder that we'd all be better off living drug-free lives. Herbs and a moxa stick are better for my body than rubbing on DMSO, injecting cortisone, or popping anti-inflammatory pills.

I consider myself a Zen warrior on the football field. That means being in harmony with my mental, physical, and spiritual self, yet still being able to crash into an opponent with the force of a truck. The only way for me to get to that state is through moderation and balance in my life, which my various forms of healing provide me. Only when I am truly balanced, with a clear mind, can I will myself back to health.

I once asked Kareem Abdul-Jabbar how he was able to play professional basketball into his forties at such a competitive level. "You have to be able to center yourself, to let all of your emotions go," Kareem advised. "You carry every year in your mind, your body, and your soul. Find somebody or something who can take you away from that, to give you a fresh outlook on what you're doing. Don't ever forget that you play with your soul as well as your body." Abdul-Jabbar prescribed yoga and chiropractic treatments. Nolan Ryan, who threw the seventh no-hitter of his career at age forty-four, has spoken about the importance of moderation in prolonging an athletic career. He prescribes basics like nutrition, proper sleep, regimented weight training, cardiovascular conditioning, and stretching and relaxation exercises.

To achieve that balance, I must first be completely relaxed. When my healers work on my body during the football season, those sessions are the few hours that I forget about my responsibilities, problems, and pressures. My treatments are my time to unplug the phone and dim the lights. I find that when my body feels better my mind feels better. Being completely relaxed makes the treatments more effective. You shouldn't fight anything that's going to make you feel better. Accept it. For example, in my acupuncture treatments, Steinke placed the first needle on the top of my head. The second was inserted right between my eyes to relax the mind and face. If I felt anything at all, it was only a little prick. Then I usually fell asleep.

Sessions with Elliott and Winter gave me a chance to recharge my emotional batteries. They became my trusted friends. They saw me at my most vulnerable moments and understood my body's weaknesses better than I did.

"How do you feel?" they would ask at the beginning of each appointment.

"Oh, a little tight," would probably be my first response. "You know, that was a tough game."

And then I would get around to telling them that my body just didn't respond as quickly to injuries anymore and that I was frustrated because nothing seemed to make me better. Finally I would admit that I was worried that my strained hamstring or sprained knee could be worse than the doctors had let on. They often sensed what I was feeling without my saying it. I trusted they wouldn't share my problems, concerns, or fears with anyone else.

The warmth and gentleness of a human touch is such a stark contrast to the brutality on the football field. It is the most important aspect of healing. The human touch allows me to *feel* emotions that I only *experience* on the field. That hit. That bruise. The exuberance of an interception. The disappointment of defeat.

We all carry a lot of emotions in our bodies. Fear gets trapped in certain areas, and the energy won't flow. Often when Elliott gives deep-tissue massage, his patients begin crying because he stirs up so many emotions. The yoga people will tell you that my hamstring problems represent anger and that my knee problems in December 1990 were a physical manifestation of stubbornness, pride, and fear.

Winter knew I dealt with physical pain better than emotional pain. Emotional pain has a greater effect on me, and I keep it well hidden. She worked on my muscles intuitively, going with what she sensed was happening even if she couldn't feel it with her hands. She watched my face to see if I grimaced, and she made note of how my body tightened. "Breathe! Breathe!" she would yell. I was tempted to hold my breath because the massage hurt so much, but I knew that would only make me pass out.

For the deep-tissue massage, Winter worked within my pain threshold and then counterbalanced that with lighter strokes to erase the memory of the pain. Not that it helped. I still wanted to kick her ass. Many nights, long after she had stopped deep massage in my hamstrings and moved on to other areas of my body, I would still be grimacing.

When it came to working on my emotional and spiritual sides, Winter also relied on her intuition. She meditated over the injured area and performed "energetic work" that aligned my chakras and aura. The aura, as she explained it to me, is the energy that surrounds my body, and the seven major energy points within the aura are called chakras. For example, the first chakra is located at the base of the spine, and it's the survival chakra; the fourth chakra, or heart chakra, is the emotional center. Stress or trauma can damage the chakras, which in turn will distort energy flow in the body and lead to physical or psychological problems. Winter said that cleaning out my chakras and balancing my energy flow went a long way toward healing me physically.

A couple of weeks after I had sprained my knees against the Giants, Winter sensed dark energy around them. Anxiety. Doubt. Fear. The end of the road. The injuries had brought home the point that my career was coming to an end, and that night my emotions radiated from my knees. Winter didn't feel my emotions from a spasm. She picked them up on another level. Thirty minutes later she completed the massage and then aligned my chakras. Winter grounded herself, connecting her energy to the earth, and then she grounded me. She focused all of her energy into focusing my energy. She balanced the chakras that were too open or too closed and cleaned out my aura. She sent healing energy into my body. For several minutes, she touched me slightly at various points right above my skin.

"What are you doing?" I asked.

"Some energy work," she said.

"Well, whatever it is, it sure feels good."

5 | SUPER BOWLS AND SUPER MEN

THE BEST TEAM EVER Super Bowl XIX had all the comforts of a home game. It was played at Stanford Stadium, about ten miles from our Redwood City training facility. Our practices were held at exactly the same time, and in exactly the same place, as they had been all season. We weren't required to check into our team hotel until Friday. I could entertain my house guests, Dallas Cowboy defensive back Dennis Thurman and Houston Oiler quarterback Warren Moon, eat dinner in front of the television in my den, and wake up in my own bed. Everywhere I went I bumped into 49er fans who wished us good luck. Stanford Stadium offered an air of familiarity, too. I had played there during my days at USC and back then I had always found that field to be in perfect shape. When George Toma, the Super Bowl XIX groundskeeper, boasted that the field conditions were the best he had seen in his many years in the business, I felt reassured that this too was a good omen.

The bigger the game, the more relaxed I like to be, and certainly with all of the pregame hype I felt the fewer distractions the better. The experts had predicted it would be almost impossible for the 49ers to contain the wide-open passing game of the Miami Dolphins, who had averaged 32 points a game. Quarterback Dan Marino and wide receivers Mark (Super) Duper and Mark Clayton, who were tagged the Marks Brothers, represented instant offense. Everybody talked about Marino's quick release and the fact that he had thrown seven touchdowns in two playoff games and had set NFL season records with 48 touchdowns and 5,084 passing yards. The Marks Brothers totaled 144 catches and 26 TDs during the regular season.

That was all fine and good but we had the best defense in the NFL. Didn't it matter that free safety Dwight Hicks, strong safety Carlton Williamson, cornerback Eric Wright, and myself had been selected to the NFC squad in the Pro Bowl, the first time in history an entire defensive backfield had come from the same team? Didn't it matter that the 17–1 49ers had the best record in pro football? And didn't it matter that our defense had allowed one touchdown in playoff victories over the New York Giants and the Chicago Bears, and that we had sacked their quarterbacks fifteen times?

Still our secondary would be under intense pressure. Bill Walsh and defensive coordinator George Seifert subjected us to two weeks of tedious and exhausting mental preparation. We studied game film after game film of the Miami offense, and it was an exercise in humility. There was Clayton jumping over defensive backs to make great catches and Duper burning guys with his blazing speed. They absorbed punishing blows and bounced back every time. We spent hours and hours perfecting our pass coverages, coming up with new ways to disguise our defenses and trick the Dolphins with different alignments.

I purposely kept a low profile in the days leading up to Super Bowl XIX. The 1984 season had been a topsy-turvy one for me, and to be honest, I'm not sure I deserved to be on the Pro Bowl team. It started with my preseason negotiations with the USFL's Arizona Wranglers that never materialized. Then a badly sprained ankle, a bruised big toe, and a dislocated shoulder knocked me out of all or parts of seven games. The injuries affected my pass coverage, so Walsh decided to have Hicks and me switch positions in the ninth game of the season. Hicks, who had been a Pro Bowl safety three straight years, had never played cornerback in his life. I had played free safety once since college days when Hicks left the team in 1983 because of a contract dispute. Neither of us was thrilled about the move, and I worried that it might hurt my relationship with Hicks and ruin our continuity in the secondary.

Although I had recovered from my injuries and would start in the Super Bowl at cornerback, there was another reason for me to shy away from the media. The last time we had played the Dolphins in 1983, wide receiver Nat Moore had beaten me on 24- and 19-yard touchdown receptions in the first half, and we wound up losing 20–17. Moore had preyed on my aggressiveness. I had taken my eyes off him for an instant to glance at Marino, and the next thing I knew Moore was open downfield.

For days after that game I couldn't go ten minutes without thinking about Moore's touchdowns. I vowed that it would not happen again, and I didn't want to discuss the subject with anybody.

To redeem myself and go for the payback, as we used to say at USC, I played a psychological game with the Dolphin receivers. The problems that I had experienced in Super Bowl XVI—frigid weather, isolated hotel, overheated rooms and 6 A.M. wake-up calls—had taught me to turn negatives into positives. The key to winning big games is not dwelling on the whys. Instead, come up with a response that shifts the focus away from the problems, as Walsh had done the week of Super Bowl XVI when he claimed the NFL was trying to do everything to help the Cincinnati Bengals win. The Dolphins' passing attack would only become a distraction if I allowed it. At the daily press conferences, I portrayed the image of being resigned to the fact that I couldn't cover Duper or Clayton. No, there's just no way I can stop them. No way. I wanted the Dolphins to read my remarks and believe I wouldn't be a factor in the game.

Lowell Cohn, a columnist for the *San Francisco Chronicle*, called my bluff. He wrote: "All week, Lott has been coming on like the poor soul of the 49er secondary—'What, me cover guys like Duper and Clayton?' Despite being the highest-paid defensive back in the NFL, Lott has bad-mouthed his own abilities and frequently said Dolphin receivers have little to fear from him. But the real-life Ronnie Lott is no doubt-stricken neurotic from a Dostoyevsky story who happened to wander onto a football field. He believes he can knock the socks off any wide receiver in the NFL."

In my heart I knew what I could do. I had extreme confidence in our defensive game plan, and I had the utmost faith in my teammates. We had more talent and depth than we had had on our first Super Bowl team. We had twenty-four new players, including several veterans who were getting an opportunity to win their first Super Bowl ring. Men like defensive tackle Gary (Big Hands) Johnson, formerly with the San Diego Chargers; defensive tackle Manu Tuiasosopo, from the Seattle Seahawks; running back Wendell Tyler from the Los Angeles Rams, and tight end Russ Francis from the New England Patriots. They were all big contributors during the regular season, overachievers with plenty of personality.

Tyler's story was remarkable. He played with the Rams in Super Bowl XIV and a month later was involved in a serious automobile accident in West Virginia. He suffered a dislocated hip, and the doctors said he had only a small chance of coming back. Through rigorous rehabilitation, he learned to walk and run all over again. In 1984 he set a 49er season rushing record with 1,262 yards.

Francis, on the other hand, was off-center. He had taken up pro wrestling following in the footsteps of his father, Gentleman Ed Francis, who grappled as a good guy in the 1950s. Russ stopped wrestling because he said he couldn't take the pounding. He also loved to skydive and to fly his 1942 open-cockpit biplane around the Hawaiian countryside. In his own way, Francis was our 1984 version of Hacksaw Reynolds.

And speaking of Hacksaw, he and defensive end Fred Dean were still around, providing us with their leadership. Reynolds, thirty-seven, once again spent Super Bowl week handing out printed sheets to the media explaining the origin of his nickname Hacksaw. This time, he also told stories of the house he had built on the island of San Salvador. There, he said, he lived on conch fritters, peas-and-rice dishes, and fresh-baked bread, and to pass the time lifted weights and took nuts and bolts off cars. What would we have done without Hacksaw's comic relief?

Reynolds kept us relaxed and it showed in our locker room on Super Bowl Sunday, starting at the top with Walsh. The calm look on his face reminded me of the scene in the locker room at Super Bowl XVI when Walsh and half the team burst through the door about two hours before kickoff after their bus had been delayed in traffic. Greetings, guys. No need to worry. Everything is under control. This afternoon Walsh was sprawled on the locker-room floor with his back against an equipment bag and his hands behind his head.

"Remember, they've got one of the greatest passers of all time," Walsh said. Then he paused. For effect. "But they haven't seen our defense."

"Are you ready, Bill?" Hicks asked.

"Yeah, it's just taking too long," he replied.

"We'll knock down a door and get 'em right now!" Hicks proclaimed.

Walsh remained calm even after he studied the Dolphins during the pregame warm-ups.

"This isn't going to be so bad," he said. "They aren't as big or as physical as we are. We're quicker and more explosive. . . . Hey, guys, you know it isn't like this is your first high school game and you're afraid the coach is going to put you in."

Unfortunately, not everybody had taken his cue from Walsh. Wright worked himself into such a state over the Dolphins' passing game that he began screaming, hollering, and jumping around during warm-ups. By the end of the pregame introductions he was so juiced I found him in tears on the sideline. The episode made me angry. Why did we allow the secondary to take so much crap before the game? Wright, after all, had only been beaten for one touchdown the entire season.

As expected, Marino came out throwing and, I have to tell you, he looked unstoppable. On the Dolphins' first possession, he completed four of five passes to set up a 37-yard field goal by Uwe von Schamann. On their next possession it was boom, boom, boom, boom, boom. Marino went 5-for-5 and tossed a 2-yard touchdown pass to tight end Dan Johnson. The Dolphins led 10–7 at the end of the first quarter.

Marino had picked on Wright a couple of times, and when he came off the field after the Miami touchdown, I put my arm around him and told him to relax. "Challenge those guys," I said. "You're the best cover guy we have."

The Dolphins had surprised us by using a no-huddle offense and that kept us from immediately changing from our basic 3–4 defense to our nickel defense. We needed another down lineman to put more pressure on Marino. After Miami scored, we stayed in our nickel package for the rest of the game. Dean and Dwaine (Pee Wee) Board attacked from the ends, and tackles Big Hands Johnson, and either Jeff Stover or Michael Carter blasted from the inside.

The key was Johnson outmaneuvering the Dolphins' Pro Bowl center Dwight Stephenson. We decided to bull-rush Stephenson, which kept him from helping out his guards on pass protection, and that enabled Johnson to shoot the inside gaps and get into Marino's face. That defensive strategy corralled Marino in the second quarter. Miami punted on its first three possessions and Marino completed just one pass for four yards. Punter Reggie Roby got off poor kicks, giving us excellent field position each time, and we scored three touchdowns to take a 28–10 lead with 2:05 left in the first half.

Even though the Dolphins added two more field goals, making it 28–16 at halftime, I wasn't worried. I was fully confident we could continue to put pressure on Marino. There were a number of things from the first half that showed we had gained control of the game. The Dolphins made only one of six third-down conversions. In the second quarter, Wright deflected a third-down pass to Duper to stop a drive, and I knocked away a third-down pass to Clayton in the end zone. We knew the Dolphins had absolutely no rushing game.

The pressure from the front four, combined with our constantly changing pass coverages, continued to fluster Marino in the second half and made him hold the ball a little longer than he wanted. On the Dolphins' opening series, Board sacked Marino for a loss of nine yards, and on the Dolphins' next possession Tuiasosopo and Board sacked Marino on consecutive plays. I noticed that Marino was throwing the ball high, at times letting it go before his receivers had turned around. Our defensive linemen told me that Marino was turning his back as soon as he released the ball, hoping to avoid being hit. Clearly we had him rattled.

Our secondary stopped Miami's next two drives, proving once and for all that Marino and the Marks Brothers were not invincible. Clayton ran a post-pattern on Wright on a second down from the San Francisco 27. Most other defensive backs would have been burned, but Wright got an unbelievable jump on the ball. He broke on Marino's release and made a leaping interception at the 49er 1 to kill Miami's threat with 3:27 left in the third quarter. The next time he had the ball, Marino was sacked by Johnson for a 12-yard loss back to the Miami 9, but he rebounded to march the Dolphins to the San Francisco 21. On the next play he rolled right and threw to tight end Joe Rose in the end zone, but Williamson picked off the pass with 10:45 remaining in the game. There would be no more scoring by either team. We crushed the Dolphins 38–16. When it was over, we had held Duper and Clayton to seven catches for 103 yards and no touchdowns. My old buddy Nat Moore gained 17 yards on two receptions. Although he threw for 318 yards, we sacked Marino four times and intercepted him twice.

Montana and the 49ers' offense had been reduced to an afterthought in all of the hoopla over Marino and Duper–Clayton. Given all that, we rolled up a Super Bowl record 537 yards in total offense and Montana directed us to scores on five straight possessions, which enabled us to go from a 10–7 deficit to a 38–16 lead with a little more than six minutes remaining in the third quarter. Throughout the years, whenever the press has hyped the opposing quarterback, Montana has taken it as a personal challenge and inspired himself to new heights. Here he completed 24 of 35 for a Super Bowl record 331 yards and three touchdowns. No interceptions. He also contributed with 59 yards rushing and one touchdown. For that Montana was named the game's Most Valuable Player.

Coming into this contest, the least talked about part of our offense had been the running game, and we certainly proved to the Dolphins we had talent in that department too. Tyler set up two of our TDs with his running and led all Super Bowl rushers with 65 yards. He caught four passes for another 70 yards. Roger Craig became the first player in Super Bowl history to score three touchdowns. He rushed for 58 yards and one touchdown, and caught seven passes for 77 yards and two TDs. Craig and I had roomed together at the hotel, and what I'll remember about him from Super Bowl XIX is how wired he was the night before. He spent a couple of hours being his own chiropractor, aligning what seemed to be every bone in his body, beginning with his toes and ending with his neck. I was watching TV and hoping to fall asleep, but every time the sportscasters would mention the Super Bowl, Craig would yell and adjust himself more loudly. "Yeah, let's play!" *Crraaackkk.* "Oh, man, tomorrow's going to be great!" *Crraaackkk.* "I can't wait!" Come to think of it, Craig's lucky he survived his own adjustments.

In retrospect, the 1984 49ers were the best team I played on in my decade with the organization. We had 49 solid players and could use every single one in critical situations. We finished with an 18–1 record, the best single-season record in pro football history, and that afternoon at Stanford Stadium we proved to ourselves, and to the rest of the world, that we were indeed something special.

THE END OF THE WALSH ERA

The warm Miami air was filled with tension during the week of Super Bowl XXIII. On Monday night, rioting broke out in the predominantly black section of Overtown after a police officer shot and killed a black motorcyclist. Buildings and cars were burned, and over a three-day stretch nearly 400 people were arrested. Even though we were staying at an airport hotel eight miles from Overtown, the rioting wasn't far from our minds. I met with our team adviser Dr. Harry Edwards, a sociology professor at the University of California in Berkeley, to discuss the situation and figure out if there was any way that the 49ers could help temper the violence. Edwards concluded that the problems in Overtown were deeply rooted and NFL players were not qualified to step in as mediators. We decided the 49ers should solely concentrate on the Super Bowl. By Thursday the rioting stopped.

"Even though some people consider it the toy department of life, the Super Bowl is important," Dr. Edwards said. "It's part of the human experience. Both the Super Bowl and Overtown are part of the human drama."

All the same, what happened in Overtown made some of the goings-on in the "toy department" seem insignificant.

For example, wide receiver Jerry Rice, who had played on a tender right ankle most of the season, twisted it again in a practice session. Bill Walsh expressed concern about his chances of playing in Sunday's game. I wasn't worried because a few hours after it happened Rice was out dancing at a Miami nightspot with me, linebacker Keena Turner, and cornerback Eric Wright. I assure you Rice had all the right moves on the dance floor. Sprained ankle, huh?

Next, our cornerback Tim McKyer stirred things up in Wednesday's media session by comparing the 49ers and the Bengals to "a Mercedes and a Chevy." He predicted "We're going to blow these guys out," and pointing to his right ring finger, he said, "The Super Bowl ring is already as good as there. It's gonna look nice, don't you think?" According to McKyer, the 49ers would win 28–10. He apologized the following day but didn't take back what he had said.

"I guess I ticked a lot of guys off," McKyer said. "I was asked questions, and I gave answers. This is Tim McKyer, and this is me. This is America, isn't it?"

I doubt anybody else on the 49ers considered the Bengals pushovers. They had fashioned a 12–4 record after finishing 4–11 in 1987, the biggest regular-season turnaround in NFL history. The Bengals were an offensive machine with quarterback Boomer Esiason, the NFL's Most Valuable Player, firing passes to a group of gifted receivers. They led the league in rushing with perennial All-Pro tackle Anthony Munoz blasting holes for James Brooks and Ickey Woods, the rookie sensation with the hippety-hop Ickey Shuffle touchdown dance.

The only real drama in the "toy department" surrounded the persistent rumors that Walsh would step down after the Super

Bowl. I sensed that Walsh was worn thin from the 1988 season, but he repeatedly refused to address retirement questions because he didn't want to distract himself or the players from the game. In my opinion, Walsh's greatest achievement in his decade of coaching the 49ers was getting us to this Super Bowl. We had rebounded from a disappointing 6–5 record and two straight midseason disasters, a 24–23 loss to the Phoenix Cardinals, in which we blew a 23-point third-quarter lead, and a 9–3 loss to the Los Angeles Raiders.

We had also endured an emotionally draining quarterback controversy. Walsh originally created the situation when he benched Montana for the first time in his career in the third quarter of our 36–24 NFC divisional playoff loss to the Minnesota Vikings that ended the 1987 season. When Montana went to the bench, he had completed only 12 of 26 for 109 yards and one interception. He had been sacked four times. We trailed 27–10, our only touchdown coming on strong safety Jeff Fuller's 48-yard interception return, when backup quarterback Steve Young took over. Young rushed for a game-high 72 yards and scored on a 5-yard run. But it wasn't enough.

Had injuries and spinal surgery in 1986 finally caught up to Montana? Did he not have the quickness to avoid the pass rush? Had he lost his nerve and his touch? Those were the questions the media asked after the game—the 49ers' third consecutive playoff loss since Super Bowl XIX—and throughout the off-season. There were rumors of Montana being traded to the San Diego Chargers for two first-round draft picks and a starting player. The Chargers reportedly offered running back Gary Anderson, but the 49ers wanted linebacker Billy Ray Smith and that apparently killed the trade.

Then Walsh created more problems in our 1988 training camp when he hinted that the starting quarterback job was up for grabs. "We may have a quarterback controversy," Walsh told the media in London after one of our practices prior to our preseason game against the Miami Dolphins. He said that he expected Young to be stiff competition.

In my mind, Walsh manufactured the quarterback controversy to take himself off the hook for our horrendous playoff defeat to the Vikings. We should have been in the Super Bowl after the 1987 season but Walsh ran us into the ground in practices in the two weeks prior to the Vikings' game. Eddie DeBartolo, Jr., had been so disgusted after the loss that he stripped Walsh of his title as team president. Walsh later admitted that he and DeBartolo didn't speak for almost two months. I also believed that Walsh conjured up the quarterback controversy as a way to motivate Montana. Walsh believed that Montana needed to be pushed. No one pushed himself to greater heights than Montana. Sometimes it seemed that none of his accomplishments were good enough.

Montana started our season opener in 1988, and despite playing with a bruised right elbow he led us to a 34–33 victory over the New Orleans Saints. Walsh jumped on the Montana bandwagon after the game, insisting there had never been any doubt as to who was the starter. However, Montana's elbow was so badly swollen after the game and throughout the following week that Young got all the snaps in practice. Montana, who also suffered from the flu, didn't take a snap until Saturday. Young started against the New York Giants the next day, but their powerful defense made him look inexperienced and a bit hesitant. Instead of throwing the ball, Young repeatedly reverted to running. The score was 10–10 at halftime. Walsh put Montana in in the second half, and although he had problems under the heavy rush, he managed to pull out a 20–17 victory with 42 seconds left, connecting with flanker Jerry Rice on a 78-yard touchdown pass.

Over the next several weeks Montana alternated flashes of competence with moments of struggle, and Walsh slowly began to retreat. The quarterback controversy escalated in our eighth game after Montana had problems on offense in a 10–9 loss to the Chicago Bears on Monday Night Football. Our pass protection broke down, and Montana was roughed up by the Bears' defense. Late in the fourth quarter, Walsh brought in Young, hoping his running ability would get us untracked. It didn't, and the next day Walsh told reporters at his weekly press conference that he was going to have Young share more time with Montana. Walsh claimed Montana was fatigued and needed a rest. That was news to Montana, who was visibly upset when reporters informed him of the decision before Walsh could.

Montana hadn't seemed tired to me. He had stuck to a strict workout regimen since returning from back surgery. Every time I turned around, it seemed that Montana was working out on the StairMaster. I believe the real motivation behind the decision was that Walsh wanted to further justify having pulled Montana from the 1987 divisional playoff game. Our next opponent, after all, was the Vikings. Young's incredible 49-yard touchdown run with less than two minutes to go, gave us a 24–

21 victory over Minnesota. Asked if Young would be the starter the rest of the season, Walsh replied "Anything's possible." That comment prompted Montana to say he was sure the 49ers were trying to trade him. I can't remember ever seeing Montana so depressed as he was during that time.

Playing musical chairs at quarterback was also splitting the team apart. I heard some of my teammates say they thought Young should be the starter, and Montana had to hear the grumblings, too. Reporters would ask him all the time to comment on anti-Montana remarks made by "unidentified teammates." *San Francisco Chronicle* columnist Glenn Dickey rode Montana hard. After reading Dickey's harsh criticism you would have sworn Montana was a third-string quarterback. He can't handle pressure. He has no escapability. He doesn't run to his left anymore. Because I seldom saw Dickey at our training facility, I wondered where he was getting his information.

Young then faltered in our loss at Phoenix, and a week later Montana found himself starting again against the Raiders. We played poorly and that brought out the boo-birds in droves. But Montana rebounded with a great game on Monday Night Football against the Washington Redskins. He threw two touchdowns and ran for another in our 37–21 victory. Montana never looked over his shoulder again. We won three of our next four games and continued our rampage through the playoffs, destroying the Vikings 34–9 and the Chicago Bears 28–3.

Although Montana declined to discuss the quarterback controversy in depth during Super Bowl week, Walsh continually insisted that the time off had been the major difference in the season. Naturally, Montana strongly disagreed and probably still does to this day.

Because of the rough road to Super Bowl XXIII, I decided to savor every moment that happened on and off the field. That was something I hadn't done at our other two Super Bowls. One night Miami Dolphin linebacker Hugh Green and his wife cooked dinner for me on their boat, and another night I hung out with Michael Jordan and several of his Chicago Bulls teammates after their basketball game against the Miami Heat.

"Man, you won't believe it," Jordan said. "Ickey Woods was at the game and did his shuffle right on the court."

"You've got to be kidding," I replied.

Woods led the Bengals in rushing with 1,066 yards and had scored 15 touchdowns. As far as I was concerned that would be the last time Ickey would shuffle in Miami. I had studied films of him for two weeks, and I hadn't seen any free safeties make a good straight-on hit. When Woods rambled into the secondary, guys just brought him down from the side. Why hadn't anybody laid any wood on this guy? I felt as though Woods thought he had a big red S on his chest. I was determined to hit him full speed. I wanted to make sure he remembered me.

As I walked through the tunnel leading to the field at Joe Robbie Stadium for the pregame warm-ups, I saw Los Angeles Dodger Manager Tommy Lasorda and we exchanged a few words. I checked out singer Billy Joel and his wife, model Christie Brinkley. Joel was going to sing the national anthem. Offensive tackle Harris Barton said that he had seen comedian John Candy. I had always looked at the Super Bowl as a game, never perceiving it as the entertainment event that it is. This day I realized I was an actor on a stage.

Super Bowl XXIII started on a sour note. Our left tackle, Steve Wallace, broke his left ankle on the third play of the game, and on our next series Cincinnati's All-Pro nose guard Tim Krumrie twisted his left ankle almost 360 degrees, shattering two bones in his leg. Parts of the field were wet and slippery, but that didn't bother Woods, who managed to grind out 27 yards on his first four carries. I was disappointed that I hadn't been able to leave my imprint on him. Near the end of the first quarter Woods ran into my sights. I felt like I was watching a big fat fastball coming right at me. I unloaded on Woods with a vicious hit, right on the sweet spot, and I'm sure that had something to do with the fact that he gained only 10 more yards before halftime.

Woods wasn't the only offensive star who had a hard time generating some offense. With the exception of Rice, who caught three passes for 58 yards, nobody else seemed to be in rhythm. Montana had mediocre statistics, completing 9 of 16 for 114 yards. He had been sacked twice and appeared to be pressing. Esiason was equally ineffective with 4 of 12 for 48 yards. The score at halftime was 3–3. There hadn't been such a low-scoring first half in a Super Bowl since the Pittsburgh Steelers led the Minnesota Vikings 2–0 in Super Bowl IX.

With the score tied 6–6 and less than a minute to go in the third quarter, the Bengals went ahead on Stanford Jennings' 93-yard kickoff return. Montana brought us back on our next possession, connecting with Rice on a 14-yard touchdown. The Bengals broke the tie with 3:20 remaining in the game on a Jim Breech 40-yard field goal, making it 16–13.

I cursed myself on the sideline for not being able to come up with a big play on the Bengals' go-ahead score. "We're going to lose the game," I said, hanging my head dejectedly. Cornerback Don Griffin noticed how upset I was, and he came over to try to make me feel better. "We're not going to lose this, Ronnie," Griffin said. "You've got to believe we're going to win."

For that to happen we had to go 92 yards. If anybody could get us there it would be a superhuman quarterback named Montana. I had witnessed his heroics since my freshman year at USC, when he helped Notre Dame beat us 49–19. Whenever the situation got tight he never cracked. He always went with the flow. Also, for good luck, he happened to be wearing his jersey from Super Bowl XIX. His wife, Jennifer, had secretly packed it in his bag the night before, and he hadn't discovered it until he got to the locker room.

To start the drive, Montana strung together three completions, an 8-yarder to running back Roger Craig, a 7-yarder to tight end John Frank, and a 7-yarder to Rice. Then he handed off on two running plays to Craig, who got us a first down on our own 35. He found Rice on the left sideline for 17, then hit Craig for 13, giving us a first down on the Cincinnati 35. On the next play Montana brought the team to the line without a huddle and began barking out the play. He yelled so hard that he began to hyperventilate. He threw the ball over the head of Rice and out of bounds and gestured to the sideline for a timeout. Walsh waved him off, not realizing there was anything wrong, and fortunately by the time the offense broke the huddle for the following play Montana had recovered. His pass to Craig was wiped out when center Cross was caught for being an ineligible receiver downfield.

Now there was about a minute remaining in the game. Facing a second-and-20 from the Cincinnati 45, I was thinking, if we can pick up another 15 yards, we can be in position to attempt a field goal, and if successful, send the game into overtime. Montana called for a square-in pattern to Rice. Bengal cornerback Lewis Billups and safety Ray Horton double-teamed Rice, with strong safety David Fulcher helping them out. But Montana's pass was perfect, covering 13 yards, and Rice broke away to gain 14 more. Another 8-yard completion to Craig put the ball on the 10.

Montana called timeout with 39 seconds left. After conferring with Walsh, they decided on a play called 20 Halfback Curl X-Up. Rice started in motion to the left, acting as a decoy. Craig, the primary receiver, ran a curl pattern up the middle but he got caught in traffic. Wide receiver John Taylor, who hadn't caught a pass all day, ran straight to the end zone, and Montana found him for the game-winning 10-yard touchdown. We had beaten the Bengals, 20–16, for our third Super Bowl victory in eight years, the most dramatic of our world championships. Rice, who had caught 11 passes for 215 yards, was named MVP of Super Bowl XXIII. Had Rice not had such a great game, Montana would have won his third MVP trophy based on his 23 of 36 for a Super Bowl record 357 yards.

In the postgame interviews, Walsh was asked if he had coached his last game. He couldn't answer the question and, according to some of my teammates, he seemed to be near tears. It wasn't until four days later that he announced his retirement. Walsh persuaded the 49ers to pick defensive coordinator George Seifert to succeed him, and it was decided that Walsh would move into the front office as vice president of football operations. I was in Honolulu preparing for the Pro Bowl when I heard the news, and I must admit that I had ambivalent feelings. Mostly, I was hurt that he hadn't informed the players of his plans or even bothered to say goodbye. I wished he could have met with us and told us man to man, "Hey, we've had some great memories, but it's time for me to move on." Instead, he wrote me a short note. The gist of it was, if I ever needed anything I shouldn't hesitate to call. A note? After eight years? I was disappointed; I always expected a lot from Walsh.

Though there were many times I didn't agree with him, and I know there were just as many times he didn't agree with me, I believe we always respected each other. He did a fantastic job of building and coaching the 49ers. He controlled every aspect of the organization. From how the buses were set up, to the function of the equipment man, to building a special entrance for the media at the Santa Clara facility, to deciding whether or not players could sit on their helmets during practice. He had a remarkable eye for talent and had a keen understanding of the defensive side of the game. Walsh genuinely tried to better our lives off the field by setting up a program for the players to go back and get their college degrees. We were the first team in the NFL to institute random drug testing. He was a leader in hiring black coaches and held seminars in training camp for top black prospects.

However, when it came to personal, one-on-one relationships, Walsh had a difficult time communicating from the heart. He was calculating and controlled with his emotions. I wanted him to exude the warmth and compassion that my USC coach John Robinson had displayed, but that wasn't in his makeup. With his multiple role as the coach and the man in charge of personnel and contract negotiations, he elected not to form close bonds with the players. That was hard for me to accept. Whenever former NFL players Ahmad Rashad, an NBC commentator, and Joe Theismann, an analyst with ESPN, were in town to gather information for their broadcasts, they played tennis with Walsh. After their matches, it never failed that Rashad and Theismann would remark to me, "Isn't Bill a great guy? I wish I had played for a coach like that." That hurt me. I remember thinking, God, why can't he deal with us the way he deals with them?

In my eight years with Walsh, the two of us never had a heart-to-heart talk. And, keep in mind, as the 49er defensive captain for four years I was one of the players he would call to his office to get a pulsebeat on the team. We only had surface conversations about the mood of the players, or business matters like my contract. I regret that we never sat down and talked about life. We never laughed together.

I used to walk past the door to his offensive meetings, stop and listen to Walsh diagramming plays, and wonder what it would be like to be inside soaking up his offensive strategy. Walsh seldom got close to defensive players. He was obsessed with his offense. I can remember Walsh walking into only one defensive secondary meeting and that occurred the day after our preseason opener in 1981. The rookie secondary had repeatedly blown coverages and missed tackles. "I don't want to see anybody tackling people by the jerseys," Walsh hollered. That scared the hell out of me.

At the time I was drafted in 1981, Robinson had told me, "You're going to enjoy playing for Bill Walsh. He's a super guy. He loves the game. And he's a true players' coach." And back then Robinson was right. Walsh loved coaching that season, and he had a good sense of humor. He was warm, open, and genuine. Greeting us in a bellhop uniform when we checked into our hotel for Super Bowl XVI was right in character.

But after that first Super Bowl, Walsh began to change.

The following season, he discovered that several 49ers were using drugs. He became frustrated that he couldn't save them from the evils of cocaine. There were moments he seemed overwhelmed. He couldn't understand why players would waste the financial opportunities that pro football had given them. In the meantime, the national media started referring to Walsh as an offense "genius" because of our victory in Super Bowl XVI. The more recognition Walsh received, the more inflated his ego became and the more he was under the microscope. The media probed into his private life, and Walsh grew distant and unapproachable. At times, he turned into a basket case, and there were some moments that I actually felt sorry for him. Here was a man who had languished for a decade as an assistant coach in the NFL, a man who had been passed over many times for a head coaching job, and now, when he was finally recognized for his offensive system, he wanted to crawl into a shell.

A friend of his once told me, "Walsh doesn't want anybody to know him. He doesn't want you to figure him out." I think that was because he was afraid people would find out that he wasn't a genius. Designing his offense didn't come easily. Walsh had to work hard at it. He was painfully methodical. He wasn't Einstein or Mozart. And he knew that.

An NFL assistant coach described him as a motherfucker, but said that was why he was successful.

"You've got to be a motherfucker to survive in the NFL," the coach explained to me. "If you don't protect yourself, then you're going to have a tough time staying on top. You can't worry about how the players feel. You've got to be able to cut them in their prime. The people you think are going to keep you on top won't be able to because the business of football changes too quickly."

The turning point in my relationship with Walsh came the day after the 1982 finale against the Los Angeles Rams. We led 20–7 at halftime, but the Rams battled back to win 21–20, knocking us out of the playoffs. On Monday morning, I showed up at our training facility for the final team meeting before breaking up for the year. We took physicals, cleaned out our lockers, left off-season addresses, and tied up other loose ends. Still in shock from the Rams loss, some of us walked around the locker room like zombies. "I can't believe we lost that game" was the refrain. Around noontime, we gathered in our main meeting room to listen to Walsh make his final remarks for 1982. We waited and we waited. Finally, a 49er official announced that Walsh wouldn't be in to speak to us that day. "You guys can take off, and we'll see you next year," he said.

I was concerned about Walsh. Had there been an accident? Was something wrong with his family? However, the next morning, I learned that he hadn't shown up because he was too emotional to face us. The loss to the Rams, the 3–6 record in a strike-shortened season, and the drug problems had devastated him. From that moment on, I wondered whose side Walsh was on. Who was the real Bill Walsh? And most of my teammates wanted to know the same thing.

I have always believed that when you're the captain of the ship, you go down with the ship when it sinks. You do not fluctuate. In 1981, everything had been wonderful. We had reached the top of the mountain, and he was a coaching genius. Then we lost to the Rams, and he didn't want to be around us. Robinson had always been consistent. He lived and died with the USC Trojans. God, all Walsh had to do was show up and say, "I'll see you guys next year." Period. Because he hadn't done that, I doubted him as a leader—my leader and the leader of the 49ers—for the rest of my career.

It saddens me that Walsh never knew what made his players tick. If he had really known Montana, and understood how to motivate him, he never would have put him through the quarterback controversy. How well would Walsh have coached if Vince Lombardi had been breathing down his neck? He started a defensive backs controversy in 1988, too, pitting me against cornerback Eric Wright, one of my closest friends. He announced that Wright would start at free safety. Walsh claimed that this position would put less strain on Wright's groin area, which he had repeatedly irritated in the quick stops and turns he made at cornerback. But I knew what his real motives were. I was going through contract negotiations at the time, and he was trying to pressure me into signing quickly. It didn't work.

There was one incident with Walsh that still bothers me. I suppose it was his way of trying to motivate me, but in actuality he screwed with my head and tore up my heart. We had lost the 1985 season opener to the Minnesota Vikings, 28–21. The Vikings' aggressive defense caused seven turnovers to end our 9-game regular season winning streak. In the fourth quarter I was burned on a 44-yard TD catch by rookie wide receiver Hassan Jones that tied the score at 14–14, and I missed a tackle on running back Darrin Nelson that set up another score. Walsh summoned me to his office the next day and said, "Ronnie, we're going to test you for drugs."

I was shocked. "Why? Because I messed up on two plays?"

Bill persisted. "We're going to have to test you."

My stomach churned. "Bill, you've got to be kidding me. You know I don't use drugs."

That was the worst moment of my NFL career. To think that anyone would accuse me of playing under the influence of drugs. Come on. Just because I made two bad plays? I would never jeopardize myself or my football career in any way. I love the game too much. I left Walsh's office in tears. I locked myself in my condominium and pulled the plug on my phone. I didn't want to speak to anybody. I cried all night and barely slept.

The next morning, I decided to confront Walsh about the accusation. I couldn't let something like that slide. I raced to the 49er facility and asked Ray Rhodes, the defensive backs coach, and George Seifert, the defensive coordinator, to meet me in Walsh's office. I wanted them to witness the conversation because I didn't want this drug accusation to be something that only Walsh and I knew about. Down the road I didn't want him to deny that it had happened.

I was boiling with emotion. I was so choked up I had a hard time spitting out the words.

"Look, Ray and George and Bill, I want all three of you guys to hear me say this," I said. "I have never played a game on drugs. And I never will. If you want to test me every day from now on, go right ahead. But I promise you I'll never test dirty."

Rhodes and Seifert seemed surprised by what I was saying. I took the look on their faces to mean that they had never suspected me of using drugs, and that the whole idea of testing me was something they were hearing for the first time. Walsh, meanwhile, just stared at me as if to say, "I can't believe this guy is doing this."

I let all three coaches know in no uncertain terms that wherever this accusation started, or however this drug testing idea came up, these lies would stop right now. I wanted Walsh to understand the type of person I was. If he was going to insinuate that I made mistakes because I was using drugs, I wouldn't stand for it, and I wouldn't let it linger. I am an upfront person. I don't like deceiving people, and I don't like to be deceived. By the way, the 49ers didn't test me, and the accusation was never made again.

Less than six months after Walsh retired, a story broke that he was leaving the 49ers—and he did on July 10, 1989—to join NBC Sports as a commentator. This is what I told the media at the time: "Will I miss Bill Walsh? My response is Bill Who? That's how he would handle it. Life goes on. . . . He's a good guy. I respect him. But we've got a season to play. I don't think we'll miss him."

FELLOW WARRIORS I don't mean to sound unappreciative, but after playing in four Super Bowls I can honestly say I do not consider any of them the biggest or most meaningful game of my career. It is purely the challenge that drives me on Super Bowl Sunday. The pursuit of the goal. In my opinion, the Super Bowl has been turned into a spectacle by the NFL, and the only difference in the game from year to year is the city in which it is held and the number of accredited media representatives.

My biggest game was my first collegiate start as a freshman at USC against Washington State in 1977. That game made me feel that I belonged. The most meaningful, our 45–14 victory over the Dallas Cowboys in 1981, which proved that the 49ers could no longer be considered a bunch of losers. We took off the shackles that Sunday. In case you're wondering, my most exciting moment in sports came in a basketball game in 1979. The nine minutes I played at guard that night for the USC Trojans against UCLA in Pauley Pavilion were as thrilling as any I have experienced in pro football.

In Super Bowl XXIV, we needed to prove to ourselves and to the public that we could win a Super Bowl without Bill Walsh as our coach. We did that in awesome fashion by destroying the Denver Broncos, 55–10, in the Louisiana Superdome in New Orleans. How's this for domination? We led 13–3 after the first quarter, 27–3 at halftime and 41–10 at the end of the third quarter. It was the largest margin of victory in a Super Bowl and the most points scored in the forty-year history of the 49er franchise in the NFL. In winning Super Bowl XXIV we joined the Pittsburgh Steelers as the only team in NFL history to win four Super Bowls. The Steelers won Super Bowls IX, X, XIII, and XIV.

If Walsh had been our coach and not George Seifert, we never would have scored as many points. Once we had a comfortable lead, Walsh would have reverted more to the ground game to make the point that we had a balanced attack. Seifert tried to project an air of calmness during the game, but I sensed he was nervous because he allowed the offense to keep bombing away. He badly wanted a decisive victory to leave his own mark as head coach of the 49ers.

Once again Joe Montana was superb, completing 22 of 29 for 297 yards and a Super Bowl record five touchdowns, and that earned him a third Super Bowl MVP Award. Have you ever stopped to think about his career Super Bowl statistics? They're incredible: 83 of 122 for 1,142 yards and 11 TDs. Montana has never thrown an interception in a Super Bowl.

I should have been elated by our victory, but I wasn't. We had clearly shot down the notion that it was only Walsh's system that had won it for the 49ers all those years. The size of our hearts had just as much to do with our success. When I walk away from the game, my hands will be clean. Walsh didn't make me; I gave it *my* all. Why did I feel so depressed and defeated? The truth is, we had crushed the team that my best friend played for. That in itself was my story of Super Bowl XXIV.

Denver Bronco safety Dennis Smith and I had always fantasized about playing against each other in the Super Bowl. Super Bowl XXIV fulfilled that dream. When the 49ers started to build a commanding lead, however, I could see that his head wasn't in the game, and after I was replaced in the third quarter, I made sure not to make eye contact with Smith from the sideline. At the final gun I ran across the field to see him, and he appeared to be in a fog. The pain in his eyes almost made me wish we could play the game over. It was Smith's third Super Bowl defeat in four years, and it bothered me that the Broncos' worst loss of the bunch occurred against the 49ers. There was nothing I could say to Smith except, "I can't believe it turned out this way."

Football goes a lot deeper than X's and O's. Growing up in a military family, and moving from Albuquerque to Washington, D.C., to San Bernardino and finally to Rialto, I had purposely not made close friends because I wanted to protect myself from the hurt of one day having to say goodbye. But that changed a few days before my freshman football season at USC when I gave Smith a ride home from our first practice. We became best friends, and over the years we shared everything. We had swigs of 7-and-7s as rambunctious freshmen. We celebrated our being first-round NFL draft picks. We had dinners at the Pro Bowl. We encouraged each other to battle back from injuries. He always joked that he was "a poor man's Ronnie Lott," and I teased that I couldn't cover receivers man-to-man the way he did. Somebody once told me that you're only going to have two true friends in your lifetime. Smith is one of mine.

We were together the week of Super Bowl XXII in San Diego

before the Broncos lost to the Washington Redskins, 42–10, and he spent time with me in Miami the following January for Super Bowl XXIII against the Cincinnati Bengals. I hung out in my hotel room with Smith after that game instead of hobnobbing with the revelers at our team victory party.

"Ronnie, I'm really happy for you. You guys did it," Smith said that night. "Maybe we can pull one out next year."

From the middle of the 1989 season on, as the 49ers and Broncos kept winning, we took turns calling each other and dreaming out loud about meeting in the big dance. Smith would complain that the Broncos hadn't won previous Super Bowls, and then I would remind him that his team had beaten us in each of our three regular-season games in the 1980s. We had dinner one night the week of Super Bowl XXIV, and I was a guest for his segment on a Denver TV show. He grilled me with some pretty tough questions. At the close of the show, he asked if I was going to come over to his locker room and congratulate him after the Broncos' victory. Why not? We're best friends.

How could anybody have prepared us for things to work out the way they did? The night of Super Bowl XXIV I knew better than to phone him, and at the Pro Bowl a couple of days later, we hardly broached the subject of the loss. I knew from past experience as roommates at USC how much we both suffered after losses. As collegians we wanted to be alone in our apartment. Friends had to drag us to a party after we lost to UCLA in the last game of our senior year. I had heard via the grapevine that he was so upset after the Super Bowl that he had left the locker room without speaking to the media. It wasn't until almost a month later that we discussed the game, but even that conversation didn't last long.

"I can't believe it happened," Smith was still saying. "I can't believe we played that bad."

I know that Smith will always look back on his three Super Bowl experiences with disappointment and feel that a part of his career was incomplete. Until his dying day he'll be asking, "Why couldn't we win the Super Bowl?" I have worked hard for all of my achievements, but sometimes I feel a little guilty about my good fortune. I know that Smith doesn't hold it against me, but I can't help asking, why have I been so lucky?

Smith showed a lot of character when he stood up at my wedding reception on March 2, 1991, and in front of a crowd that contained Montana and some of the 49er coaching staff, addressed the Broncos' Super Bowl XXIV debacle. "Somebody told me that as the best man, I have to get up and tell some jokes," Smith began. "Oh, yeah, the Super Bowl—there's a joke. . . ."

Smith wasn't the only man whose character was tested by the events of Super Bowl XXIV. To me that game will always represent the strength, courage, and determination of Joe Montana. He had battled back from spinal surgery in 1986, survived a quarterback controversy that began in the 1987 playoff loss to the Minnesota Vikings and continued throughout 1988, and during the week of Super Bowl XXIV he had been at the center of controversy. Roberta Baskin, a television reporter in Washington, D.C., had reported that three white quarterbacks had tested positive for "high levels of cocaine" during the past ten years but her story claimed that they were never punished by the NFL and their names were never revealed. Baskin said the purpose of her report was to point out the inconsistencies in the NFL's drug testing policy, since twenty-six of the thirty players who had been punished since 1987 were black. Well, the 2,500 media members jumped all over her story, and Montana, who hadn't been named in the report, was forced to defend himself against the alleged drug charges. He had been down this road before, in the mid-'80s, fighting drug rumors at that time, too.

"It makes me mad, but what can I do?" Montana said to the media four days before Super Bowl XXIV. "I know it's untrue, that's why I'm not worried about it. They have tried to say this before about me, and I attacked it and challenged it. There's no telling what this does to you and your family. They don't take that into consideration."

Addressing these allegations took more courage than he would have to muster on Super Bowl Sunday. If he hadn't responded, he would have carried it with him. Montana keeps a lot of his emotions inside. You can tell a person's true character by how he responds in a critical situation away from his normal environment.

People always ask me, "What's Joe Montana really like?" When I tell them he's shy, they always seem surprised. They can't believe he's a regular Joe. He's a family man who loves to play with his three children. I think when his career is over, he'd be happy being with his kids all day long. His wife Jennifer keeps him loose for big games by taping snapshots of the kids in his playbook. Underneath she writes silly captions. Montana loves kids. On road trips, he sometimes spends his free time visiting with children who are suffering from life-threatening diseases. These children have said that if they could have one wish it would be to meet Joe Montana. He works with the Make-A-Wish Foundation of America to make their wishes come true. Montana understands the importance of the wishes, and he spends quality time with each child. Talking to these kids is difficult for Montana. I know how he feels because I've been in the same situation. There is no way you look a sick child in the eye and not be touched.

In my mind, the Kingpin is the reason we were able to be The Team of the '80s. He is one guy who could have spun away from us and gone on to be rich and famous. He never became bigger than the team. He hasn't changed since 1981. He's extraordinary but ordinary. A normal guy. You'd never see him pull his Ferrari into a reserved parking space in the front of the 49er training facility. Most of the time he drives a suburban-family-type-car to work. The only time he acts like a superstar is when he's in the heat of battle.

Although he receives and answers hundreds of fan letters each week—the mail carriers deliver them in large plastic tubs—Montana has no conception of his place in the world. It doesn't register that he is better known than three quarters of the presidents of the United States. Granted, being in public with Montana isn't quite like the rock-star mania that surrounds Magic Johnson and Michael Jordan—they can't even go to the movies without having to sign autographs in the dark. From time to time, however, I have seen people go berserk around Montana. Like the day after Super Bowl XIX. The 49ers heading to the Pro Bowl were sequestered in an airline club at the San Francisco International Airport. When it was time to board the flight to Honolulu, we opened the door and were blinded by dozens of flashbulbs. He was swamped by autograph hounds. It's interesting to see how three of the biggest superstars in professional sports handle the commotion they create. I base my observations on the times I've been with them. Magic goes with the flow. He relishes the attention. He enjoys socializing with Hollywood stars, and parties at his house almost always include the big names from the entertainment world. Jordan is more down-to-earth. Always a gentleman, I think he just puts up with fame. He could easily live without it. Montana gets very uncomfortable when people fuss over him. When he's eating in a restaurant with teammates and a steady stream of people ask for his autograph, he might pretend to us that he's irritated but I know that he's embarrassed.

I don't think I truly understood his international appeal until we spent a week in Tokyo for our preseason game with the Los Angeles Rams in 1989. Everywhere I went, from the subway to an automobile factory, when the Japanese found out I played professional football, they nodded knowingly and asked, ". . . Ah. Joe Montana. Do you know Joe Montana?" It was overwhelming.

By the way, this is how I knew Joe Montana:

He was one of the biggest practical jokers on the 49ers. In training camp, he was notorious for stealing any bike that wasn't chained down. He would hide them on the roofs of buildings or hang them from trees. He did a hilarious imitation of our squatty nose tackle, Jim Burt. He knelt on the floor, put his shoes under each knee, and then crawled around the locker room yelling, "Hi, I'm Jim Burt." He adopted the Hank Williams, Jr., song from the opening of Monday Night Football as our official theme in 1989. He darted around the locker room a couple hours before games, grabbed players by the shoulders, shook them and sang, "Are you ready for some football?"

When Walsh was coaching, Montana always used to make some smart-aleck remark about our play selection. It kept our offense focused and loose. "That stupid son of a bitch. What does he want to run that for?" Montana would say after a play had been signaled in from the sideline. Then he would step into the huddle and say, "The old man is panicking. He's losing it, boys. We've got to do it ourselves."

But when I reflect on Montana many years from now, what I'll remember most is the courage he showed in 1986 when he returned to action eight weeks after surgery to remove a ruptured disk in his back. To me, that was the greatest feat of Montana's illustrious career. I visited him in the hospital the afternoon of his surgery on September 15. He was woozy and pale but remarkably upbeat. He was trying to talk and be friendly. Same old Joe.

"Relax, man. You don't have to say anything," I told him. "Save your energy."

When I returned for another visit two days later with wide receiver Dwight Clark, Montana seemed even better. He was chattering on, boasting about all the exercise he was getting.

"So they're letting you move around already?" I asked.

"Yeah, I'm walking to and from the bathroom," he kidded.

As we were getting ready to leave, the nurses suggested he

accompany us to the elevator to stretch his legs. Montana seemed eager to demonstrate his progress.

"I've got to walk a certain amount every day," he said. "This will be great. Let me show you how well I'm doing."

That's when reality struck. First of all, Montana had trouble getting out of bed. It took a couple of nurses to sit him up and lift him to his feet. Just that little bit of movement seemed to exhaust him. He looked so fragile, I was afraid to touch him. Montana began to walk us down the hall, taking tiny steps, moving inch by inch like a 100-year-old man. Every part of my body was feeling for him. I was frightened. Montana had no fear in his eyes. He never did. He only showed concern. But there wasn't any concern in his eyes either. He was actually thrilled to be walking so soon after surgery.

When we finally reached the elevator, I was quite upset. Montana said happily, "Thanks for coming. I'll see you guys." The elevator door closed, and I felt like crying. I thought, my God. This guy's never going to play again.

How badly did I underestimate Montana? After the back surgery, and including the 1990 season, he threw for at least 3,000 yards in three different seasons, won the NFL passing title, was named MVP of the league, and guided us to two Super Bowl victories.

Some of the sweetest moments I spent with Montana came after the last two Super Bowls when I dropped by his hotel room to share some pizza and have a glass of champagne. Instead of celebrating with a restaurant dinner of fine New Orleans cooking, he went back to his room, put on a white shirt and tie, and hosted a room-service feast for forty family members and friends.

I've always felt that Super Bowl victories should be celebrated quietly, with the people you love. It should come as no surprise that I've never been moved to tears of jubilation after Super Bowls, and I don't get excited until I slip on the diamond championship ring. The feeling I have is one of serenity and humility. For a few minutes I walk real gingerly, bow to the gods, and say, thank you. Then it's time to party.

After Super Bowl XXIV, I asked my contingent of loved ones to meet me back at my hotel room. It was the first time I had ever been with my parents, brother Roy, and sister Suzie the night of a Super Bowl victory. Also with us were my attorney Leonard Armato and his father; my future wife Karen Collmer and her brothers; my son Ryan; former USC teammate Eric

Scoggins, and my godparents Chuck and Eva Young. I raised a glass of champagne and toasted them one by one, citing the help each had given me during my career and what they had meant to my life. Without them, I couldn't have been on four Super Bowl championship teams. At that moment, I felt very lucky.

6 THE QUEST FOR THREE-PEAT

MY WORLD AND WELCOME TO IT: A Season Diary

Here are my reflections, recorded during my final season with the San Francisco 49ers, as we tried to win three consecutive Super Bowls:

JUNE 1, 1990
LIHUE, KAUAI

WHY THREE-PEAT?

Eddie DeBartolo, Jr., the most generous owner in professional sports, really outdid himself this time. He flew the entire 49er organization—management, players, coaches, and staff, as well as their spouses, significant others, and dates—to this magnificent tropical paradise for a six-day "family" vacation. The all-expenses-paid trip was to celebrate our fourth Super Bowl victory and back-to-back world championships in 1988 and 1989. DeBartolo gave each of the players a total of $1,100 to spend on meals, which were free to begin with.

The Westin Hotel in Kauai is situated on 800 lush acres, featuring a reflecting pool with every species of swan and a wildlife sanctuary in a man-made lagoon. Mahogany launches float past six islands of flamingos, kangaroos, gazelles, zebras, monkeys, and wallabies. Scattered throughout the halls of the hotel are $2.5 million worth of paintings, sculptures, and ceramics from the Far East. My room overlooked a huge 26,000-square-foot swimming pool with four cascading waterfalls.

It wasn't unusual for DeBartolo to shower us with gifts and perks. He wore his heart on his wallet. For Christmas in 1989 he sent every player's wife or girlfriend a $500 gift certificate from Neiman-Marcus. Players who signed with the 49ers as Plan B free agents were welcomed with large fruit baskets. When linebacker Jim Fahnhorst's wife, Kim, gave birth to twin boys in 1989, DeBartolo sent a huge flower arrangement that weighed almost 70 pounds. I joined Mr. D in Las Vegas for boxing title bouts, and he picked up the tab. A couple of times he flew me to grand opening galas for his shopping malls in various parts of the country.

DeBartolo's Super Bowl victory celebrations were much more grandiose. Following our 38–16 victory over Miami in Super Bowl XIX, he invited a group of players to his home in Youngstown, Ohio, and had a Rolex watch waiting for each of us. After our 20–16 victory over Cincinnati in Super Bowl XXIII he flew every coach, player, and front office staff member to Youngstown for two days. The focal point of the weekend was a charity dinner for 750 people that raised more than $200,000. He hired the pastry chef from the Beverly Hills Hotel, the head chef from the Mayfair House Hotel in Miami, and four other nationally known chefs. Their gourmet meal consisted of lobster, smoked salmon, fresh pasta, Belgian endive salad, and homemade chocolate candy. We danced to the music of Jeffrey Osborne.

The first night in Youngstown, DeBartolo hosted a dinner for us at his restaurant, Paonessa's, and when we returned to our hotel rooms we found a treasure chest of little goodies: a portable compact disc player, cologne, perfume, Godiva chocolates, champagne, and a fruit basket.

DeBartolo's generosity always left me speechless. I felt intimidated by his wealth and uncomfortable about socializing with him because he was my boss. There was a perception among the 49er players that if you hung out with Mr. D, he would give you extra money. I never wanted Mr. D to think I was mooching off him, and I never wanted to put myself in the position of being bought. I turned down many of his invitations over the years because I was too nervous around him. I know he felt snubbed, but I was too shy to walk into his office to explain my actions.

Other than a fair contract, all NFL players really expect from an owner is support, and DeBartolo proved he would do everything it took to win. I thought it was great that Mr. D greeted the players on the field at Candlestick Park after each victory, shaking our hands and adding pats on the back. Our embraces over the years left Mr. D's expensive clothes sweaty and muddy, so he had to carry a white towel for protection. Slumped on a bench in the locker room after losses, Mr. D always looked pale, disheveled, and wrung out, as though he had played the game along with us.

The Kauai vacation was DeBartolo's most special gift to us. It was wonderful that he acknowledged our extraordinary accomplishment, since we were only the second team in NFL history to have won four Super Bowls. The most unforgettable moment occurred the night we received our Super Bowl rings. Following dinner and the premiere of our 1989 highlight film, coach George Seifert called each of us to the front of the room, one by one, and handed us a small leather box. When I opened it, my heart skipped a beat. This Super Bowl ring was larger and classier than the three previous rings we had received. It featured four football–shaped marquise diamonds situated on a cluster of forty-four smaller diamonds. My name was engraved on the shank, along with 88 BACK TO BACK 89, 17–2 (our record), and a rendering of the Golden Gate Bridge with the four Super Bowl Lombardi Trophies representing the years 81-84-88-89 replacing the bridge towers. Yes, this Super Bowl ring was a monument.

For the first time, I allowed myself to reflect on our accomplishments. Winning championships had always seemed similar to eating candy. Every time I took a bite I'd say, "Dang, that's sweet. Gimme some more. I want more lollipops. That's good stuff." I never relaxed long enough to give myself a pat on the back and say, "Great job, Ronnie." I never watched replays of our Super Bowls, and I only wore one of my Super Bowl rings at public appearances where I thought fans might want to see it. My attitude had always been, okay, the game's over. I gave my best effort. Now what? How can I give more?

After the ring ceremony, Huey Lewis and the News performed, and we all jammed with them. Lewis, a 49er fanatic who lives in the Bay area, is one of our good-luck charms. Practically every time he sings the national anthem before our home games, we win. Montana, Clark, Riki Ellison, and I sang background vocals on his group's hit "Hip To Be Square," and so I wasn't surprised when Lewis called Montana to the microphone to sing a duet in Kauai. To dog Joe, Huey stepped back from the microphone during an old song, "It's All Right," and he exposed our quarterback's off-key singing.

I floated back to the room with my Super Bowl ring on my finger. "This has got to be the greatest moment of my life," I told my girlfriend Karen Collmer. "A dream come true." I hadn't only been part of a great evening, but I'd been part of a unique football team. Now it was time to start thinking about winning a third consecutive Super Bowl.

The day after we received our Super Bowl rings, more players talked openly about the concept of three-peat. I knew the 49ers would be traveling through a long, dark tunnel in quest of three consecutive Super Bowl championships, and I believed that talking about the quest would make it seem much less scary. That's the way we had approached repeating as world champions in 1989. Prior to that season, I drove to Oakland to watch the Los Angeles Lakers play the Golden State Warriors, and I hung out with Magic Johnson and Byron Scott after the game. I quizzed them about their mental approach to winning consecutive NBA Championships in 1987 and 1988.

"Just talk about the concept," Scott advised. "Don't be afraid to talk about it. It'll give you more confidence."

Magic added, "We kept telling ourselves, 'We can do this. It's not the coaches or the owner. It's us.' The players have to make up their minds to do it."

In the 49er era under Bill Walsh, nobody wanted to talk about repeating. During minicamps and training camps the season after Super Bowls, we were programmed to parrot the cliché "We're just happy to be here." I remember seeing an interview with Washington Redskin coach Joe Gibbs after his team had beaten the Denver Broncos 42–10 in Super Bowl XXII. "What about next year?" the sportscaster wanted to know. "Can you do it again?" "Let's just enjoy the moment," Gibbs replied. "Let's not worry about next year."

Well, after my talk with Magic and Scott, I impressed upon my teammates that we had to say "back-to-back" and "repeat" over and over again until we believed we could do it. After Super Bowls, you must set your goals higher than you think imaginable because it's too easy to be satisfied. If we had adopted the Let's-not-worry-about-next-year approach, we never would have repeated. If you can believe it, the mind can achieve it.

I realized we would be climbing a different mountain in 1990, and it would be steeper and rockier than any we had encountered before. We would need to get comfortable with the word "three-peat." We would have to think about it while running hills and lifting weights. Sweat it into our minds. Burn it into our hearts. We had to remember that we couldn't recapture the euphoric feeling we had January 28, 1990, in New Orleans after Super Bowl XXIV. That only existed on film.

The day after Super Bowl XXIV, we had thrown ourselves back into the hat. We had become one of twenty-eight teams. In 1990, we would be building a new company. Sure, we still had the same framework and attitude, but the technology had changed. The employees were all a year older, and the elements wouldn't be the same. Rain. Wind. Injuries. Monday Night Football games. AstroTurf games versus grass fields. AFC Central opponents. A bye in the fourth week. It would be important for me to remind my teammates constantly that we would not be a great team until the end of the season.

I was sure the press would ask, why aren't back-to-back Super Bowls enough? Why isn't winning four Super Bowls satisfying? Well, my response would be, why wasn't I satisfied with one championship? And why isn't this season, this minute, or even tomorrow enough for me? Champions have insatiable appetites. There are a lot of unanswered questions in life, a lot of whys that will never be understood. All I have to dwell on right now is figuring out a way to win in 1990.

WEEK 1

Ragin' in Cajun Country

I have never been one to venture out of the hotel on road trips. My excuse is that I'm on a business trip and not on a vacation. An unusual experience in New Orleans the last week of my rookie season in 1981 has a lot to do with my hermit existence. The Saturday afternoon before that Saints game, the rookie defensive backs—Eric Wright, Carlton Williamson, Lynn Thomas, and myself—snuck out of the hotel to explore the world-famous French Quarter. As we walked down Bourbon Street, a man raced toward us.

"I'm going to kick your butt," he yelled. "I'm going to kick your butt."

We quickly realized he was speaking to a guy in front of us.

"Stop, I've got a gun," the man in hot pursuit screamed. He thrust his hand into his pocket. "I'll shoot you."

They were going to face-off right in front of us.

"Oh, no, this guy's going to start spraying bullets," I shouted. "Hit the dirt!"

Lying face-first on the street, we braced for gunshots, but instead we heard laughter. When we looked up, the guy pretended to shoot an imaginary gun formed with his fingers into the air.

"Man, let's get inside," I said. "The bars will be safer."

We checked out Pat O'Brien's Bar, but it was so crowded we left. At the second watering hole, Wright insisted we grab a table and buy a beer.

"No, they're going to charge us a lot of money," I said. I was beginning to feel guilty that we had left the hotel. The other defensive backs agreed with Wright. "Come on, just one drink," Thomas said. Added Williamson, "It's not going to kill us. This is the first time we've gone out on a road trip."

Maybe they were right. We had been so serious all season, why not take one afternoon off? A pretty lady, tall and well built, with long flowing hair, sashayed over to our table.

"Buy me a drink, guys?" she asked, cocking her hip and thrusting her chest into our faces.

"No, don't buy anybody a drink," I said.

Wright rolled his eyes. "A round of Coca-Cola," he said to the bartender. "Five Cokes, please."

The lady was cordial and not a bad conversationalist. She told us about some New Orleans hangouts to check out. When the drinks came and she reached for her soda, I noticed that she had the hairiest knuckles I had ever seen in my life. Wow!

"Eric, let's get back to the hotel. Let's bolt," I said, motioning to the hands.

"Uhhh . . . yeah . . . guys," Wright stammered. "Aren't we going to be late for meetings or something?"

We politely excused ourselves, said goodbye to her—or was it really him?—and hailed a cab. We wound up driving around and around the streets of the French Quarter. About twenty minutes and twenty dollars later, we reached our hotel, safe and sound.

That was enough of Bourbon Street to last my entire career.

As we arrived at the Louisiana Superdome for our Sunday morning practice, we reminisced about the last time we had played there. On January 28 we had crushed the Denver Broncos, 55–10, in Super Bowl XXIV. I thought about that day, too, and at the same time I remembered that during almost every game I had played in the Superdome, I had sustained some kind of injury. I erased the past from my mind and focused on playing football indoors.

Playing in a domed stadium can get you juiced up and easily take you out of a game. It's like being trapped in the middle of a crowded dance floor for three hours, listening to blaring disco music. You have to scream at the top of your lungs to converse with the person next to you, and even then there's a good chance neither of you will hear a word of what has been said.

The Superdome and Seattle Kingdome are the loudest domed stadiums in the NFL. Each has its own personality. If I stand at midfield with my eyes closed, I immediately know which stadium I'm in by the timbre of the crowd. The Kingdome sounds like a busy airport, with jet planes taking off nonstop. The Superdome has a Bayou flavor with plenty of Cajun accents and "hoo dey" cheers.

To help condition ourselves to the noise level in domed stadiums, Bill Walsh blasted hard rock and heavy metal tapes over the public address system at our practices on Friday afternoons and Saturday mornings. That exercise taught me it was useless to try and tune out the clatter. That would only mean I was admitting to a distraction. I decided it was better to perfect alternative forms of communication such as hand signals, and to train myself to believe I had the noise conquered. Walsh invented a slogan, "Let's see if we can make the crowd go home before the game's over," which he used in his pep talks prior to our games in domed stadiums.

Temperature and air quality indoors are the two things I can never prepare myself for. The lack of air circulation creates a thick haze of cigarette smoke over the field. At times it becomes almost impossible to breathe, much like jogging in the middle of a smoggy Los Angeles day. By halftime I crave the air in the locker room, and coming back onto the field in the third quarter I notice myself breathing more deeply, straining to inhale any spare molecules of unpolluted oxygen. I wind up coughing by the end of the game. The air in the Superdome is hot, heavy, and humid, a reflection of the New Orleans climate. It's debilitating to perform in. I sweat profusely. To overcome the elements in the Superdome, I need to drink a couple of quarts of water before and during games.

In the days leading up to the Saints game, I spent a lot of time visualizing aggression on the football field. I conjured up pictures of brutal, bone-jarring collisions and images of 250-pound muscled missiles soaring through the air. Each season I need to recondition my mind to the violence of football in the NFL. I just can't step on the field on game day and expect my competitive juices to flow. I gradually build my anger and fine-tune my concentration throughout the week before the first game. It's a powerful crescendo. As far as physical conditioning goes, I don't reach top form until a month into the season.

I've never believed that winning the season opener makes a difference in the outcome of the year. After all, you don't get to the Super Bowl unless you win the last game. But this year I changed my tune. The Las Vegas oddsmakers listed us as a 4-to-1 shot to win the Super Bowl, followed by the Los Angeles Rams and New York Giants at 7–1. Walsh picked us to go all the way, too.

A part of me worried that that was a bad omen. Walsh's pick put tremendous pressure on coach George Seifert. Would he buckle under it? Would we? Because of Walsh's proclamation of the 49ers' greatness, if we failed to three-peat the Seifert critics and doubters would come out of the woodwork. I thought Walsh might be trying to jinx Seifert. If we were to win Super Bowl XXV, our second without Walsh, wouldn't that prove that the 49er players were just as much responsible for the team's success as Walsh?

For the 49ers to three-peat, I felt we had to set the tone for 1990 right from the start. It was imperative that we wage a physical and victorious battle against the Saints. We needed to deliver a strong message to the NFL that we were a force to be reckoned with. I wanted to play kamikaze football by recklessly throwing my body into the pile to finish off tackles. The fact that the game was on Monday Night Football would make our job easier.

For onfield intensity, games on Monday Night Football are

surpassed only by Super Bowls. Sunday afternoon games, by comparison, seem like ladies' teas. As a kid, I loved to watch Monday Night Football. I was a huge fan of Howard Cosell because I admired Muhammad Ali. When Ali was stripped of his heavyweight title for refusing military service because of his religious beliefs in 1967, I liked the fact that Cosell defended him. (I finally got to meet Cosell a few days before the AFC–NFC Pro Bowl in January 1984, while dining at a Honolulu restaurant with Los Angeles Raider running back Marcus Allen. The Raiders had just beaten the Washington Redskins, 38–9, in Super Bowl XVIII, and Allen had been named the Most Valuable Player when he rushed for a Super Bowl record 191 yards. Cosell walked over to our table and introduced himself, but I would have recognized his staccato voice if I had been blindfolded.

"The two Trojans from USC," he uttered, in typical Cosellian tones. "Ronnie Lott. Number 42. Marcus Allen. Super Bowl MVP."

Allen and I laughed. Dang, I thought, this is Howard Cosell.)

With quarterback Bobby Hebert unsigned, John Fourcade was getting his chance to open the season as the Saints' starter. Hebert, a star in the defunct United States Football League, had thrown 50 touchdown passes in the preceding three seasons with New Orleans. He had been a free agent, and after failing to negotiate a new contract with the Saints or force a trade, he was now threatening to sit out the entire 1990 season.

On the other hand, Fourcade, twenty-nine, was a journeyman, having been cut or traded nine times while toiling in the Canadian Football League, the USFL, and the Arena Football League. When the Saints signed him as a replacement player during the 1987 NFL strike, he was teaching high school in Marrero, Louisiana. Fourcade hadn't enjoyed success since he was at the University of Mississippi, where he smashed a number of passing records held by Archie Manning, who is, ironically, the Saints' all-time passing leader.

Rarely do I watch any more game film than what is required in our team meetings. Our right guard Harris Barton and inside linebacker Matt Millen pore over videotapes at the 49er training facility within hours after that day's game. Safety Dave Waymer arrives at the office at 5:30 A.M. on weekdays, makes coffee for the rest of the employees, and shoves tape after tape into the video machine. I don't have the patience to fish for tendencies and offbeat quirks of my opponents. As an instinctive player, I prefer to get inside their heads.

However, I made an exception with Fourcade. Knowing he was a journeyman told me that plenty of other people had discovered flaws in his game. I made it a point to search for his shortcomings. Any time I face a quarterback for the first time, I study his feet, his poise in handling the ball, and his confidence in the huddle. I had specific questions about Fourcade. How does he play when the game is tight? When the Saints are behind? Does he scramble if they're losing? Will he throw when the team is ahead? In films, Fourcade showed me that he hadn't learned to use all of his offensive weapons. I noticed he had a tendency to leave the pocket under pressure, and most of the time he didn't give his offensive linemen and receivers a chance to follow his lead. I know that inexperienced quarterbacks can't scramble and see the entire field at the same time. They're too busy concentrating on the pass rushers coming at them.

Under coach Jim Mora, the Saints' strategy is to minimize offensive mistakes and win with a physical defense. The 49ers' strategy? Put some heavy pressure on Fourcade. Disguise coverages. Force him to make decisions early.

Both teams struggled on offense in the first half. The Saints led 9–3 at halftime. Joe Montana had thrown an interception, setting up one of Morten Andersen's three field goals. Fourcade had only completed 6 of 16 passes for 86 yards. For me, it was kamikaze football all the way. When I popped wide receiver Brett Perriman on the Saints' second offensive series, Monday Night Football commentator Dan Dierdorf called it "a major-league kiss." In the second quarter, I jerked my knee into Perriman's head after riding him to the turf, which Dierdorf felt would further intimidate the Saints. I tipped a pass intended for halfback Dalton Hilliard and jumped over the back of tight end Hoby Brenner to try to get at another ball.

Montana opened the third quarter by fumbling at the Niners' 11-yard line on the second play. Then Fourcade's bloop pass intended for tight end John Tice was intercepted by cornerback Darryl Pollard in the right corner of the end zone. At first the officials did not allow the interception, but instant replay showed that Pollard did indeed have his feet in bounds when he made the diving catch.

Montana took over on the 49er 20, and the game turned ugly. Saint free safety Gene Atkins was penalized 15 yards for unnecessary roughness with a late hit. Saint rookie defensive end Renaldo Turnbull was flagged for a head slap. Thanks to 26 yards in penalties from the Saints, Montana hit tight end Brent

Jones three plays later with a 4-yard touchdown pass, putting us ahead, 10–9.

Witnessing the Saints' aggressiveness turned up the fire in me even more. Twice in the next Saints' possession, I nailed Hilliard so loudly that Dierdorf remarked about the impact of the blows. I noticed Fourcade telegraphing his passes, looking directly at the receiver he would throw to. On third-and-12 from the San Francisco 23, I stepped in front of wide receiver Lonzell Hill, being careful not to bump into him, and made the interception. I returned the ball 15 yards. I was so overcome with excitement and an adrenaline rush that I began hyperventilating and gasping for air. On the sideline, I had to put a plastic cup over my mouth and suck in some oxygen from a tank.

I opened the fourth quarter with a crushing tackle on wide receiver Eric Martin, who had just caught a 16-yard pass from Fourcade. I hit him high, hoping to jar the ball loose, and our helmets collided. For a second I was in a fog. Three series later, I popped Hilliard so hard that he coughed up the ball. Our strong safety Chet Brooks recovered. I was probably more surprised than anybody that Hilliard fumbled the ball. He's a hard-nosed guy. One of my earlier hits, however, had bruised his shoulder, and I think that may have had something to do with the fumble.

With less than two minutes to play and New Orleans ahead, 12–10, Mora made a questionable decision. The Saints were on their 41 with a third-and-five. Instead of keeping the ball on the ground to take time off the clock, Mora called for a pass. Fourcade overthrew Perriman down the middle. The Saints were forced to punt with 1:41 left, and that was more than enough time for Montana, the best two-minute quarterback in football. He drove the 49ers 60 yards in seven plays, and Mike Cofer kicked a 38-yard field goal with nine seconds remaining to win the game 13–12.

Fourcade tried a desperation Hail Mary pass, but I picked it off, giving me 50 interceptions for my career. Generally speaking, on passes that end up being intercepted, the ball seems so small when it leaves the quarterback's hands. Then it becomes larger than life and right on top of me. At that moment time stops, and the catch shifts into slow-motion. I tell myself, "Don't drop it!"

In addition to the pair of interceptions, I finished the Saints game with seven tackles, broke up three passes, and forced one fumble. That is kamikaze football.

Afterward, several of my teammates complimented me on my performance and predicted that I'd have a great season. I appreciated their kind words, but I was bothered by the fact that I had been out of position on too many coverages. Furthermore, I suffered a nasty thigh bruise on my left leg. It had occurred on the first interception, when I was hit by a Saint helmet. The swelling made it look as if I were wearing an inflatable knee cast.

I had badly wanted to win this game to relieve that three-peat pressure. Come to think of it, most of my teammates appeared somewhat relieved, too, especially Seifert and Montana, who had been sacked six times. That night the noise in the Superdome had been louder than at any time I could remember. Montana was so hoarse from barking out signals that he eventually lost his voice and had to gargle with medication. Right tackle Steve Wallace couldn't hear Montana over the crowd of 68,629 and was penalized for four false starts.

When the media gathered around my locker, I divulged the extra incentive behind my kamikaze performance. It had nothing to do with three-peat. Ira Miller, the longtime 49er-beat writer with the *San Francisco Chronicle*, had written a story three days before our Saints game suggesting the 49ers wouldn't three-peat because our team chemistry had taken a beating. Miller singled me out as being the most unhappy, claiming I was upset the 49ers had placed my friends Keena Turner, Eric Wright, and Riki Ellison on the unprotected Plan B free agent list the preceding spring, and that I had gotten perturbed again when the team waived and resigned Turner right before the season. Miller implied that I hadn't played well in our preseason games because I wasn't into playing football anymore. Wrote Miller: "Ronnie Lott was the player most affected by the fallout, and what happened to his friends seems to still bother him. There is a certain spark that hasn't been lit in Lott yet."

Well, that story made me absolutely crazy. It drove me nuts. It wasn't true at all.

"My thoughts were based on Ira Miller, who said my spark wasn't there," I told the media. "Those things inspire you to play that much harder, because I don't want my teammates reading something like that and saying I'm not giving 110 percent."

My purpose in the preseason has always been to get myself in fighting shape. If I tried to play kamikaze football, I'd never make it to the regular season. Tonight, my mission was to show my teammates in no uncertain terms that I will always give them 110 percent. I am totally involved in the common goal. Sure, I cherish my off-the-field friendships, but on game day my teammates are the most important people in the world. I'll do anything for this team. I'll play my heart out for it.

WEEK 2

The Comforts of Home

It was great to be back home at The Stick. The home opener stirs up the same pride, anticipation, and confidence as the first day of school. You're all decked out in your new shoes and ready to meet the school year head-on. An NFL home opener might not have the tradition of baseball's Opening Day, but for me, coming back to Candlestick Park at the start of the season is like opening night on Broadway. There's nothing like a premiere in front of your family and friends.

I always shake the hand of the little man in the players' parking lot. I look forward to being teased by Bob and Harvey, who work in the clubhouse. "Where's Squeaky?" they kid me. "Where's your pal, Squeaky?" (Squeaky, in case you don't know, is 49er cornerback Eric Wright, who in his high-pitched chirp regularly gives them a hard time.) I couldn't wait to see my loyal buddies, the season-ticket holders in the end zone, who lifted my spirits every time I touched the pylon in front of them for good luck in the warm-ups.

For nearly my entire career, I have used the same locker at Candlestick. Assigned by Chico Norton, the 49er equipment manager emeritus, my locker is located in the area across from the training room where all the defensive backs dress. Wright has always occupied the locker to my right. If I were to arrive on game day and discover that somebody had moved me to another locker, it would throw me for a loop. My locker is like a security blanket.

In the early '80s, the defensive backs would sit on stools in front of their lockers and crack jokes before games. George Seifert, then the defensive backs coach, tried to inundate us with last-minute reminders. Watch out for this. Don't forget about that. Yeah, George, we got you. We got you. He'd walk away satisfied, then we would burst out laughing. When Seifert was promoted to defensive coordinator in 1983, he would send his successor, Ray Rhodes, over to do his dirty work. "Man, tell George to relax and leave us alone," we kept telling Rhodes.

The 49er locker room is separate from the one used by the San Francisco Giants. I often sequester myself in front of a television in the Giant clubhouse early on Sunday mornings to watch the NFL games that are being played on the East Coast. Pictures of Giant greats Willie McCovey and Willie Mays adorn the walls, along with some amusing signs like the one over the showers: No Dick Watching.

Once my teammates and I were saying prayers in the Giant clubhouse when Mays walked in on us. "What are you praying for? They used to throw 100 mph pitches at my head all the time," Mays said.

That was my introduction to Willie Mays, who autographed a baseball for me that day. As long as we're on the subject of baseball players, our good luck charm in 1988 was Cleveland Indian pitcher Tom Candiotti, who volunteered as an equipment assistant after we had a 6–5 record. Candiotti, a cousin of Ted Walsh, our assistant equipment manager, helped hand out jackets at home and on the road, and we went on to win Super Bowl XXIII. Since then, I've religiously worn the lucky Indian cap Candiotti gave me.

Of course, you might say I need all the good luck charms I can get while grappling with the diverse winds at The Stick. The howling Hawk whips in from the nearby Pacific Ocean, separating into tiny tempests as it collides with Bay View Hill directly west of the stadium. A study once commissioned by the city of San Francisco showed the gusts at The Stick could reach velocities of 62 mph. The weather bureau has estimated that the winds there shift as much as 180 degrees during a game.

I've learned the hard way that the wind is different from one end zone to another. And I've seen it shift on each change of possession. On coin tosses, for example, we've chosen to defend a certain goal so we'll have the wind with us in the third quarter. But when that time comes, the wind is blowing in the opposite direction. I've seen footballs blown backward on field goals and punts, and I've heard the gales whistling through the ear holes of my helmet. I never stop checking the wind. Forget about studying the flag at the top of Candlestick. I pick up the grass in front of me and throw it in the air, because the Hawk is always different at groundlevel.

I have only one complaint about The Stick. None of the 49ers has ever enjoyed playing there in August and September during the baseball season. Running from soft grass onto hard dirt, where the baseball infield is, can be hazardous, and it is a definite disadvantage to defensive backs who have to react to receivers on that part of the field. All of the guys are fearful of falling on the dirt because it's as hard as cement. You ought to see some of my nasty bruises from the infield at The Stick. One season, I even managed to trip on the metal hook that anchors the bases and sprain my big toe.

Sure footing is a prerequisite when it comes to playing the Washington Redskins because each one of their wide receivers is a game breaker. Art Monk, Gary Clark, and Ricky Sanders, who are collectively nicknamed the Posse, each gained more than 1,000 yards in 1989. Since we hadn't played the Redskins last season, I studied films of their 1990 preseason games and looked at our games against them from previous years. I disregarded the Posse's statistics. You can't take into account what they accomplished in the past because the makeup and attitude of this year's team is different. Besides, the truly great receivers learn new tricks from year to year.

Although the Redskins had put in a few new wrinkles since the last time we played them, the offensive philosophy of coach Joe Gibbs hadn't changed. His is a ball-control offense designed to get receivers open. The Posse create openings by making decisions on the fly. During my career, I have faced four different starting quarterbacks who have paraded through the Redskins' lineup, and experience has taught me that putting pressure on the quarterback disrupts Gibbs' entire offensive system.

Before the game, our outside linebacker Charles Haley broke into one of his rousing pep talks, reminding us to stay focused, and he promised to lead the defense by example. One of the most ferocious pass rushers in the NFL, Haley, 6-foot-5, 230 pounds, is an intensely emotional man. His mood swings are more violent than mine. One minute he's turning cartwheels on the 49er practice field and kidding Joe Montana and me about our receding hairlines. The next minute he's trashing the locker room at Texas Stadium, out of touch with reality and throwing chairs. One side of Haley apologizes to opponents for injuring them, while the other side pulls pranks that hurt his own teammates. Once, without warning, he grabbed flanker Jerry

Rice and lifted him high in the air. Rice kicked and screamed, pleading to be returned to the floor. After Haley obliged, Rice ripped a fire extinguisher from the wall and tried to hit Haley with it. Several players had to pull them apart to keep them from mauling each other.

The various sides of Haley, coupled with his propensity to ramble on with his opinions on racism, have made him one of the most misunderstood 49ers. People look at the outside of Haley rather than what is in his heart. The 49ers go out of their way not to promote Haley to the national media or to local business groups. In the organization's mind, he's a loose cannon who could embarrass the team. There have been times defensive coordinator Bill McPherson couldn't deal with Haley, so he asked me to communicate for him. Some days the coaching staff says, "Whatever you want, Mr. Haley." Other days, I've seen them screw him. Like the final regular-season game of 1989 against the Chicago Bears, when Haley and defensive end Pierce Holt were tied for the team lead in sacks with 11½. Incredibly, Haley was pulled in the second half. That hurt him deeply. To me, it was very clear that somebody wanted Holt to win the sack title. (In the end, both finished with 11½ sacks.)

I am reminded of what comedian Richard Pryor once said about boxer Leon Spinks. Everybody made fun of Spinks because he didn't speak well, was missing a couple of front teeth, and had had a somewhat tumultuous life out of the ring. But Leon's the heavyweight champion, Pryor said, so let's be thankful for that. Let's not chip away at what he doesn't do well. Let's be proud for what he is able to do. The 49ers ought to adopt that attitude with Haley.

Regardless of how anybody else on the team feels, I love Haley's craziness. He's not difficult to figure out at all: he isn't comfortable with fame, money, and big-city living. The second youngest of four sons, Haley grew up in the tiny town of Gladys, Virginia. The family lived in a three-bedroom house with no electricity, indoor plumbing, or phone. A fat, awkward kid, Haley made twenty dollars a day working at local farms, picking tobacco, hauling corn, and baling hay. He'd give half his earnings to his parents, then spend the rest on boxes of cornflakes. At age thirteen he took up football to get back at the kids who made him feel bad for being overweight. "I used to just like hurting people," Haley says. "Because that was the only way I could get back at them for making fun of me." He wasn't heavily recruited out of high school and finally signed a scholarship with Division I-AA James Madison University in Harrisonburg, Virginia. He wasn't invited to the NFL Scouting Combine after his senior year, so the 49ers discovered him on blurry black and white game films provided by James Madison. Walsh drafted Haley in the fourth round in 1986, and now, at twenty-seven, he's among the highest-paid players in the NFL. Imagine the adjustments he has had to go through.

True to form, Haley's pep talk fired us up against the Redskins. After allowing six sacks the week before against the New Orleans Saints, our offensive line was superb. Montana wasn't sacked once, and tackle Steve Wallace, who had been flagged for four false starts against the Saints, didn't have any penalties. He completely controlled Charles Mann, the Redskins' Pro Bowl defensive end. Montana threw to eight different receivers, completing 29 of 44 for 390 yards and two touchdowns in our 26–13 victory. He surpassed John Brodie to become the 49ers' career leader in passing yards with 31,654. From 1957 to '73, Brodie totaled 31,548.

Defensively, we were outstanding. The Redskins reached the San Francisco 20-yard line on three drives but came away with only one touchdown. Two big defensive plays stick out in my mind.

On the first possession of the third quarter, with the 49ers ahead 20–10, quarterback Mark Rypien drove the Redskins to the San Francisco 15. Chip Lohmiller attempted a field goal, but Haley leaped into the air and blocked the kick. I played on special teams from 1981 to '87, and I can tell you there's no art to blocking field goals. It's all desire.

On the Redskins' next series, they moved from their own 30 to the San Francisco 1 in just four plays, and we stopped them from scoring a touchdown. Gerald Riggs, a 232-pound running back, pounded over right tackle on first-and-goal, but he was met by linebacker Mike Walter and strong safety Chet Brooks. On second-and-goal, the Redskins lined up in their "Heavy Jumbo" formation with four tight ends, including one in the backfield. Riggs tried to burst up the middle but couldn't get past nose tackle Jim Burt.

I think that the first two downs of a goal-line stand are the most important. The majority of defensive players adopt a defeatist attitude right from the start. They'll say, "They have four downs to go one yard. We can't stop them." But I approach goal-line stands as great momentum changers. By demoralizing the opponent's offense, you give your own defense the upper hand.

On third-and-goal, Matt Millen, our 245-pound inside linebacker, was charged up, shouting encouragement as we lined up. All of his hours of watching game films had paid off. As Rypien stepped up under center, Millen immediately recognized the play, yelling out, "Bootleg! Bootleg!" Rypien faked a handoff and tried a quarterback bootleg, a play we usually have trouble with. He took off to his right, and I shot in from the left corner, heading straight for him. Together Millen and I smothered the play. It's so easy for safeties to get drawn into the fake of the quarterback on bootlegs. If you watch the ball instead of focusing on the area of the defense the quarterback is running to you're sunk. The Redskins kicked a field goal. We were all so excited, we didn't want to come off the field.

As well as we had played on defense, I had critical words for the secondary after the game. I was angry that rookie cornerback Eric Davis made a careless mistake on a 35-yard completion to Monk. Davis wasn't playing deep enough in his zone, and Monk slipped behind him. I can try to get everybody lined up in the right spot, but it's up to them to make the plays. I had thought we were coming together as a secondary, but now I wasn't convinced.

WEEK 3

The Man in Black

In a poll conducted by the *San Francisco Chronicle* in 1990, the majority of 49ers said that the last coach they would want to play for is Jerry Glanville. Well, that's not how I voted. Mike Ditka of the Chicago Bears, Bill Parcells of the New York Giants, and Glanville of the Atlanta Falcons are at the top of my list of favorite NFL coaches. They are honest, tough, demanding, and fiery on the sideline. They don't take crap from anybody. Over the years, their players have shown personality and emotion. I think I could thrive in their hard-nosed systems, and I hope they feel the same way too.

A few years ago, Ditka said I was the best safety who ever played the game. I'll always remember that compliment because Ditka is a man I respect. He played in the NFL for twelve years with the Bears, Philadelphia Eagles, and Dallas Cowboys, and in 1988 he became the first tight end to be enshrined in the Pro Football Hall of Fame.

Parcells introduced himself prior to our playoff game at Giants Stadium on December 29, 1985. He shook my hand and said, "I like the way you play." That day, my other hand was wrapped in a protective pad because I had crushed the tip of my pinkie against the Cowboys the preceding Sunday. For most of the Giants game, I caught myself saying, "God dang, Parcells told me I was a pretty good football player. I can't believe he said that to me." After I missed a tackle on running back Joe Morris, one of my first thoughts was that Parcells had been blowing smoke to keep me from focusing on the game. After that, I promised myself to make only small talk with coaches before games, limiting it to, "Hi, how are you doing?" Whatever they said to me had to go in one ear and out the other.

I first met Glanville during my second season in the NFL in 1982. He had been with the Falcons since 1977, first as the defensive backs coach for two years, then as coordinator of the punishing, sacking "Gritz Blitz" defense. "Hey, Number 42!" Glanville shouted across the field. "You're a hell of a player."

I had no clue who he was, but I politely said thank you. In fact, it wasn't until he took over as head coach of the Houston Oilers in 1986 that I connected the name with the face, and since then he has always told me, "I wouldn't mind having you on our team."

I had always wondered what that would be like, so I've asked two of my 49er teammates, running back Spencer Tillman and tight end Jamie Williams. Both played for Glanville at Houston. The reviews were mixed. According to Tillman, Glanville preached kamikaze football, beginning with the first day of training camp. "Everybody's got to be around the ball by the end of the play," Glanville would tell his players. "I don't want anybody just standing there. You've got to go in after 'em." However, Tillman also called Glanville the prince of left-handed compliments. "You made a helluva play yesterday on special teams," Glanville once told Tillman. "I love you more than I did yesterday. Of course, I didn't love you much yesterday." And, when a highly paid player made a good play, Tillman said Glanville would yell downfield to an assistant, "I think we ought to keep him around another day so he can make a payment on the Jag."

Williams, on the other hand, thought Glanville was mostly hype. For the longest time, Williams joked that Glanville dreamed of being just like him. That is, a 6-foot-4, 245-pound black man with dreadlocks who goes by the name of Spider Man. But then Glanville countered by kidding that Williams found his dreadlocks hanging from a horse's butt, and after that Williams wasn't in the mood to joke too much.

Oiler quarterback Warren Moon, a close friend of mine, has always said that Glanville was outlandish, but that he was a decent coach. Moon never really appreciated Glanville's act, especially his House of Pain creation at the Houston Astrodome. It was a good theme, but it got out of hand. All those late hits and personal fouls by the Oilers only provoked overly aggressive behavior from opposing defenses, and unfortunately Moon was one of the victims.

For the most part, I get a kick out of Glanville's routine. He has left tickets at the Will Call window for Elvis Presley, James Dean, Buddy Holly, W. C. Fields, and the Phantom of the Opera. Before a game against the Pittsburgh Steelers in 1989, he limped onto the field, claiming he had been bitten on the foot by a water moccasin. In keeping with his bad-boy image, he dresses completely in black for games, right down to his custom-made cowboy boots. Whereas most NFL coaches prefer to play quiet games of golf in the off-season, Glanville competes in drag racing and has gone on cross-country trips on his motorcycle. If that's what it takes to get the most out of his players, then I agree wholeheartedly with Glanville's comic approach.

The NFL needs coaches with personality and charm, like Glanville. In recent years the league has legislated a lot of the fun out of pro football. After former New York Jet defensive end Mark Gastineau popularized the Sack Dance, the NFL created a 15-yard unsportsmanlike conduct penalty to stamp out premeditated celebrations that taunt opponents. The league's higher-ups have managed to standardize towels, headbands, gloves, and shoes, too. Now every player on a team must wear the same color shoes, and no personal messages can be written anywhere on the uniform. What happened to the fun?

The color rule is ridiculous. Because the 49ers voted to wear white shoes this season, I had to ditch the black soccer shoes I had worn since 1986. That rule is hazardous to my health because playing in soccer shoes puts less strain on my knees.

The NFL should spend its energy on serious issues like negotiating a collective bargaining agreement with the players (we haven't had one since 1987), perfecting its drug testing policy, and pushing teams to hire more minorities for head coaching and front office jobs. Why not let the fans vote on shoe color and end zone dances?

One reason pro basketball enjoyed increased popularity in the 1980s is because the fans felt so much more a part of the game. They can easily identify with the players. They sit closer to the action, and they can actually see the faces of the athletes. They feel the emotion, experience the pain and the happiness. They also enjoy the brilliance of superstars like Magic Johnson and Michael Jordan. Fans can't "touch" NFL players because they are hidden underneath helmets and their protective gear. There are so many more players on the football field than on the basketball court that it keeps fans from getting to know them. Who wants to watch a bunch of faceless robots? Give me some flash and pizzazz.

Like (Neon) Deion Sanders, the jewelry-laden Falcon cornerback who has come close to matching his flashy image on the field. Sanders' mass of gold chains seems to lift him to another level. In his first NFL game in 1989, he returned a punt 68 yards for a touchdown. Five days earlier, he smashed a home run and two doubles for the New York Yankees in a game against the Seattle Mariners. With his speed and hands, I think he could be an All-Pro. The only question is, how badly does he want it?

There isn't a Neon Deion type player in San Francisco, and I think one of the biggest myths about the 49ers is that a wild and crazy guy couldn't exist here. Although the 49ers have never had a pure showboat, Bill Walsh did sign some eccentrics such as linebacker Jack (Hacksaw) Reynolds, linebacker Tom Cousineau, and tight end Russ Francis. Cousineau was one of the first players in the NFL to pierce his ear, back in the days when it was only the rage of artists and rock stars. Francis was a free spirit who once jumped from a sixth-floor balcony into a swimming pool on a dare from Pittsburgh Steeler linebacker Jack Lambert. Francis marched to the beat of his own drummer in practice, buckling his chin strap behind his helmet and making one-handed catches. In training camp, he used to sneak out of the dorm in the middle of the night and drive off on his motorcycle. Other times, I would look out the window and see him working with his lasso. With Francis, in his laid-back Hawaiian style, you never knew what to expect.

Even outspoken Tim McKyer, a cornerback from 1986 to '89 who was traded to the Miami Dolphins, fit in with the 49ers. He had a couple of nicknames. A faction of the team called him Tin Man and Cowardly Lion, after the characters in *The Wizard of Oz*, because they believed he lacked heart and courage. McKyer referred to himself as the Blanket, and along with cornerback Don (the Quilt) Griffin, formed The Cover Brothers. I miss his outgoing personality and his ability to speak his mind. His antics were a welcome relief.

While these characters at times drove Walsh, the perfectionist, up a wall, the realist in him understood that oddballs helped team chemistry. They relieved a lot of tension. Bottom line, as long as the guy can play, who cares if personality takes over a room?

Neon Deion can play, all right, but don't judge his skills and intelligence on a major lapse that he had in the third quarter of our game with the Falcons. He underestimated the strength and speed of our tight end Brent Jones. A lot of folks in the NFL are guilty of that. The 6-foot-4, 230-pound Jones doesn't appear to be a fluid runner. Because his legs move in all different directions, we call him Gumby. He is one of the best tight ends in the game when it comes to running with the ball after the catch. I admire his ability to deal with adversity. The Pittsburgh Steelers selected Jones in the fifth round of the 1986 NFL draft out of the University of Santa Clara, and then he was waived after injuring his neck in a car accident. In 1987 the 49ers signed him as a free agent, and he had to spend two years battling knee injuries.

Sanders, who is only 5 feet 11, 187 pounds, made the mistake of hitting Jones in the torso when he should have grabbed him by the legs. Jones straight-armed Sanders and ran away from him for the game-winning 67-yard touchdown in our 19–13 victory. Jones finished the game with five catches for 125 yards, and he wasn't the only 49er receiver to have a good day. Jerry Rice had eight receptions for 171 yards, including a 35-yard TD in the third quarter, and Mike Sherrard, who had come back from a broken leg to make his first NFL start since 1986, caught four passes for 75 yards.

One other note. The game ended with a controversial turnover in the final seconds and Glanville was, well, Glanville, hotly contesting a call by referee Jerry Seeman. We were ahead, 19–13, with the Falcons threatening to score. On second-and-six from the San Francisco 29, Falcon quarterback Chris Miller had no timeouts left. He took the snap from center, bobbled the ball, and without gaining complete control spiked it into the ground to stop the clock. However, Seeman said that Miller had never controlled the snap and ruled it was a fumble. Instant replay, which I'm not a big fan of, supported Seeman. Fortunately, 49er defensive end Pierce Holt had the presence of mind to fall on the ball, and we took over on the 29 with four seconds left. Glanville was irate. He blew his stack. I don't think he even shook Seifert's hand when he left the field.

WEEK 4

Over the Moon

Imagine the sight of two ocean liners racing each other.

Well, that's what popped into my mind the other day after a practice when Steve Wallace and Bubba Paris, our mammoth offensive tackles, competed against each other in a who's faster race. Our linemen were finishing their conditioning drills, lumbering back and forth across the width of the practice field, when Wallace and Paris bolted from the rest of the group. There they were. Feet thumping. Arms pumping. Thighs flapping. Stomachs bouncing. Once they got going, Wallace sprinted past Paris but pulled up lame and limped off the field with a strained groin, much to the displeasure of coach George Seifert.

"What the hell are you guys doing?" Seifert yelled.

Playful escapades in practice are not unusual. Quarterbacks Joe Montana and Steve Young engage in a ridiculous game of tossing spools of adhesive tape into the air, hoping to get them to land on the crossbar of a goalpost. At Saturday morning practices, the offensive linemen like to pretend they're quarterbacks and wide receivers, sending each other downfield for long passes. The Wallace–Paris battle of the bulge helped to break the monotony of practice.

Wallace, our starting right tackle, stands 6 feet 5, 276 pounds and has a somewhat graceful stride. To us, he is simply "Big Sexy." A cool dresser with a cool attitude, he glides when he walks—and you should see him on the basketball court; he trots like a wide receiver. If he were smaller, he probably would have been a great defensive back.

Paris, on the other hand, runs like a guy carrying a baby grand piano on his back. His plump thighs make him waddle like a duck. At 6 feet 6, he ballooned to 380 pounds at minicamp in May but then dieted down to 330 for the start of the regular season. It goes without saying that Paris loves to eat. And eat. And eat. And eat. Split end John Taylor calls him Chicken Hawk because of his love for fried chicken. And if he's not stuffing his mouth, he's using it to pontificate.

When he was drafted in the second round from Michigan in 1982, Paris weighed only 290. He had great balance and mobility and could have become an All-Pro tackle. But for some unknown reason, Paris has never wanted to go the extra mile. Bill Walsh didn't help by harping on his weight in public to the media. One season he promised to give Paris a giant-screen television if he reached a weight under 300 pounds. Walsh made a big deal about the contest in front of the whole team and kept us all posted about the number of pounds Paris had lost. Walsh ended up auctioning the TV at the end of the season because Paris hadn't even come close to the magic number. Montana bought it for $3,000 and the money was donated to charity. Walsh had humiliated Paris in front of everybody. I felt sorry for Bubba. I've spoken to him about losing weight, and so have several of my teammates. We're worried about the possible long-term effects on his health. Because offensive line coach Bobb Mc-Kittrick used a platoon system at two positions in 1989, Paris alternated at left tackle with Wallace. For the 1990 season McKittrick is using both of them full-time, which I'm not so sure is a good idea. But that remains to be seen.

This was our third straight week of preparing for the run-and-shoot offense. We didn't have a game the Sunday before because it was the NFC West bye week. Playing the run-and-shoot is like competing in an endless track meet. It's a two-minute drill, over and over. It's you-go-long playground football, with four wide receivers. The run-and-shoot isn't only a physical grind. It's mentally taxing, too. The ball is always in the air and that has made me a little punchy. After our game against Atlanta I felt like the sweaty catcher in that Rolaids commercial, who becomes nauseated while studying a film of Oakland A's outfielder Rickey Henderson stealing bases. That catcher knows he is in great need of relief because Henderson can run at will. I get a sick feeling in my stomach knowing that if the offense makes the right reads the run-and-shoot can't be stopped.

When I used to watch Jim Kelly direct the run-and-shoot with the USFL's Houston Gamblers in 1984–85 I was intrigued by the offense. In the NFL, the Washington Redskins have played a version for years, using one running back and four wide receivers on third down. Before the 1990 season, I thoroughly quizzed Houston Oiler quarterback Warren Moon about the fundamentals of the run-and-shoot, and I asked June Jones, the former quarterbacks coach of the Oilers, to teach me how the receivers read the defense. The biggest mistake coaches and players make on defense is trying to stop every offensive weapon. You can't do it. The key is not to panic. Just line up and cover your man. You never hear players on either side of the ball complain about physical punishment after playing a run-and-shoot team: Don't forget to hit hard.

The one drawback to the run-and-shoot is that it doesn't take enough time off the clock. It would be great if you used it until you got far enough ahead, then inserted two running backs to grind off several minutes. Throwing so often gives your opponent more opportunities to come back.

In the future, I think a lot of offensive coaches will add variations of the run-and-shoot to their offensive systems the same way defensive coordinators adapted Buddy Ryan's 46 defense, which was successful for the Chicago Bears in 1985. This offense can only be pulled off with an experienced quarterback, five or six fast receivers, and a speedy running back. That's why the Oilers run the most sophisticated version in the NFL. They're the only team with all the right components.

That's for sure. The Oilers wasted no time against us, scoring on their first two possessions. Moon marched the team 65 yards in 14 plays on the opening drive. Five of his completions were to four different receivers. On our following series, Montana was intercepted by cornerback Richard Johnson at the San Francisco 30. The next play, Moon connected with wide receiver Drew Hill up the middle for a touchdown to make the score 14–0 with 5:15 remaining in the first quarter. I blew the coverage. Moon not only spied me looking in the Oilers' backfield, but he also saw that I was "squatting." In other words, positioned in the wrong spot and not playing deep enough. The deeper you are, the better the angle you have to make the play. I have always said, if you're in the middle and the ball is thrown 30 or more yards downfield, you should be able to break from sideline to sideline without a problem. It's similar to getting back to the middle of the court when you're playing tennis. The 49er coaches have always had to remind me to stay in the middle. My instincts have never changed, but now that certain skills have deteriorated, I just can't take the chances I used to.

The Oilers' game plan became evident to me rather quickly. They were going to pick on Ronnie Lott, and there's no NFL quarterback better equipped to do that than Moon. We have known each other since 1977 when I was a freshman at USC and Moon was a senior at the University of Washington. He knows me inside out. I think that helps his preparation a whole lot more than it helps mine. Hard hits only go so far. Moon has the advantage of being able to react to my aggressiveness. He knows I have the tendency to follow the ball, and as soon as he noticed I was "squatting," he looked in one direction but fired the ball the other way without turning his head.

Moon and I have spent hours talking on the beach at Waikiki during the week of the Pro Bowl. We have attended several NBA All-Star games and championship fights, and I've made a fool of myself hacking around the course in his charity golf tournaments. I'll always remember the time we went with Magic Johnson to the Marvin Hagler–Thomas Hearns middleweight title fight in Las Vegas in April 1985. Johnson took us to a prefight party in a hotel penthouse filled with movie stars. Magic knows everybody. He introduced me to Jack Nicholson, who is a big Los Angeles Lakers fan. I was awestruck, yet Nicholson was easy to talk to. All he had to tell me was that the 49ers were his favorite team in the NFL and we had a lot in common.

I have always admired Moon for his patience, wisdom, and fortitude in adapting to different cultures, leagues, and offensive systems. Moon, the Pacific 8 Conference Player of the Year and MVP of the Rose Bowl in 1978, signed with the Edmonton Eskimos of the Canadian Football League six weeks before the NFL draft because he had heard none of the twenty-eight teams would draft him. On Draft Day there were 334 players selected, none of them named Warren Moon. I believe nobody picked him because he is a black quarterback. He played in the CFL for six seasons, and during that time the Eskimos won five consecutive Grey Cup championships. In 1983 Moon threw for 5,648 yards, the most in a single season in pro football history. A year later, after shopping himself around the NFL as a free agent, he signed with the Oilers. From 1985 through 1990, Moon has had three different offensive coordinators, but he has always been one of the best quarterbacks in the NFL. It disturbs Moon that the media don't mention him in the same breath as Kelly, Boomer Esiason, and Dan Marino.

With the Oilers leading 14–7 at halftime, we decided to make some defensive adjustments. We played more man-to-man coverage to give Moon different looks and to make him hold onto the ball longer. We unleashed our inside pass rush, and it paid off. Moon was sacked twice by linebacker Charles Haley and once by defensive end Pierce Holt. He only registered 71 yards passing in the second half, and in the fourth quarter the Oilers on their two possessions were held to six yards total offense and no first downs.

Two touchdowns by John Taylor, who had missed two weeks with a bruised lower back, were the difference in the game. Both times he beat Oiler cornerback Cris Dishman. His 78-yard TD catch tied it at 14–14 and his 46-yard TD was the game winner with 6:31 left in the fourth quarter. Our 24–21 victory was our twelfth straight regular season road win. But it was costly because we lost our iron man running back Roger Craig. Craig has never missed a game in his eight years with the 49ers. This was consecutive game No. 114. The last time I saw an injury affect the mood of the team this way was in 1986 when Joe Montana had back surgery to remove a ruptured disk.

In the second quarter, Craig made one catch for a career total of 493, which broke Walter Payton's receptions record for running backs. It brought back memories of watching him struggle to catch balls in practice. Not only wasn't he used as a pass catcher at the University of Nebraska, but, to be quite honest, he doesn't have the natural grace of a Jerry Rice. We all used to laugh watching him strain to adjust his body to grab passes in practice.

Our happiness for Craig and his accomplishment quickly disappeared one play after making the record-breaking catch when he rushed for 13 yards but had to leave the game after twisting his right knee. His foot got stuck in the Astrodome's crummy artificial carpet. Craig came back to play on our next series but left again in the fourth quarter when he caught a helmet to that knee. Later a magnetic resonance imaging (MRI) test revealed several partial tears of the posterior cruciate ligament. A complete tear would have meant surgery, but in this case rest and rehabilitation was the prescribed treatment. Still, the 49ers' doctors estimated that Craig could miss as many as six games.

As far as I'm concerned, there is only one advantage to playing on artificial turf. The carpet translates into better footing, which makes players quicker and faster. Because I can gather more velocity, it allows me to deliver harder hits. However, when it comes to the turf at the Astrodome, I can't think of any benefits. It's the worst that I have ever played on in my career. Some of the seams running across the carpet are almost two inches wide, and if you're not careful you can easily stick your foot in an opening and fall flat on your face. By the way, landing on this carpet feels like falling on blacktop.

There are a lot of nasty things that can happen to your body on artificial turf. There's no injury I dread more than turf burns. They're nothing like floor burns you get in the gymnasium diving for a basketball. When your skin grazes the turf, the top two or three layers are rubbed right off. I can almost hear it sizzling. I've seen players get second-degree burns. In the worst-case scenario, infection could set in and lead to hospitalization. A weird instance occurred at a 49er minicamp a few years ago when a player burned himself on the artificial turf and later his face swelled up and he broke out in welts all over his body. One of the 49er trainers thought that perhaps the player was allergic to materials in the turf.

If I fall on my knees or slide on the field making a tackle, I get burned right through my pants and socks. Lunging for balls, I lose patches of skin on my forearms. For protection on artificial turf, I stick large Band-Aids on my knees. On my forearms and elbows, I wear rubber sleeves. Kids ask me all the time where I get them. They're actually calf supports that I have turned inside out. They're not perfect, though. To help prevent knee and ankle injuries, I lace up a new pair of high-top basketball shoes. Air Jordans, of course.

Thanks to artificial turf, I have gotten some pretty ugly scars. Turf burns often take a couple of months to heal because each week you fall, you reopen the wound. You should never wash the burns with soap and water because that will remove the healing membrane on the top of the skin. I delicately apply Neosporin, an antibiotic salve, for days on end. Immediately after the game, the trainers dump hydrogen peroxide on the raw, bloody area. That's one of the worst feelings in the world. It stings like hell. I've got to grab something to bite—a little towel, someone's arm, my own fist. Then I blow on it and dance around the training room.

WEEK 5

Airing It Out

When I bumped into several unemployed running backs in the 49er locker room on Tuesday afternoon, I became alarmed. My God, could Roger Craig's knee injury be more serious than the team is publicly admitting?

On Tuesdays, which is normally the team's day off, the 49ers bring in a number of players for tryouts. These sessions are held after the roster players have finished morning therapy treatments and have left for the day. They change clothes right in the stalls of the roster players and then head out to the practice field to display their skills to general manager John McVay, coach George Seifert, position coaches, and a few scouts. Afterward the players are quizzed about the offensive and defensive systems with which they are familiar to determine how quickly they could fit into the 49er lineup. This day I happened to see Joe Morris, the career rushing leader of the New York Giants, and Gene Lang, formerly with the Denver Broncos from 1984 to '87. The 49ers appeared to be bracing for the worst.

Usually the only way we find out who has checked in or what position is being scrutinized is from the media. Rarely will job hunters call ahead to a roster player to ask about the situation with the team or whether they would be a good fit. Now, if you do happen to see who has come in, you might say to a buddy, "Hey, guess who was here." But you sure don't tell the roster players who are insecure about their positions because they could be flipped out by the news.

I had stopped by the 49er facility that afternoon because I was shooting a commercial, and I have to admit that if I weren't so confident about my position, I might have thought twice when I saw thirty-seven-year-old Mike Haynes, the former All-Pro cornerback of the Los Angeles Raiders. I've been a fan of his since I watched him in a Pro Bowl practice on the USC campus.

I remember asking Haynes why he was able to stay crouched in pass coverage longer than any defensive back in the NFL. He said it was because he practiced and practiced his backpedaling, and that's something I never forgot. Carting himself to a tryout must be a humbling experience for a fifteen-year veteran and nine-time Pro Bowler.

"I haven't been running much, but I'm ready to play," Haynes told me. Because the Raiders had waited until the beginning of the season to release him that had made it difficult for him to hook on with another club. According to Haynes, he had asked the Raiders to move him to free safety, but they didn't give him a shot. Hold on a second. Free safety? That's my position. When Haynes said that, I wondered what the 49ers had in mind for him. Who knows? I never saw him again.

Tuesday's tryouts weren't the only indication that the 49ers were searching for help at running back. There was a rumor floating around that we wanted to trade linebacker Charles Haley and draft picks to the Raiders in exchange for running back Marcus Allen, my former USC roommate who was still a close friend. The Los Angeles Rams were reportedly also interested in Allen. I can be objective when I say he is one of the best running backs ever to play the game. He made an unbelievable move on me in his rookie year in 1982, a pirouette that left me grasping for air. Allen can run, catch, block, and throw. If he had been in the 49ers' system, he would have had seasons of 1,000 yards rushing and 1,000 yards receiving. He has such marvelous peripheral vision. I can tell he sees me faster than other running backs because when I hit him he's always fully prepared to receive my blow.

Haley, who had asked the 49ers to trade him after the 1989 season, was convinced he was going to be traded to the Raiders. And he was jumping for joy. I anticipated 49er management might ask me how Allen felt about playing in San Francisco, so I telephoned him to find out what he knew about the trade. I assured him that a lot of the 49er players would welcome him with open arms, and I offered him the spare bedroom in my home. If he did move in, I probably couldn't count on him to help with the household chores. At USC, Allen couldn't even boil water. At any rate, we discussed how he might respond if Craig ever got healthy and pushed him into a backup role. I understood how belittling it had been for Allen the past three seasons to bust his butt in training camp and start the first five or six games of the regular season, only to step aside for Bo Jackson, the major-league baseball player who once called football a hobby. The situation that was created made it tough for Allen to compete. For the most part, he handled himself professionally and didn't make waves. Inside linebacker Matt Millen, who formerly played with the Raiders, had told me that Allen's predicament had helped him mature. Allen convinced me that he could play second fiddle to Craig, if necessary, and I passed that on to Dwight Clark, the 49ers' executive administrative assistant. I figured Eddie DeBartolo, Jr., had already gotten positive feedback from his buddy O. J. Simpson, who is Allen's best friend.

Later that Tuesday I tried to examine the trade realistically. Losing Haley would really hurt the 49ers. You don't trade your best defensive player. Nobody gives up a home run hitter like Jose Canseco for a superstar who is on the back end of his career. But, more important, the 49ers needed to keep Haley and his personality because we had lost cornerback Tim McKyer when he was traded to the Miami Dolphins in April 1990. Our locker room hasn't been the same since. These guys are talkative practical jokers, who can keep a team from becoming too uptight.

By Saturday morning, picking up a veteran running back through a tryout or trade became a moot point. When I showed up for practice at Atlanta–Fulton County Stadium, I couldn't believe my eyes. There was Craig, dressed in full workout gear, running stride for stride with Dr. Michael Dillingham, the 49er orthopedic surgeon. After days of bad news and the diagram in the newspaper of his bad knee, Craig looked as if he were 100 percent healthy. "Don't count me out," he called over to me with a big smile. Then he started weaving and cutting, and I almost fell over. Seifert stepped away from one of the practice drills and looked dumbfounded. I'm sure that scene changed the minds of the 49er front office about a trade.

Craig has the amazing ability to will himself to health. In the locker room after games, he always looks as if he's been in a cage with a tiger. There are thick red and brown stripes, the imprints of opponents' facemasks, crisscrossing his broad back and muscled rib cage. Deep, dark gouges from turf burns cover his elbows, knees, and forearms. Scratches from being stepped on in pileups scar his hands. He says he can sense internal bleeding from all the bruises and blows because his body temperature is warm for several hours after games. He can't eat and has trouble sleeping. On the day after a game, while everybody else is jogging to loosen up the kinks and work out the soreness, Craig runs four laps around the field and eight 100-yard dashes at three-quarter speed. It takes two chiropractors and a massage therapist to get him ready for the next kickoff. He spends about $300 a week to keep his body more or less healthy.

Relentless determination has also made Craig one of the best running backs in the NFL. When he came to the 49ers as a second-round draft pick from Nebraska in 1983, he didn't know how to work hard in practice. Running back Wendell Tyler pointed out to Craig that offensive linemen always finished their blocks and quarterbacks didn't stop in the middle of their play fakes. "Whenever you get the ball," Tyler told him, "run the length of the field. Pretend you're scoring."

In 1986, Craig was plagued by a strained hip and bruised ribs and an ulcer caused from taking anti-inflammatory drugs. The following season he had difficulty making the transition from fullback to halfback, and according to the Bay area media, Craig had lost a step. That was nonsense.

Craig is the most hyperactive of all the 49ers. He trains like a competitor in the Iron Man triathlon, incorporating long bike rides and four-to-eight-mile runs along steep, winding horse trails in Woodside, California, into his workouts three days a week. On other days he sprints uphill and does interval training at a local track. Cornerback Eric Wright, who has worked out with Craig, calls him a machine because once he starts, he can't stop himself.

Craig has attacked off-field endeavors, acting and modeling, with just as much verve and vigor. He's the best-dressed 49er, by far, straight from the pages of *GQ* magazine, with a fully coordinated outfit for every occasion. Before the 1990 season, he posed for a department store in a sexy Calvin Klein underwear ad that appeared in the Bay area newspapers. Later it became a popular poster, and I burned my bikini briefs. From now on I'll stick to basic white Fruit of the Looms. I don't want to embarrass Calvin Klein.

I gave Craig lots of grief about the poster, with the crowning blow coming at the San Francisco Chamber of Commerce Kickoff Luncheon several days before the start of the 1990 season. Craig was emotionally wrapped up in a speech when I snuck in front of the podium and unfurled the underwear poster, which was just off the presses. He fought to maintain his composure but ended up stuttering and stammering. At that point I turned around and showed the poster to the crowd. They went wild.

Although he cultivates a sophisticated, flamboyant image, there's a simplicity and naïveté to Craig which often gets him into trouble. After he finished this morning workout in Atlanta, I pulled him aside.

"Rog, please don't do anything foolish," I said. "Do what's best for you. Don't do it for the team. This is your career you're fooling around with."

On game day, when our coaches and doctors persuaded Craig not to suit up, I was relieved. He was disappointed he wouldn't play against the Falcons because he was only four games away from matching what many consider the record for consecutive games started by running backs. Jim Brown had started 118 straight while playing with the Cleveland Browns from 1957 to '65. Craig toyed with the idea of starting, playing briefly, and then coming out of the game, but he figured that would taint the record. Besides, why risk further injury? By kickoff he was upbeat, laughing and kidding around on the 49er sideline. He mouthed, "I'd give anything to play today. Anything!" straight into a CBS Sports camera.

I think Seifert and offensive coordinator Mike Holmgren had another reason for keeping Craig on the bench. Three weeks before, when we played the Falcons at Candlestick Park, our offense ran 19 sweeps, and 62,858 fans booed loudly. At the end of the game, they yelled, "No more sweeps. No more sweeps." The chanting bothered Seifert, and without Craig in the lineup, Holmgren said we would be forced to diversify our offense and throw the ball more. Sweep or no sweeps, nobody could have predicted the field day Montana and Jerry Rice had in our 45–35 victory over the Falcons.

Montana threw for a career-high 476 yards and six touchdowns, and Rice caught five touchdowns, tying the NFL record held by a pair of tight ends, Kellen Winslow of the San Diego Chargers and Bob Shaw of the old Chicago Cardinals. In all, Rice had 13 catches for 225 yards. Would you believe that Montana and Rice were not satisfied? A couple of times during the game, Montana shook his head and said with all seriousness, "God, Ronnie, I missed a throw." I thought to myself, yeah Joe, but the rest of them were right on target. Montana never focuses on the positives or basks in glory. If he says he wasn't perfect, he truly means it.

Rice cited four or five mental mistakes and claimed that he had only made two in our 55–10 blowout of the Denver Broncos in Super Bowl XXIV, where he and Montana connected on three touchdowns. A perfectionist who is awfully hard on himself at times, Rice cried on the bench after dropping two passes his rookie year. At the time I put my arm around him and said, "Lighten up. Football's meant to be fun." Just as perfect in practice, Rice will pretend he's about to go out of bounds on each catch, no matter where he is on the field, landing in a tippy-toe stutter step. Nobody on the team spends as much time in front of the mirror. Before the pregame warm-ups, and before the kickoff, Rice combs his hair and checks his uniform. I wouldn't want to kick dirt on Rice's number 80 jersey.

Why did Montana and Rice have such a magnificent game? It was the result of Montana and the 49er offensive system forcing the Falcons' defensive backs into impossible situations and just dumb mistakes. Each time the Falcons blitzed, they left corner-back Charles Dimry one-on-one with Rice. Montana also sensed he was "on" with Rice. It's as if Montana said to himself, "Okay, so you're hot today. Let's go with you." He always knows the right guy to get the ball to at exactly the right moment. When Montana is in sync with Rice, they begin reading a defense together before the play unfolds.

Montana and Rice never once had shit-eating grins during their aerial attack nor did they make disparaging remarks about Dimry. Our defensive backs could sympathize with Dimry's dreadful performance. Our jobs are so black and white: Either you make the play or you get burned. There's no in-between.

Watching Dimry brought back memories of the 1985 season for me when I called myself "One-A-Day." Like the One-A-Day multivitamin. I must have given up a touchdown a game in the early part of that season. Those outings toughened me up and helped me develop a thick skin and short memory. Now I couldn't help thinking, why doesn't Dimry give himself a chance to make a play? It looked to me that he foolishly believed he could stop each move Rice made as well as every pass thrown to him. It's better to try to slow down a receiver. For instance, concentrate on taking away the out pattern but permit him to catch the slant. Let's face it. Rice is so good, he is probably going to beat you for a touchdown no matter how you try to stop him. A defensive back can count on his heart being in his throat all afternoon.

After a while, Dimry became a sitting duck. I almost felt sorry for him. Why didn't one of Atlanta's coaches tell him not to get into a foot race with Rice? They should have told Dimry to get

Listening to defensive coordinator George Seifert while chilling out at halftime against the Miami Dolphins in 1986. *(Photograph copyright by Michael Zagaris)*

Coach Bill Walsh congratulates me in 1984. *(Photograph copyright by Michael Zagaris)*

Owner Eddie DeBartolo, Jr., and the 49er Five, the only players who were members of all four Super Bowl championship teams. Left to right, Eric Wright, Mike Wilson, Joe Montana, Keena Turner, and me. *(Photograph copyright by Michael Zagaris)*

A sideline strategy session with the defense in the third quarter of the NFC Championship Game against the Chicago Bears on January 6, 1985. *(Photograph copyright by Michael Zagaris)*

Owner Eddie DeBartolo, Jr., consoles me after our emotional 7–3 victory over the New York Giants on Monday Night Football in 1990. *(Photograph copyright by Michael Zagaris)*

Shaking hands with Joe Montana as the clock ticks down in our 23–0 NFC Championship victory over the Chicago Bears, sending us to Super Bowl XIX. *(Photograph copyright by Michael Zagaris)*

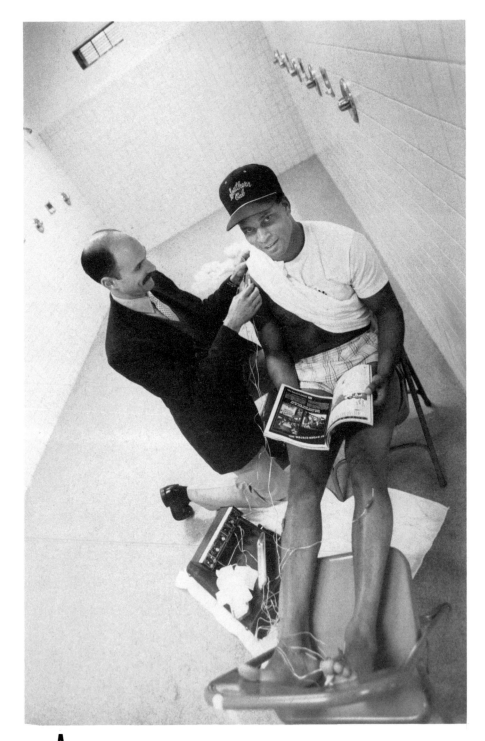

A last-minute acupuncture treatment before a game. *(Photograph copyright by Michael Zagaris)*

Focusing on my assignments in the locker room at Joe Robbie Stadium prior to Super Bowl XXIII against the Cincinnati Bengals. *(Photograph copyright by Michael Zagaris)*

George Chung, my karate instructor, puts me through Zen warrior training. *(Photo by Anthony K. Chan)*

My second interception against the New Orleans Saints in our 1990 season opener. It was the fiftieth interception of my career.
(Photograph copyright by Michael Zagaris)

A Bobo Growl.
(Bill Fox Sports Photos)

Upending New York Giant wide receiver Stephen Baker in a 34–24 victory on November 27, 1989. *(Bill Fox Sports Photos)*

After tackling a New Orleans Saints player, I found a helmet in my hands in a 30–17 victory on December 11, 1988.
(Bill Fox Sports Photos)

Jubilation! I set a 49er post-season record for longest interception return with a 58-yarder for a touchdown in our 41–13 victory over the Minnesota Vikings on January 6, 1990. *(Photograph copyright Mickey Pfleger, 1990)*

himself in a position to make the tackle. Maybe the coaches kept feeding Dimry to the lions to toughen him up.

One horrendous game, or even one critical mistake, can devastate a defensive back. You become a favorite target of offensive coordinators. Those mistakes are recorded on game films forever. And oh . . . the endless negative publicity! Just think of the dozens of times that Dallas Cowboy cornerback Everson Walls has had to answer questions about how Dwight Clark outmaneuvered him to make The Catch in the 1981 NFC Championship Game. If Dimry had asked me for advice, I would have told him to try and forget about it. Focus on your next opponent when the game plan is put in on Wednesday or you'll be playing back on your heels. Feed on your mistakes today but don't let them feed on you tomorrow.

In all fairness, Dimry wasn't the only defensive back on the field who had a rough afternoon. The Falcon receivers repeatedly found openings in our secondary. It's becoming clear that cornerback Don Griffin is our only strong coverage back. Of course, playing a zone defense against the Falcons' run-and-shoot, I expected their receivers to make catches. The problem is we were just too passive. Falcon wide receiver Andre Rison caught 9 passes for 172 yards and two touchdowns. In our first game with Atlanta, he caught 11 passes for 128 yards, all in the second half. One of the NFL's bright young stars, a Jerry Rice wannabe, Rison calls himself Showtime, with his touchdown dance the Highlight Zone. He loves to taunt opponents during games, calling it "trappin" or "talkin' smack," and he has been known to spike balls in the faces of defensive backs. He wouldn't dare try that with me—or at least I hope he wouldn't. What separates Rison from other receivers is his ability to change his speed in patterns. Just when you think he's at full speed he can turn it up a notch. He's a great leaper, moves well laterally, and has excellent body control.

Right before halftime, I pulled my left hamstring while chasing him, and that sent me into a panic. Four weeks of practicing for run-and-shoot offenses had aggravated my hamstring. Twice, I found myself lined up on Rison man-to-man, and I thought, if their quarterback Chris Miller throws to him, I'm dead. Luckily, he never realized I was hurt and didn't go to Rison either time. I would have been running for my life.

WEEK 6

Stealing a Win

I guess I had just better resign myself to the fact that I'll never figure out Bill Walsh. He was at the 49er facility this week to gather information to use in his role as a commentator for NBC Sports, which was televising our game against the Pittsburgh Steelers on Sunday.

"Hey, Ronnie," Walsh said, smiling and catching up to me as I walked out to the field. "I want to talk to you about an investment deal."

I was caught off guard. He had phoned a few days earlier, but I hadn't had a chance to return his call. I was surprised he wanted to talk about something other than football. I had expected Walsh to inquire about my pulled hamstring. Nice of Bill to look out for my future, I thought, but I wish he had spoken to me about investment deals earlier in my career. That way I wouldn't have to work after I retire. Nevertheless, I listened to Walsh's proposal but politely turned him down because I don't have the money to invest with him right now.

I once asked Walsh's pal Mike White, a longtime college and pro football offensive specialist who is now the quarterbacks' coach for the Los Angeles Raiders, why Walsh rarely came to the facility to watch practice.

"Bill feels a little nervous around you guys," White said.

"What for?" I replied. "We're going to treat him just like any other NFL-coach-turned-TV-commentator."

In recent years, my conversations with Walsh have never been more than football chitchat. How's the team doing? Pretty good. That guy looks like a decent player. Yeah, he's helped us out a lot this year. That was the extent of it.

One of the most bizarre, out-of-the-blue phone calls I ever received on a road trip came from Walsh. We were in Tampa to play the Buccaneers the second week of the 1989 season, his first year out of coaching. The day before the game, around lunchtime, the phone rang.

"Hello Ronnie. This is Bill Walsh. I saw you against the Indianapolis Colts last week. You looked good. You were moving around really well."

All right, who's the smart aleck playing games with my head? "Thanks for calling, Bill, I really appreciate it," I said and hung up, convinced that one of the 49er players had pulled a prank.

Still unsettled by the call a few hours later, I cornered linebacker Keena Turner in the dining room. I knew Walsh was fond of Turner and that they occasionally met for lunch.

"Guess who called me," I said to Turner. "Bill Walsh."

"He called me too," Turner replied. So maybe this was legit, after all. But then again knowing that they had kept in touch since Walsh retired, the call to Keena wasn't any surprise. When I told Joe Montana that I had received a call, however, Montana said, "Bill called me too." And then, tackle Bubba Paris, who overheard me speaking to Montana, chimed in with, "Yeah, I got a call from Bill."

At first I had thought it was a nice gesture that Walsh would take the time to call me, but then I asked myself, why would he phone all these guys and all on the same day? I thought about the story former 49er safety Dwight Hicks told me of seeing a lonely-looking Walsh at a charity dinner the spring after he retired and how Walsh had kissed him on the forehead for no apparent reason. I remembered Turner telling me of a phone conversation he had with Walsh several months after he had retired, how Walsh paused to keep Turner on the line a little longer and then said, "I love you." Here we go again. Walsh was "communicating" without actually communicating. Was he trying to mend burned bridges? Did he regret having been so detached from us when he was our coach? Was he sorry he never got closer? Did he miss the players but wasn't able to say so?

I found it rather ironic that NBC had decided to send its No. 1 broadcast crew of Dick Enberg and Walsh to the Pittsburgh-49ers game. The Steelers were the NFL team that Walsh had had the most trouble with, although we had only played them three times during his era. Our only blemish in our 18–1 season in 1984 was the 20–17 loss to the Steelers. Walsh was so stubborn about his offensive system that he would stick to his script of plays despite playing right into the hands of the Steelers' defense. Pittsburgh has always been a black-and-blue team. Every time you line up against the Steelers they check your balls. They want to see how tough you are. The toughest wide receiver I ever faced played for the Steelers. But it wasn't John

Stallworth or Lynn Swann. Ever hear of Weegie Thompson? Well, he blocked the hell out of me in our 1984 game. The Steeler coaches had told him I had a sprained ankle, so Thompson cracked down on it, time and again, keeping me from pursuit on the Steeler running plays. At the time, the 6-foot-6, 210-pound Thompson was only a rookie fourth-round draft pick out of Florida State. I admired his commitment to winning.

I've always felt that if the Steelers, The Team of the '70s, played the 49ers, The Team of the '80s, Pittsburgh would win. Each one of Pittsburgh's four Super Bowl championship teams had better talent. I still don't feel the Steel Curtain defense has gotten enough credit. Mean Joe Greene. L. C. Greenwood. Jack Lambert. Jack Ham. Mel Blount. Those guys won games single-handedly. They kicked ass and took names every single play. And they had class. During the week of the Pro Bowl following our first Super Bowl, wide receiver Dwight Clark and I were hanging around a bar on the beach at Waikiki when Blount and Lambert toasted our championship. That impressed me. To receive congratulations from guys who had won four Super Bowls was pretty special. They could have said, "Hey, one Super Bowl victory is no big deal." Instead, they kept buying us rounds of a concoction called Tropical Itch. Everything you can think of is in that drink. All I can remember is painting my hotel bathroom with Tropical Itches.

Although I knew my hamstring wasn't strong enough for me to play against the Steelers, I still dressed in my full uniform and went through warm-ups on Sunday. I hadn't practiced all week, but in an effort to get back on the field I had subjected my left leg to every form of treatment imaginable. Massage. Acupuncture. Chinese herbs. Electronic stimulation. Saunas. Whirlpool baths. And even something called hit pills, which were given to me by acupuncturist John Steinke. The hit pills contained a mixture of ginseng, frankincense, and myrrh, and the medicine helped reduce the swelling in my hamstring. Unless I was absolutely needed I wouldn't see action. There was no reason to risk further injury. I kept my helmet at the end of the 49er bench just in case.

Watching this game from the sideline would be draining. For me, there's a big difference between standing on the sideline in full uniform and being in street clothes. Any time I am suited up and not playing my body undergoes physiological changes. I get overheated and start to sweat. My heart rate accelerates as if I've actually been on the field making plays. Sometimes I even get butterflies in my stomach. It's not unusual for me to lunge toward the field and contort my body as if I were tackling. After watching a game in uniform I am physically and mentally exhausted, and in the past I have noticed myself panting as I walk off the field.

Normally, if I'm not playing I keep a very low profile. Leaving the field with Turner after the pregame warm-ups, he said he sensed a lethargic attitude among our players. "The team is flat," Turner said. "We're too comfortable. I don't see hunger in guys' eyes."

Usually the best place to get a handle on the mood of a football team is in the locker room while players are getting dressed. If they seem to jump into their uniforms like Superman they're ready to go. Your uniform should create self-worth. It should make you stronger and more powerful. I had been so wrapped up trying to block the pain out of my left hamstring I hadn't noticed the locker-room mood. Once Turner tuned me in, I sensed a lack of intensity. It's really hard to get psyched up every week for a regular season game, especially after winning four world championships. It's like new toys under the Christmas tree. You tear the wrapping from the box, play with the toy every day, and then the excitement wears off. Most NFL teams hit a lull around the fifth or sixth game of the season. That's when the starters' bodies begin to break down and the bench-warmers start complaining that they're not being allowed to contribute. Turner chose not to speak to the team and he insisted I deliver a pep talk. I decided to do it because I was in my uniform. In street clothes I wouldn't have been effective at all.

"You can't go out there like the Oakland A's did in the World Series, losing to the underdog Cincinnati Reds in four games," I told the team. "You can't believe that just because you're the reigning world champions you'll knock these guys off. They aren't going to lay down for you. Every time you step on the field, you have to earn respect. Each and every one of you has to believe you can win the game all by yourself. Don't be like the A's, who said, 'Oh, Jose Canseco will get the hit' . . . or, 'Rickey Henderson will make the play' . . . Don't ever fake your way through a game and tell yourself, 'Hey, Joe Montana will find a way to win the game.' I promise you, Joe can't win game after game all by himself. Do your job to the best of your ability. Strive to be the best."

It was obvious, based on the way we played in the first half, that few players had taken my pep talk to heart. The 49er defense allowed quarterback Bubby Brister to complete 9 of his first 13 passes, and our tackling was very sloppy. Montana was intercepted twice in the first half, and we were extremely fortunate to go into the locker room at halftime with a 10–7 lead.

A 20-yard field goal by Mike Cofer put us ahead, 13–7, in the third quarter, and that led to one of the most bizarre plays you'll ever see in a football game. In fact, it would have been chronicled as one of pro football's all-time blunders had we been playing in a Super Bowl. Here's what happened. On Cofer's ensuing kickoff, Pittsburgh's Barry Foster for some unknown reason did not field the ball. As it rolled toward the end zone Foster simply froze, and none of the other Steelers attempted to pick up the ball. I had never seen anything like it. A kickoff is a free ball. It only has to travel 10 yards before the kickoff team can field it. If this had been a punt, the ball could have been downed. If it had rolled into the end zone, it would have been brought out to the 20-yard line. Our Mike Wilson recovered at the 5-yard line.

Ordinarily, the Steelers would have cornerback Rod Woodson as the deep man on kickoffs, but he had asked for a rest after being on the field during our field-goal drive, which had lasted almost eight minutes. Later Foster admitted that he had blanked out. His mistake didn't shock me. I am sure there are a lot of players in the NFL who don't know the most fundamental rules of the game. Learning the rules only for your specific position isn't enough. NFL players have played long enough to know the object of the game is to get the ball, hold onto it, and score. It's like putting down $100 in front of an eleven-year-old. Don't ask questions. Go after it.

Three plays after Foster's blunder, 49er fullback Tom Rathman scored on a 1-yard run. It charged up our defense and changed the momentum of the game. On Pittsburgh's next possession, defensive end Kevin Fagan stopped fullback Merril Hoge for a 4-yard loss, and then Haley sacked Brister on consecutive plays, the second one resulting in a fumble. Defensive end Pierce Holt recovered on the Steeler 17, and Rathman again bulled in from the 1, which made the final score 27–7.

Until Rathman's two touchdowns, the 49ers had been the only team in the NFL that hadn't scored a rushing TD in the 1990 season. I had always maintained that when Rathman was involved in our offense we were practically unstoppable. He will set the tone by how hard he runs, doing bodily harm to tacklers and breaking his facemask in his fury.

Rathman had been suffering from gout for several weeks, and the infection eventually lodged in his elbow. When he feels well he's the most enthusiastic 49er during our pregame introductions. A real wild man. He runs with his knees high, leaps into the air, pounces on players' backs, and throws his arms in all directions.

Off the field, Rathman looks like a down-home farm boy, in a crew cut and blue jeans, somebody who just stepped off the set of the TV show "Hee Haw." He grew up in Grand Island, Nebraska, which is in the middle of nowhere. I call him Woody after the gullible bartender on the hit show "Cheers." Other 49er players refer to Rathman as "Bonehead" because his crew cut makes his head look square. His long, drawn out Midwestern accent always makes me laugh. "Okay, fellas," Woody always says before games, "let's kick some aaaaass."

With the victory over Pittsburgh our record went to 6–0, and the NFC West race was essentially over. The Atlanta Falcons, Los Angeles Rams, and New Orleans Saints all had 2–4 records. In 1984 and 1987 we also had a comfortable lead in the standings, but Walsh taught us to disassociate from the rest of the teams in the division and to compete against ourselves. He insisted we perfect our skills. Everything had to be precise, right down to the most minute detail. Coach George Seifert took a different approach. He emphasized that the victories we get now will pay off in the end by having the best record and, therefore, home-field advantage in the playoffs. Our 6–0 record made me nervous. I preferred Walsh's approach. We weren't clicking. We were winning ugly.

WEEK 7

Hard Knocks

Wide receivers are the most easily intimidated players on the football field. I love to play on their emotions. Their bodies and minds are always exposed. A good receiver will try to make a catch every chance he gets, but too often the quarterback doesn't throw the ball to the right spot.

The pass is either too high, too low, too far in front, or too far behind. On an incomplete pass I always study the body language of a receiver. How upset is he at the quarterback? Knowing that, I'll move in for the kill. If a pass is thrown too high and I know there's no way a receiver can catch the ball, I run right next to him and get as close as I can without bumping him. Just to let him know that I'm waiting for him the next time around. I'll note if a receiver is frustrated by passes that are thrown too far in front of him. The receiver who won't dive for balls because he's afraid of getting hurt is the one I'll be particularly physical with. Knock him around on routine pass routes because he's the man I can take out of the game quickly. He'll hear footsteps before the other receivers.

By practicing against the 49er receivers, I have learned what it takes to agitate players at this position. After we won our first Super Bowl, the defensive backs reported to training camp in the summer of 1982, more confident than ever. During pass coverage drills Lynn Thomas would still say, "Bank's closed." Saladin Martin would taunt, "Shut 'em down today." One of the most easily agitated 49er receivers was tight end Russ Francis. One afternoon Francis, a newly acquired veteran All-Pro, was repeatedly strong-arming Verlon Redd, a rookie free agent safety from the University of Hawaii who was trying to make the team.

"Man, what are you doing?" a fed-up Redd finally asked Francis.

To get Redd to fight back, I yelled, "Light 'em up! Got to go in there and light 'em up!" On the next pass play, Redd demolished Francis. He angrily lashed out at Redd, pushing his chest up into the kid's face. Five defensive backs quickly swarmed around Francis, as if to say, "This is our neighborhood." Suddenly Francis turned on me. "You'll learn! You'll learn one day," he shouted.

"Why are you talking to me? I didn't do anything to you," I snapped. "You should be talking to him. He knocked the shit out of you. I don't have to learn shit. This is how we play here."

Over the years I have engaged in a couple of heated shouting matches with flanker Jerry Rice. One time, one of the defensive backs was covering him aggressively in a passing drill, and I screamed, "Way to shut him down."

That rubbed Rice the wrong way. "Why don't you come out here?" he replied.

"Man, I'm not even talking to you," I said. "I'm talking to the damn defensive back."

On the next play, Montana sent Rice on a seam pattern. I ran as hard as I could, as if I were going to blow right through Rice. Just lay him out. At the last instant I backed off. It was kind of fun to watch the anger in Rice's eyes turn to fright.

The eyes of a receiver can be revealing. After a play, I look at his eyes to see if I have hurt him. When a receiver breaks the huddle I watch his eyes to detect excitement. Sometimes the eyes tell me if his number has been called. Often when I'm stride for stride with a receiver, he'll look back to the quarterback as if to say, "Hey, the ball's coming my way." That's an old trick. If his eyes are not opened wide and focusing, the receiver is faking me out. If a defensive back turns his head ever so slightly, he gives the receiver that split second to get open.

What do wide receivers see when they look into Ronnie Lott's eyes? They may see that I look pissed off, or a little crazy, but nothing more. Defensive players rely on their emotions to lift their level of performance, but they can't wear these emotions like a suit of clothes. During a game, I don't want opponents to know how I'm feeling or what I'm thinking. If I give up a long pass, I react like a veteran pitcher who gives up a big home run in a tight game. I shake it off. Give me a new ball and let's move on to the next batter.

We play the Cleveland Browns on Sunday, and I get a kick out of competing against their outstanding wide receiver Webster Slaughter. His body language is among the most obvious and revealing of any receiver in the NFL. His game is 100 percent enthusiasm. Since their quarterback Bernie Kosar isn't an outwardly emotional player, the Browns look to Slaughter as their spiritual leader. He reminds me of a fast-talking bobble-head doll. I won't be drawn into debates with him because I know he's talking big stuff to fire up his team. He experiences so many ups and downs in a game. Patience isn't a word in Slaughter's dictionary. One minute he's happily prancing around the field because Kosar has thrown the ball to him. Then he's pissed off because he's not part of the action. To play on his emotions, we decided to double-cover him because we figured he would start complaining if Kosar didn't throw the ball to him at the beginning of the game.

A big part of our defensive game plan also focused on disrupting wide receiver Brian Brennan at the line of scrimmage and forcing him to change his routes. He's such a clutch third-down guy, a consistent, dependable receiver who reminds me of Steve Largent, the former Seattle Seahawk great who is the NFL's all-time leading receiver with 100 touchdowns and 13,089 yards. And we wanted to pressure Kosar up the middle to flush him out of the pocket and make him throw on the run. Playing behind an offensive line with four new starters, Kosar had already been sacked 20 times for minus 125 yards coming into the game.

To me, Kosar is the most unfairly criticized quarterback in the NFL. He's an easy target for sportswriters because of his unconventional sidearm delivery and awkward running style. A sportswriter once said Kosar resembled a giraffe on Quaaludes. Kosar is an intelligent bookworm who graduated with honors from the University of Miami in three years with a double major in finance and economics. I think he opens himself up to attacks from the media because he shies away from in-depth interviews.

My description of Kosar is that of a nimble contortionist, in both the mental and physical sense and, in my mind, that is why he's one of the most difficult quarterbacks to defense. While the flight of Kosar's sidearm passes don't look any different from normal throws, his unusual delivery allows him to thread the ball underneath and between onrushing defenders. Kosar can move his body in one direction and throw the other way, making it impossible to read his shoulders, which is one way to determine the direction of a quarterback's passes. Because defensive backs don't know where the ball is going until it's in the air, it's hard to get a good break on Kosar's throws. That's one reason why Kosar has the lowest interception percentage in NFL history. The experts rave about the quick release of Miami Dolphin quarterback Dan Marino, but he telegraphs his passes. I can pick up where his throws are headed because he squares his shoulders to the area he's going to. That gives defensive backs a better chance to make a play.

Our defense gave Kosar fits, and a string of bad luck in the second quarter pushed Slaughter over the edge. It started when cornerback Eric Davis belted Slaughter, forcing him to fumble, and to sulk and pout. I recovered the ball and returned it to the Cleveland 41, which led to a 49er touchdown, putting us ahead 14–0. Slaughter's misfortune continued on Cleveland's final possession of the quarter. First, he raced into the end zone with a 32-yard catch, but a penalty nullified the touchdown. What followed was more dejection. Three plays later, another Slaughter reception was ruled incomplete by instant replay. The next pass sailed off Slaughter's hands. With about a minute to go until halftime, Slaughter had only managed two catches for 30 yards. He was not a happy camper. He threw his hands in the air, stomped his feet, and shook his head. He was so frustrated that when he lined up on the San Francisco 19 on a third-and-nine, he got into a scuffle with cornerback Eric Wright. He jerked Wright's facemask and was flagged for unsportsmanlike conduct. We kept the Browns from scoring.

At halftime, I reminded our defensive backs to keep Slaughter pissed off. Run next to him when he's not involved in the play. Nudge him. Stare into his eyes. Follow Slaughter all the way back to the huddle if you have to. Violate his space. Throw Slaughter's rhythm off. Get him thinking, "Leave me alone! Get off me!" instead of thinking about football.

In the Browns' first possession of the third quarter, Kosar overthrew Slaughter as he ran across the middle, and I snared the pass for my fifty-first career interception. Two Cleveland series later, with the 49ers leading 17–3, coach Bud Carson replaced Kosar with backup Mike Pagel. It was the first time in Kosar's career that he had been benched. The benching caught our defense by surprise. Pagel bought himself more time with his mobility and picked apart our zones. He threw two touchdowns in the final 10 minutes to tie the score at 17–17 with 1:10 left on the clock.

Carson's move may have been a useful quick fix for the Browns at the time, but in the long run I feel that benching a star quarterback during the course of a game can only drag a team down. It is very divisive and keeps the entire team from playing as a unit. It allows doubt to creep into the players' minds. I saw it happen with the 49ers in 1988 during our quarterback controversy. One faction wanted Joe Montana to be the starter, another group preferred Steve Young. The psychology of playing quarterback is enough to drive you bananas without having a backup breathing down your neck. During the game, a quarterback gets in a rhythm, with his brain rapidly clicking through a sequence of plays and counterplays. It's better to keep a quarterback in the rhythm and let him play through a bad slump. Football isn't like baseball, with its parade of relief pitchers. Kosar's benching represented a move of desperation by Carson. There had been rumors that he would be fired. Carson's stress showed on his face. He looked haggard. The Browns' players couldn't help but sense his emotions. It's like hanging out with a buddy who's on death row. You can feel he's getting ready to die.

Meanwhile, Montana had one of the poorest performances of his career against the Browns, completing fewer than half of his passes, but I'm sure it never occurred to George Seifert to replace him with Young. For the second week in a row, Montana had passed for less than 200 yards. A bruised finger suffered during the pregame introductions while slapping high fives as he ran through a gauntlet of teammates was partly to blame, as were the howling Candlestick Park winds.

"The ball is taking off," Montana told me on the sideline. "I'm having a really tough day."

How tough was it? So tough that Montana opened up our final drive with two straight incompletions. On the first, split end Mike Sherrard was penalized for pass interference, sending us back to our own 18. Montana refused to panic. On third-and-14 from the San Francisco 24, he hit Sherrard on a 35-yard pass, which put us on the Cleveland 41 with 38 seconds left. Three plays later, Mike Cofer's 45-yard field goal with five seconds remaining gave us a 20–17 victory.

If you ask Montana what comes over him when his back is against the wall, he can't describe it. He probably concentrates better but he's not really sure. Some of Montana's coolness under pressure is innate and mystical, but a lot of it is practice. He has prepared himself well for pressure-packed situations like this. At least once a week during the regular season, the 49er first-string offense practices against the first-string defense, until the offense gets it right. In training camp, both the offense and the defense work against the clock in four-, three-, two-, and 1:40-minute situations with officials. We fine-tuned offensive drives and conditioned our defense to fight to get the ball back. (It was always so competitive. The winners had their curfew extended that evening by an extra hour to midnight.) Bill Walsh trained us to understand how to use the clock and always to have a sense of where you were on the field. Great preparation will overcome any obstacle, Walsh preached, and it will win more games than talent. The players who function well in crucial situations will make the difference.

After the game I blasted the team in the newspapers and on TV. I was using reverse psychology to keep everybody's feet on the ground. I claimed that the 49ers weren't a great team. Hell, how could we be? We couldn't even put our opponents away. I was hoping to put some more fire into our guts to stoke up our intensity.

When Sherrard appeared at the 49er facility on Monday morning, we received some bad news. He had fractured the fibula in his right leg while making that big catch on the game-winning drive when he was tackled by Brown cornerbacks Tony Blaylock and Raymond Clayborn. It was the same leg he had broken twice before as a member of the Dallas Cowboys. The 49ers had signed Sherrard as a Plan B free agent in 1989 and, because he was still rehabilitating his leg, placed him on the physically unable to perform list for the regular season. We nicknamed him the Erector Set. I made it a point to sit down and talk to Sherrard, making sure he would feel a part of the team. When you're not playing, people never get to know you.

The 49er team doctors told Sherrard he would be out six to eight weeks. I tried to be positive. "You're going to be back, Mike," I told him. "You'll be back before the end of the season." Sherrard appeared upbeat, but he had to be wondering if his bones were brittle. Dr. Michael Dillingham assured Sherrard that wasn't the case, and he told the media, "I don't think this in any way reflects a tendency toward brittle bones. It is the same leg, but a different bone from his previous breaks. I think the injury he sustained was enough to cause this kind of thing."

Later that day, I asked myself if I could handle three broken legs in four years the way Sherrard has. How would I deal with something like this? I would like to think I have the mental toughness. I've always contended that players who come back from serious injuries or rebound from drug and alcohol problems are mentally stronger than everybody else on the field. If Sherrard could muster up his fortitude one more time, it would make him a formidable receiver and a confident man. I believe that many players are afraid on the football field because they haven't had to deal with injuries, being tackled hard, or getting hit while catching a pass over the middle. Their fears protect them from the unknown. Once they have had these experiences, they are likely to say, "That wasn't so bad. Now I can go about my business."

In a sense, Sherrard might be lucky. After coping with this broken leg, I am sure he'll be able to say, "Whatever life dishes out I can handle." Nothing can intimidate him anymore.

WEEK **8**

Winning's Not the Only Thing

We should have been hungry to play the Green Bay Packers. They were the last team to beat us, 21–17, back on November 19, 1989, and I will never forget how upset George Seifert was after that game. We had beaten ourselves by committing 4 turnovers and 10 penalties and allowing 6 sacks. This year in training camp, Seifert made us watch films of that horrible loss three times, and during our preparation for this game he harped on the theme "We owe these guys."

I don't know if any of the 49er players felt as nostalgic about the trip to Green Bay as I did. For sure, nobody is as big a pro football history buff as I am. Going to Green Bay was like taking a journey back in time. The Packers were the only modern-day team to have three-peated, when they won three straight NFL championships in 1965–66–67 under the legendary Vince Lombardi. I have fantasized about playing for Lombardi. He asked each of his players to go the extra mile. That's something I have prided myself on. The 1967 Packer team produced six Hall of Famers—Bart Starr, Ray Nitschke, Herb Adderley, Forrest Gregg, Willie Davis, and Willie Wood—and even today the town of Green Bay still proudly calls itself Titletown U.S.A. The Packers complex is located on Lombardi Avenue. The Packers are a community-owned corporation consisting of 1,856 shareholders, none of whom receives any cash dividends on his initial investment.

When we landed at tiny Austin Straubel Field, the pilot of our jumbo jet slammed on the brakes because the airport's lone runway wasn't built for such a large airplane. The lobby in our motel was jammed with fans, and the local newspapers and the Green Bay TV stations were loaded with information on the game. The Packers and the state high school football championships were the social events of the weekend in Wisconsin.

Stepping onto Lambeau Field, I experienced the chills. Perhaps it's the same feeling a major-league baseball player gets while playing in Yankee Stadium. There is so much history inside the green-and-gold walls. An incredible winning tradition that dates all the way back to the early 1930s. The intimacy of

Lambeau Field makes it the most perfect football stadium in the NFL. It's small, with a capacity of only 59,543, and the fans appear to be sitting right on top of the action.

But the ghosts of championships past weren't enough to get the 49ers going. For practically the entire first half we played as if we hadn't gotten our wake-up call. The offense was flat and out of sync, and we had to punt on our first four possessions. Trailing 10–0, and with 38 seconds left before the half, Packer coach Lindy Infante made a move that put us back in the game. Infante opted for a squib kick on the ensuing kickoff because he said there was a stiff wind blowing in the face of his kicker Chris Jacke. Harry Sydney returned the ball to the San Francisco 41. Three plays later, Joe Montana found John Taylor on a 23-yard pass in the end zone.

That touchdown gave us the momentum we so desperately needed. There are three key stages in a game where I believe you have to gain your momentum. The first drive, the one right before the half, and the drive at the end of the game. Scoring right before the half gives a team a huge psychological boost. You go into the locker room feeling good about yourself. Hey, we can get in the end zone! It takes the enthusiasm out of the opponents and gives them something to think about for the twelve-minute intermission between halves.

Our momentum carried us right through to the opening minutes of the fourth quarter when we went ahead for the first time in the game. Tight end Brent Jones caught a 6-yard touchdown pass to put us on top 17–10.

I knew we couldn't relax because the Packers' Don Majkowski to Sterling Sharpe passing combination is one of the most dangerous in the NFL. Majkowski is gutsy and confident, and earned his nickname Majik Man when he rallied Green Bay to victory five times in the fourth quarter in 1989. Majik is a fashion statement. He wears skin-tight uniform pants and a specially tapered number 7 jersey, and he spats his shoes and ankles with white adhesive tape. With his eye black, and long blond-streaked hair streaming out the back of his helmet, Majik resembles hard rocker Alice Cooper.

Infante's offensive system, a controlled, short-passing game, is tailor-made for Majkowski's never-say-die attitude. Majik shows no fear in catapulting his 6-foot-2, 197-pound body up-field, scrambling over linebackers and running through safeties. If you pressure Majkowski, he'll run sideways and then upfield. Then he'll run sideways again. Majkowski doesn't plant his feet and balance his weight before throwing the ball, which makes his passes difficult to anticipate. That keeps defensive backs guessing and makes them a step late.

Sharpe is the Packer receiver Majik goes to in a bind. A fearless acrobat, he has a strong upper body and powerful legs, which make him tricky to bring down. A defensive back can easily bounce off when delivering a hit. It's important to wrap him up with your arms. Before the 1988 NFL draft Bobby Beathard, now the general manager of the San Diego Chargers, referred to Sharpe as the best college player in the country. I had seen Sharpe on TV while he was at South Carolina and I felt confident he would be a successful NFL receiver because he seemed to understand the pro passing game and how to read various kinds of zone defenses. My prediction on Sharpe proved to be accurate. In his first season with the Packers he set a rookie record with 55 receptions. In 1989 he had 90 receptions for 1,423 yards, the most by any receiver in the sixty-nine-year history of the Packer franchise.

On the Packers' first possession of the fourth quarter, Majik marched his team 53 yards in nine plays, setting up a Jacke 37-yard field goal to cut our lead to 17–13. The key play in this drive was a 37-yard catch by Sharpe. Cornerback Don Griffin had the coverage, and Sharpe leaped into the air to grab the ball, laying his body out and making a spectacular catch.

Montana countered with a dazzling 64-yard touchdown pass to Jerry Rice, but Majik brought the Pack back again, moving the team 72 yards in seven plays in just 2:06. He threw a 17-yard touchdown pass to Sharpe in the left corner of the end zone, reducing our lead to 24–20. It was Sharpe's second touchdown of the game, and both times he had beaten cornerback Eric Wright.

The lack of a running attack puts pressure on a defense, so when we were unable to string together an extended drive and eat up the clock, the Packers gained possession at the Green Bay 19 with 2:12 left in the game. In our defensive huddle, I reminded everybody to stay alert, to get to the football, and to lie on the ballcarrier after the tackle to eat up the clock. Every second counts. In crunch time I become very conscious of keeping my teammates from cracking under pressure. I point out every situation they could encounter, and I go out of my way to encourage them. If they stay calm and think positively, the pressure will not get to them. At moments like this, I try to come up with the big play. I know a big hit can change the momentum. How can I get the ball back to Montana as quickly as possible? That big hit occurred on what turned out to be the Packers' final possession. Majik completed a 7-yard pass to wide receiver Perry Kemp. Johnny Jackson and I crushed Kemp, forcing a fumble, and Wright recovered. The game was over for the Packers.

Afterward, my teammates gathered in the center of the locker room for the postgame prayers. We were still unbeaten with an 8–0 record, and with a 16-game winning streak, we were only two victories away from tying the NFL record held by the Miami Dolphins and the Chicago Bears. Satisfaction on our teammates' faces did not sit well with Charles Haley and me. To us, this game marked the fifth time in 1990 that we had to come from behind to win, and it was the fifth victory decided by six points or fewer.

Haley simmered in front of his locker. Then he erupted.

"If you think this is what it's going to take to get to the Super Bowl, then this team is in for a long year, a very long year," Haley yelled. "Let's get our act together. We've got to play much better than this."

Seifert, who had maintained a low profile this season, quickly stepped in front of the team and downplayed Haley's comments.

"Charles, that's all well and good," Seifert said. "But I think you guys have got to start having more fun. You should enjoy these goddamn wins. You work too hard and play too well to come in here and complain about them."

Have more fun? What was this carefree approach all about? Once again, our running game had been unproductive. Against the Packers, we rushed for a total of 34 yards on 20 carries, the 49ers' lowest rushing total since November 16, 1980, the day we gained only 23 yards against the Miami Dolphins. Back then, I was a senior at USC and the 49ers were on an 8-game losing streak. It was hard to believe that Montana and rookie running back Dexter Carter were the team's leading rushers against the Packers with 13 yards apiece. Roger Craig, in the lineup after missing three games with a knee injury but still not 100 percent, managed only eight yards on five carries.

Yet Seifert's let's-have-some-fun-around-here sentiment was echoed a few days later in a letter I received from owner Eddie DeBartolo, Jr.

Dear Ronnie:
The season is half over, and thanks to your style of play, we continue that special 49ers mystique that has won us the

respect of both our fans and our detractors. Even though we are only halfway home, I feel you deserve a special note of praise for accomplishing what no one thought we would, or could!

Keep up the great work, and thank you for bringing all of us a step closer to making NFL history.

Sincerely,
"Mr. D"

P.S. Aside from it all, let's start enjoying ourselves and bring the fun back into winning!

In my opinion, you can't be content with winning if you're not operating well at every phase of the game. I believe that each week our record is 0–0–0. No wins, no losses, no ties. You can't depend on the past. You have to concentrate on the future. Teams must constantly improve, set new standards, and reach higher goals. If we weren't building for something, then our record might as well be 0–8.

If you aren't executing properly, you're only setting yourself up for a fall. And then you're going to sit there and say, "Oh my God, why didn't we pay attention to that detail? Why were we satisfied with winning?" The running game wasn't clicking. I could sense that our running backs and offensive linemen were beginning to lose confidence in themselves and in each other.

I had an even bigger worry about this 49er team. Unlike any previous season, we seemed to be playing every game under an incredible mental strain. Opponents approached our games as if it were their Super Bowl. Green Bay linebacker Brian Noble put it best when he said that he'll never be in the Hall of Fame, but at least he can tell his children and grandchildren that he held his own against Montana, Craig, and Rice, some of the greatest players of the 1980s. Instead of rising to the level of our opponents, we seemed timid and complacent.

I will promise you this: Haley and I will both be pissed off each time we don't play well. We'll be pissed off because we're not going for our first Super Bowl in 1990. We're going for our third in a row. *Bring back the fun in winning?* Well, football and life are parallel. Success is never a road of happiness. It's a road of hard work and determination.

WEEK 9

Cheap Shots

It must be a lonely, empty feeling to only be able to hug those you love with one arm. I think about that sometimes when I'm with former 49er strong safety Jeff Fuller. He hasn't had the full use of his right arm since he tore the nerves on the right side of his neck making a tackle against the New England Patriots in the seventh game of the 1989 season. Even though I try to act nonchalant I can't ignore the fact that Fuller's right arm dangles at his side. When he tries to fold his hands in his lap, he has to cradle the right arm in his left and move it into position. I try to deal with the arm as just being a unique part of Jeff Fuller, but it's not easy. I know Fuller senses how difficult it is for me and the rest of the 49ers to see him helpless, and I can only imagine how difficult it is for him to be with us. He has admitted that when he visits the team, he tries to remember to wear a special brace to hold the arm in place so we'll all feel more comfortable. Every time I see Fuller I hold a glimmer of hope that he'll raise his right hand to shake mine, but that hasn't happened yet. He has shown so little improvement that it tears me up inside.

When I spoke to Fuller the afternoon before our season-opener in New Orleans, he admitted that it had been difficult to think about football since the injury. He had trouble watching games on television. He had turned down several invitations by the 49ers to attend games and defensive backfield meetings. And he said he couldn't bear to watch our Saints game from the sideline. However, his spirits lifted when he described all of the inspirational letters he had received from people who had suffered similar injuries. He told me about a man who had been to ten different doctors until he finally found a specialist in Canada who had helped him. Fuller explained that whatever nerve regeneration was going to take place would happen in the first twenty-four months. After that, it was doubtful the movement in his arm would improve. I urged Fuller to visit the specialist in Canada, and I impressed upon him that time was running out. Now, nine weeks later, in the hallway of our hotel in Dallas, Fuller admitted that he hadn't phoned the specialist in Canada.

"Jeff, you told me you were going to seek other medical opinions," I said.

"Yeah, I'm going to do it," Fuller replied. Although he was faithfully undergoing physical therapy and getting closer to writing his name, I wanted him to go further.

"Jeff, you owe it to yourself, man," I said. "This is your life, your health. You should go to all extremes to make sure your body is healthy."

Fuller had always been a superior athlete. He never had to push himself. Eddie DeBartolo, Jr., had announced that he would give Fuller $100,000 a year for life, but would that really help him get on with his life? I hoped so but I wasn't sure. Was I being unfair? Perhaps. It must be impossible to keep the faith and search for more answers when you can't understand why God chose to end your promising football career so soon. But you should never give up the fight before you've exhausted your options.

I figured that Fuller was frightened, afraid the Canadian specialist might have a discouraging prognosis, and scared to face the future without football. He didn't have a job. Football had taken up most of his life, and I wondered what he would do without it.

I was reminded of Fuller's neck injury during our game with the Dallas Cowboys at Texas Stadium. Cowboy cornerback Issiac Holt and free safety Ray Horton were each called for a facemask penalty. Both plays were cheap shots, and thankfully neither resulted in any kind of career-ending injury. Trying to rip off helmets isn't good football.

The first facemask incident occurred midway through the second quarter. On second-and-nine from the Dallas 42, Joe Montana completed a 37-yard pass to Jerry Rice. Before Rice made the reception, Holt grabbed Rice's facemask and yanked on it. He then knocked the ball from Rice's hands. The ball rolled into the end zone. At first the officials ruled an incomplete pass and a 15-yard flagrant facemask penalty, but instant replay reversed the decision to a completion, a facemask penalty, and a fumble. The ball was placed on the Dallas 2, and four plays later fullback Tom Rathman scored on a 1-yard touchdown run putting the 49ers ahead 7–3.

The second facemask incident happened in the fourth quarter. Rookie running back Dexter Carter caught a pass from Montana, and was nailed by Horton, who latched onto Carter's facemask and twisted his helmet. That was totally unnecessary. Carter was so enraged that he unbuckled his chin strap and foolishly slammed his helmet to the ground. A rookie mistake. If there's an argument, you should never take your helmet off. You're too vulnerable to being slugged. One of the Cowboys' defensive players could have knocked the daylights out of Carter and gotten away with it by arguing that he was just chasing the football. By throwing his helmet, Carter was automatically disqualified from the game.

Other than these two cheap shots, and a sensational leaping one-handed 7-yard TD catch by Rice at the back of the end zone, it was an uneventful game. We beat the Cowboys 24–6. We stayed on the ground and had 40:39 in possession time.

Football is 90 percent crazy and 10 percent physical. If I'm mixing it up with a 275-pound offensive lineman and he's punching me in the throat, my brain says, "Hey, the only way I'm going to survive against this big son of a bitch is by being crazier than he is." For Holt and Horton, facemasking could be a means of survival against crazies or perhaps a form of intimidation. Tackling by a facemask is a cheap shot and a sign of absolute desperation.

The most flagrant cheap shot I have ever seen occurred when Philadelphia Eagle safety Andre Waters, on a blitz, dove helmet-first toward the knees of Los Angeles Ram quarterback Jim Everett in 1988. In response, the NFL adopted a rule making it illegal to hit a quarterback below the knees while he's in the pocket. In a Monday Night Football game on October 15, 1990, Waters tackled Minnesota Viking quarterback Rich Gannon at his knees, and the NFL fined him $10,000. (Amazingly, no penalty was called.) Waters angered me. Shots at knees? What's going through that guy's mind?

I'll hit an opponent with whatever it takes to stop him dead in his tracks. Bring them down any way you have to. If I have to throw my shoulder, knowing that I'm risking a dislocation, I'll do it. If I have to use my little pinkie, I'll do it. Sometimes I'll even smash opponents in the head, right behind the ear hole of their helmet. Experience has taught me that if you hit them in the head, the rest of the body will follow. As unbelievable as it sounds, if I had to throw my entire body, and know that I would die tackling somebody, I would still do it. I have only one rule. Stay away from the knees if at all possible.

Throughout my career, George Seifert has repeatedly said, "If you see a running back, cut him at the knees." Well, I'm not a cutter. Never have been. Never will be. Take out somebody's knees and you could end his career. Furthermore, I have witnessed a number of defensive backs cut an opponent and wind up with concussions or neck injuries. The 49er offensive linemen have been regularly accused of leg whipping, a technique taught by offensive line coach Bobb McKittrick. They swing their legs around, cutting their opponents' legs from behind, and below the knees, and sweeping their feet out from underneath them. Leg whipping is dirty football. You're caught totally off guard, focused straight ahead on your target, and then suddenly you're on the ground with your shins burning in pain. There is no time to get out of the way because you can't see the leg whip coming. The act of being leg-whipped reminds me of the hot summer days when my childhood buddies and I would stand in a circle in the backyard and whirl a garden hose. Every time I saw the hose coming, I had to jump over it or it would knock me down. Los Angeles Raider defensive end Howie Long became so enraged at the 49ers' leg-whip technique that he chased McKittrick off the field after a game in 1985.

The bottom of piles are usually the easiest places to cheapshot a player. That's where guys get pinched and bitten, their hands get stepped on, and their nuts get squeezed. Roger Craig has come to the sideline several times with a pained look on his face. "So-and-so hit me in the balls," he'll say in a high-pitched voice, shaking his head in disbelief.

I'd like to believe that some cheap shots are accidental and not premeditated. Maybe linemen don't mean to poke their fingers in your eyes and gouge deep scratches on your cheeks and upper arms. Perhaps tight ends and running backs can't help that their forearms smash you in the stomach when the officials aren't watching. Maybe those players who come flying into the pile at breakneck speed after the whistle has blown—and wipe you out with a kill shot to the chest—really did try to veer off course. As for those nutcrackers, well, sometimes when you're trying to tackle somebody, you're just reaching out and pulling him down, and his crotch is the only place to grab.

Only once have I taken a cheap shot on purpose. In 1981 I slugged Atlanta Falcon wide receiver Alfred Jackson and was ejected from the game for the only time in my career. Jackson had provoked the attack by popping me in my face with a forearm. I have received my share of flags for late hits, but none of the hits have been meant purposely to hurt an opponent. I come flying in to finish off tackles and can't put on the brakes in midair. Chasing down wide receivers, my mind says, "Nail that sucker." All the way to the sideline. As he is sailing out of bounds, I will let up some. To avoid crashes after the whistle, I try to dive over piles, and many officials have commented about that. In Super Bowl XXIII I threw myself over a mass of Cincinnati Bengals, and then bounced and skidded on the turf a couple of yards.

"Good job, Lott," the referee said.

"Hey, where'd you learn that move?" Bengal quarterback Boomer Esiason asked. "Karate class?"

WEEK **10**

A Good Defense Is the Best Offense

Each year a different group of leaders emerges on the 49ers. So far this season our defensive linemen are setting a standard for everybody to be proud of. During my career I have been able to play cornerback and safety at such a high level because of the tough guys up front. Force a quarterback to throw the ball, and any defensive back will look like an All-Pro.

Two of the guiding lights on our line are Pierce Holt and Kevin Fagan, who I believe are one of the best pairs of defensive ends in pro football. I admire both of them for their perseverance and determination in beating the odds to make a name for themselves in the NFL.

Holt didn't play organized football until his senior year in high school. After graduation, to make ends meet he held a number of odd jobs and tried boxing, but a bad left eye killed that idea. Born with amblyopia, also known as "lazy eye," Holt only has 10 percent vision in the left eye and had trouble ducking punches. Holt phoned the NCAA to inquire about his football eligibility and was told he could play four years at a Division II school. He enrolled at Angelo State in San Angelo, Texas, and graduated in four years. Most NFL teams were turned off by his small-college background and they wondered about selecting somebody who was twenty-six years old. Holt impressed the 49ers with his performance in the 1988 Senior Bowl, and they selected him in the second round. Today there is no better inside rusher in the NFL than Holt. His slap-down, swim move scissors him quickly through offensive linemen.

Fagan is a medical miracle. It amazes me that he can play so well on a right knee that has required six operations. His forte is stuffing the run, and his hands are so quick that he can strike and twist blockers before the same is done to him. Fred von-Appen, our former defensive line coach, described Fagan's 6-foot-3, 260-pound physique this way: "You can probably strike a match on his rear end. You'd want him to be the first guy off the landing barge at Iwo Jima. Bullets would probably bounce off his chest." I tease Fagan that all those muscles make him look older than twenty-seven.

These guys are fun to be with, and you always have to be on your toes for their shenanigans. Fagan's gag on Holt, when he was a rookie in 1988, is a classic. Fagan told Holt that Tom Holmoe, my backup at safety, had played Dennis the Menace in the old television show. Holt, not sold on this bill of goods, asked Holmoe point-blank if he was really Dennis the Menace.

"Now that I'm playing football, I don't like that association," Holmoe said seriously. "That's why I don't say much about it."

A few days later, Holt tried to trick Holmoe.

"Okay, so what was your stage name?" he asked.

"Jay North," Holmoe replied.

Now Holt didn't know what to believe. For the life of him, he couldn't figure out why a tidbit like that wasn't in the 49er press guide. Holt did a little detective work, trying to verify the information with whomever he could. Finally satisfied, Holt approached Holmoe in the locker room and said, "Gee, I saw all your shows when I was a kid."

With Holt and Fagan leading the charge, our defense shut down the Tampa Bay Buccaneers. We beat them 31–7, and for the third time this season our defense didn't allow a touchdown. The Bucs' only TD came on a 65-yard interception return by cornerback Wayne Haddix in the third quarter. We put tremendous pressure on quarterback Chris Chandler, who had started in place of Vinny Testaverde. The 1986 Heisman Trophy winner, Fagan's roommate at the University of Miami, Testaverde was benched because he had thrown nine interceptions and two touchdowns in the last three games. We chased Chandler all afternoon and sacked him seven times for minus 47 yards. Time and again we flushed him out of the pocket, and he somehow managed to scramble for 44 yards.

By crushing Tampa Bay, our 18-game winning streak tied the

NFL record held by three teams: Don Shula's Miami Dolphins of 1972–73, featuring the No-Name Defense, Larry Csonka and Mercury Morris, and the George Halas Chicago Bears teams of 1941–42 and 1933–34. The streak covered regular and post-season games. It has been my impression that the attitude of the record setters in the 49er organization has always been one of: So what? We don't sit back and gloat and count yards, catches, tackles or interceptions. We always take it one game at a time.

Our victory over Tampa Bay was somewhat clouded by the fact that one of my closest friends, cornerback Eric Wright, strained the medial collateral ligament in his left knee in the third quarter. He had caught his cleats in the ground at Candlestick Park on pass coverage. The sight of him crumbling to the grass, clutching his left knee and rocking back and forth in agony, made me feel sick to my stomach.

"Oh, my God, I can't believe he's hurt," I said while running to his aid. "Not Eric. No. Please, not Eric."

Wright always wore a hard outer shell, and he only showed his emotions in extreme cases. The 49er doctors and trainers tried to talk to him but he was inconsolable, swaying and shaking as if he were in the middle of the field all by himself. "My knee. My knee," he yelled. "It's killing me." I have found that when pain first hits, the body tenses up and goes into a mild form of shock. It's important to lie still and relax. I bent over and cradled Wright's knee in my hands.

"Relax, Eric," I said. "Just try to relax. You'll only make it worse. Please relax."

Wright finally calmed down enough to be helped off the field. I felt tears coming to my eyes but I fought them off, not wanting to let my emotion flow, because if I did I knew I would lose my focus on the game. On the sideline, I found Wright in the back of a cart, getting ready to go to the dressing room for X-rays.

"Are you all right?" I asked.

"I think I'll be okay," he said, looking more pissed off than frightened.

As I walked away from Wright I felt all alone, even though I was in the area of the 49er bench with my teammates and surrounded by 62,221 screaming 49er fans in Candlestick Park. But at that moment I felt as if there were nobody out there. My body went into a mini convulsion, and I felt like throwing up.

The next time I saw Wright was on Monday morning. He was on crutches. He thought he needed surgery, but later it was decided the knee would be treated with rest and rehabilitation. Seeing Wright's plight saddened me because I knew how hard he had worked this past off-season to get himself in shape, and I had closely followed his fight to overcome a groin injury that he has battled on and off for five years. When the groin injury first occurred in 1985, Wright was the best coverage cornerback in the NFL. At first none of our doctors could pinpoint why he was experiencing pain in his groin. Wright would walk around without limping, but when he started running and cutting the pain would increase.

"Ronnie, something is hurting me," he kept telling me, stumped by the injury.

Wright played in only two games in 1986 and two in 1987. He came very close to giving up and retiring. There were some 49er players who questioned if Wright really was hurt. Others wondered why Walsh didn't release him. In fact, one day Wright had a confrontation with cornerback Tim McKyer. "You ain't nothin'," McKyer said. "You might have been great once, but now it's my turn." That angered Wright and drove him to work harder.

Finally, before the 1988 season the doctors said the pain was caused by chronic inflammation at the point where the pubic bones joined. To rehabilitate his groin area, Wright worked out with the San Francisco Ballet. But the groin problems persisted through the 1989 season, and I feared his career had come to an end when the 49ers made him a Plan B free agent in the spring of 1990. No other team signed him. In training camp this year, he had a hamstring injury and found himself on the bubble before the final roster cut. He told the media that the 49ers gave him the option to retire or be waived. He refused to retire and turned down an injury settlement, so the 49ers found a spot on the roster and instead waived rookie cornerback Anthony Shelton.

Wright and I have been through so much together. We were roommates on the road early in our careers when we were fun-loving guys. We are business partners. We are part of an elite group known as the 49er Five—along with Montana, linebacker Keena Turner, and wide receiver Mike Wilson—who are the only players to have been on all four 49er Super Bowl teams. With this latest knee injury, I couldn't help but wonder if this might be the beginning of the end for the 49er Five.

WEEK **11**

Wake-Up Call

On Thanksgiving Day, we had a typical Thursday practice. It lasted for about two hours and was detailed and spirited. The players, however, were able to leave the 49er facility by midafternoon, and I drove to Rocklin, California, to have my turkey dinner with my godparents Chuck and Eva Young. It was the first time I had seen Chuck since his heart attack in September and his subsequent surgery to install a mechanical valve, and I was delighted to find him as feisty as ever.

I had spent previous Thanksgivings with my teammates Eric Wright and Keena Turner and their families, and I had also had them over to my place. On those occasions, I prepared an elaborate meal with mashed potatoes, candied yams, and greens. I even baked a pumpkin pie. I have to admit, I cook a great Thanksgiving turkey, even if my method is unconventional. I learned my culinary skills from my dad. The night before Thanksgiving, I pop the bird in the oven, cover it tightly with foil, and set the temperature gauge to 150 degrees. About fifteen hours later I remove the foil to brown the bird, and when I see the meat falling off the bones, it's an indication the turkey is ready to be devoured. The first time my fiancée, Karen, watched me preparing the turkey for slow cooking, she figured we were doomed to ptomaine poisoning or dinner at Mc-Donald's. "Karen, just watch the master," I said confidently, and after she took her first bite she couldn't stop raving.

Traditionally, NFL teams use the Thanksgiving holiday as a time to have some fun. Coaches and veterans usually spread the word that a local supermarket is giving away free turkeys to the rookies on the team. All they have to do is show up at the store and identify themselves. Of course, the cashier at the checkout counter knows nothing about the free turkeys, and neither does the store manager, who often winds up in an argument with the players. It doesn't dawn on the rookies that they've been had until they explain the mixup in the locker room the next day.

In my rookie year in 1981, the 49er veterans passed out fliers for free turkeys, and I stopped by the grocery store that same day. But my teammates never knew I fell for their prank because

I was too embarrassed to tell them. I kept my mouth shut. This year our rookies couldn't deny going to the supermarket because we asked the store manager to take a photograph of each player in an Indian headband, holding up a rubber chicken.

I became a spokesman for the San Francisco Food Bank in 1989, and that has made my Thanksgivings even more meaningful. The food bank donates food to nonprofit agencies in San Francisco that provide an average of 30,000 meals a month to people in homeless shelters, soup kitchens, child-care centers, AIDS support groups, and spouse-abuse programs. Last week before our game against Tampa Bay I sponsored a Thanksgiving food drive which was held outside Candlestick Park, and we collected 21,000 pounds of food. During the 1990 Christmas holidays I will spearhead the second annual Tackle Hunger campaign, urging employees at 150 Bay area businesses to donate nonperishable items in any of the 600 red barrels with my picture on them. A year ago my Tackle Hunger Christmas campaign collected 61,000 pounds of food. Spend a buck or two on a can of soup or baked beans, drop it into a barrel, and you've helped somebody. It's that simple.

As a rookie I felt uncomfortable because all I had to do was write my name on a contract to receive a $300,000 signing bonus. From that day on, I have felt a responsibility to share some of my blessings with those less fortunate. Besides my work with the San Francisco Food Bank I visit hospitals, raise money for the Special Olympics, and have set up a charity to fund sports camps for underprivileged kids.

During my ten years with the 49ers, I have watched the homeless population in the San Francisco and San Jose areas increase steadily. I have supported the work of the Glide Memorial Church, which is located in the deprived section of San Francisco known as the Tenderloin. The church feeds people three times a day, every day of the year, and some of my teammates have dished up food in the church's food lines.

Believe me, it's a humbling experience to be recognized by a homeless person. I can't just ignore the person and walk away, as so many people do. It's a constant reminder that this person knows my face from watching television or reading newspapers or magazines, which are now luxuries that are no longer affordable. This could happen to any of us. Whenever I'm recognized by anybody, I am most appreciative, and I don't categorize fans by race, creed, educational background, physical appearance, or economic status. Being black, I've lived with being made to feel different because of what I am rather than who I am. I never say, "Oh, he's homeless . . ." and make a judgment or turn up my nose. To me, the homeless are just people, people who have fallen on hard times, who desperately need our help.

As I took the field for our pregame warm-ups, I knew that the 10–0 49ers were about to face the Los Angeles Rams as the only undefeated team in the NFL. I had been told the New York Giants, the only other team with an unblemished record, were about to lose to the Philadelphia Eagles 31–13. I sprinted to the far end zone to stretch, pausing only to shake hands with my friend Jerry Gray, the Ram Pro Bowl cornerback, then I raced to the 49er bench area to join our defensive backs for drills.

"Okay, let's go! We have got to make it happen!" I said, pulling them into a tight huddle at midfield. "Whatever you do in this game is going to be remembered because these guys are in the NFC West with us. You're going to play them again and again for the rest of your lives. You've got to get after them because the Rams are a big part of your career."

Following the drills, I noticed Ram coach John Robinson standing on the 45, so I strolled over to say hello. After calling him "Coach Robinson" for my four years at USC, I am still not totally comfortable with calling him John. I didn't call him by his first name until three years ago. He was ecstatic when I mentioned that I was getting married, and I told him I would be honored if he came to my wedding.

Though he has been their coach for eight years, it's hard for me to accept Coach Robinson in Rams blue and gold. I'll go to my grave detesting the Rams. I haven't liked them from the day I moved from Washington, D.C., to Southern California in 1968. I loved the Washington Redskins while growing up, but in Rialto, California, we could only get Rams games on television. I never understood why the Rams couldn't win championships with talented players like Roman Gabriel, Jack Snow, and Deacon Jones, and I thought they treated James Harris unfairly because he was a black quarterback. "Shack" Harris should have been a full-time starter. Then, when I went to USC, it was drummed into me to hate the UCLA Bruins. And what were their colors? Blue and gold.

A 49ers–Rams game generates the same kind of intensity in me that I found in the USC–UCLA rivalry. The Rams have a knack for winning games at Candlestick, 15 of the last 20 in fact, and the 49ers win practically every game in Anaheim Stadium. We've beaten them there eight of nine times since I've been with the 49ers. They are, without a doubt, our most difficult opponent because each team knows the other so well. It's like battling your brother, but in this case without any brotherly love.

These Rams looked nothing like the 1989 Rams, who had finished 11–5 and lost to us 30–3 in the NFC Championship Game. They had a 3–7 record and statistically one of the worst defenses in the NFL. I reminded myself not to take the Rams lightly, however, regardless of their record. You should never underestimate the emotions in this rivalry. To jack us up, I launched into a pep talk in the locker room, after we finished with our pregame prayer. I focused on our last loss to the Rams, 13–12, on October 1, 1989, at Candlestick Park.

"It's easy to look back on the victories we have over them, but I think we shouldn't forget the defeats," I said. "The last time they were here, they walked up the tunnel after the game and pounded on our locker-room door. That showed no class. As a matter of fact, it was sort of bullshit. Some of the Rams actually opened the door and hollered into our locker room. Now, are we going to let them get away with something like this?"

Maybe I shouldn't have said anything. We self-destructed on offense with six turnovers, four of them coming on our first six possessions. The Rams converted two into touchdowns and led 14–0 early in the second quarter. A 53-yard pass from quarterback Jim Everett to Willie (Flipper) Anderson set up another touchdown, giving the Rams a 21–7 lead with 39 seconds left before halftime. The Rams' defense had confused our offense with a formation called the Big Nickel. They used six defensive backs, and it was something our coaches hadn't anticipated. When teams throw a confusing defense at us, I occasionally talk to Jerry Rice on the sideline about the coverages, but this time I didn't say anything. I did, however, speak to a frustrated Montana. "I wish the damn coaches would wake up and let me call my own plays," Montana said. I couldn't figure out why it took us so long to adjust in the first half, and I agreed with Montana. I have never understood why the best quarterback of all time can't call his own plays and has no input in the game plan. With twelve years in the 49er system Montana knows our offense better than George Seifert and his offensive coordinator Mike Holmgren, both of whom call the plays.

With 6:05 remaining in the third quarter, Montana connected on a 23-yard touchdown pass to running back Harry Sydney, and on our following series Mike Cofer kicked a 42-yard field goal, chopping the Rams' lead to 21–17. Miraculously, we were back in the game. But that feeling of euphoria lasted only a few minutes. In the opening minute of the fourth quarter, Montana moved us to the Ram 40, and then was intercepted at the 10 by safety Vince Newsome.

On first down, Everett overthrew running back Cleveland Gary, but the Rams were penalized for a false start, moving them back to their 5. We had the Rams where we wanted them. Gary picked up a couple more yards, and they were faced with a second-and-13 on their 7. We brought in our nickel package, giving us an extra defensive back, and defensive coordinator Bill McPherson directed us to stick to a zone defense. I haven't felt confident in zone coverage all season. For a zone defense to be successful, all the defensive backs must communicate with one another. We haven't been doing a good job of it. Because of so many injuries, we can't keep everybody healthy and that forced us to use several different combinations in the secondary. Teams have scored more touchdowns on us in zone situations than ever before. I thought we were a much better team in man-to-man coverage. It made us more aggressive.

When play resumed, Everett rolled to his right, tight end Pete Holohan slipped in behind outside linebacker Bill Romanowski and made a 15-yard reception, giving them a big first down on the 22. From there, the Rams methodically kicked our butts. Nothing fancy. Just good old-fashioned smash-mouth football and perfect passing. Everett was five for five on the drive for 56 yards, but what really hurt was the way the Rams pounded the ball down our throats and we missed tackles. It seemed that every time we tried to disguise our defense, the Rams knew exactly what we were doing. Gary ran left and right and up the middle.

With less than three minutes remaining in the game, the Rams had a third-and-goal on our 1. On the next play, Gary bobbled the pitch from Everett, picked it up and scored the touchdown that clinched the game at 28–17. The Rams covered 90 yards in 17 plays and took 10:37 off the clock. Gary carried nine times. We failed to set the NFL record for consecutive victories. Our winning streak ended at 18 games.

When an opponent is grinding out yardage like that I wish the players had veto power over the coaches in the press box. So often, I sense emotions on the field that coaches can't possibly pick up. They can't see the faces of the guys in the huddle, know who's fired up and who's sitting on his heels. In crunch time, the coaches look at the situation purely from a strategic sense: we can stop them with this defense. But maybe it would have been better to work on emotions, to blitz, take a chance, roll the dice, try anything that would get us into the attack mode and let some of the inspiration out of the Rams. Several years ago, as a way to help offenses hear the plays in noisy domed stadiums, the NFL investigated the possibility of putting a microphone in the quarterback's helmet and speakers in the earpieces of the other offensive players. The technological innovation wasn't adopted, but I think that someday it would be a good idea to equip the defensive captain with a device to confer with the coaches about plays. There's plenty of time to call upstairs. All it would take is a smart player and a patient coach.

Our players were more subdued than usual, but it was hard for me to make an honest assessment of the team's emotional state because we hadn't lost in a long time. As a rule, the 49ers stay on a pretty even keel, win or lose. Having had such a winning record for so many years has kept us from getting too high with wins or dragged down by losses. I knew I wouldn't be able to get a handle on what people were feeling until we installed the game plan for the Giants on Wednesday, strapped on our jocks, lined up on the practice field, and started knocking heads. Then I'd see who was ready to give a little bit more of himself. Actions speak louder than words.

WEEK 13

Expect the Unexpected

Our biological clocks were thrown out of whack this week. After beating the New York Giants 7–3 in a hard-fought game on Monday Night Football, we had to fly halfway across the country four days later to face the Cincinnati Bengals. The quick turnaround meant an immediate shift in focus from our exhilarating victory to an ordinary regular-season road game.

My painful knees had kept me up most of Monday night. The pain in the left one was excruciating. The swelling for most knee injuries is on the front of the leg, but mine was confined to a large spot behind the left knee, and the area was giving off tremendous heat. On Tuesday afternoon I took a magnetic resonance imaging (MRI) exam, which produces a more detailed picture than X-rays. The medical technicians positioned me feet first into the narrow cylinder of the MRI machine up to my waist. People who are placed completely inside the cylinder often find the experience so claustrophobic that they are given Valium to relax. I felt confined only because the technicians told me to lie still. It would take ninety minutes for the machine to scan both knees. I tried to fall asleep but the throbbing in my knees made that impossible.

I was relieved to find out from Dr. Michael Dillingham, the 49er orthopedic surgeon, that surgery would not be required on either knee. The right knee was diagnosed as a first-degree sprain, but the left one was more damaged. The MRI showed a second-degree sprain of the medial collateral ligament plus torn cartilage, making it feel wobbly and unstable as if somebody had wrapped the kneecap in Jell-O. Still, I was able to walk without crutches. Dillingham said it was unlikely I would play against the Bengals, but I told the media not to count me out.

On Wednesday night I called on my trusty team of healers. My house resembled a rehabilitation center. Jennie Winter arrived at 6:30 P.M. to give me a massage, then John Steinke came by at eight for my acupuncture treatment. Their goal was to reduce the swelling in my left knee and keep the muscles in both legs toned. Winter stroked the left knee lightly but not deeply, because working her fingers into a fresh bruise would only create more internal bleeding. When she was finished I felt relaxed. Steinke relieved the congestion in my left knee by lancing the top of my right shoulder and sucking the blood out with a sterilized cup. He inserted needles into my scalp, my right shoulder and upper right arm, and the tops of my feet. When I stood up forty-five minutes later I had a little more movement and a little less pain in my left knee. After a good night's sleep and a visit the next afternoon with my chiropractor Bo Elliott, I felt energized.

I boarded the team plane on Friday afternoon with the idea that I might be well enough to play. I had my electronic stimulator and several bottles of Chinese herbs and linaments in my bag. Even if I had been definitely scratched from the game, I still would have made the trip. That's part of my role as one of the 49er leaders. It is especially important for a man to give his heart and soul to his team in December during the final push to the playoffs. I may be the only 49er who has attended every game in his career. Even if I am unable to play, I stand on the sideline in street clothes and sleep at the team hotel the night before home games. Just because I'm injured doesn't mean I can't lend confidence and support to the rest of my teammates.

The good feeling in my knees made me so confident that it caused me to make some stupid mistakes. On the flight to Cincinnati, I didn't ice the knees or move around the plane to keep the muscles from tightening up. After we checked into the hotel, I walked several blocks to a bar to have a beer with our third-string quarterback, Steve Bono. Before Saturday's practice both knees felt so pain-free that I decided to jog and backpedal in my street clothes on the AstroTurf at Riverfront Stadium. There were no problems. In the afternoon, I strolled across the suspension bridge linking Cincinnati to Covington, Kentucky, and had lunch overlooking the Ohio River. Then I walked a mile back to the hotel and rubbed my knees with linament.

By Sunday morning, all the physical activity had taken its toll. I awoke with swollen knees and in more agony than ever before. I asked Dillingham to reexamine my left knee.

"It looks as if the joint has opened up more," Dillingham said. "The ligament might be completely torn."

He couldn't be right. How could I have walked, run, and backpedaled on a torn ligament? I started to panic. Oh, God. Oh, God. Now I'm going to need surgery. What do I do? Dillingham told me that when the team returned from Cincinnati, I would have to take another MRI to see if his opinion was correct.

If Dillingham had told me Saturday that my left knee was not good, I would have stayed off my feet. Nobody said there was a possibility that I could hurt myself more. I am so used to pushing myself when I am injured that I need somebody to harness me by laying out all the facts. Be specific. Don't tell me to just ice my knee because then I'll think I can walk, run, and backpedal. Let me know what I can and can't do. And tell me the ramifications.

On game day, I helped defensive backs coach Ray Rhodes figure out how the Bengals were attacking us. Rhodes sat with our other defensive coaches in the press box because he was too weak to stand on the sideline, having not fully recovered from his appendectomy. It is much easier to analyze formations, shifts, and tendencies from the sideline than it is from standing deep in the defensive backfield. I tried to decipher the Bengals' snap count, and I watched to see if quarterback Boomer Esiason tipped off any plays. Esiason is one of the best at faking a handoff and throwing the ball. He is left-handed. Fortunately, we could prepare for him in practice because our backup, Steve Young, is a lefty. Right-handed quarterbacks run most of their plays to the right. It sometimes takes a little while to adjust your thinking to Esiason and pursue plays the opposite way.

Playing the Bengals on the road presented another problem. Riverfront Stadium, which is known as the Jungle, is one of the noisiest outdoor stadiums in the NFL. To communicate defensive coverages in no-huddle situations, we would have to rely solely on hand signals. Our signals usually consist of a simple gesture. A common one is a finger pointed upward. That means sky force, or safety force, when the safety's job is to contain a runner outside the linebacker.

To outsmart Bengal coach Sam Wyche, you have to search for any clue, no matter how small. You have to expect the unexpected. Wyche, the 49er quarterback coach from 1979 to '82, is by far the most creative coach in the NFL today, a master magician both on and off the field. On flights back from games we used to beg Wyche to perform magic tricks. "Magic! Magic! Magic!" we would call out to him. One of his favorite sleights of hand was pulling blouses or bras from seemingly unsuspecting stewardesses. I found out later that the women were willing accomplices. I get a kick out of Wyche's passion for football, and I admire the compassion he has for his players. He knows the chemistry of the locker room because he was there from 1968 to '77 as a journeyman quarterback with the Bengals, Washington Redskins, Detroit Lions, St. Louis Cardinals, and Buffalo Bills. Wyche is definitely a players' coach.

It takes a lot of mental preparation to play Wyche's offense. He scripts most of his first dozen or so plays and uses a no-huddle offense to keep opponents from making substitutions and using elaborate defensive schemes. What you have to do is keep hitting hard, maintain your poise, and believe they will eventually make a mistake. They can't get a first down every time. We came into this game planning to use a wide variety of defenses, but it quickly became evident that the fewer we used the better off we would be. Esiason did a good job of recognizing our defenses and attacking our weak spots. The Bengals scored on their first possession with a 7-play drive that covered 70 yards in a little more than five minutes. Esiason threw a 2-yard touchdown pass to running back Craig Taylor. Montana brought us back on the next series, using nine minutes to drive us 73 yards, and fullback Tom Rathman punched the ball into the end zone from the 1 to tie the game. That's the way it remained in the second quarter.

Both teams kept it nip and tuck in the second half. Jim Breech put the Bengals ahead 10–7 on their first possession of the third quarter with a 38-yard field goal. We came right back with fullback Harry Sydney scoring on a 3-yard touchdown run. The Bengals retaliated on the following series with a 1-yard run by Ickey Woods to go up 17–14. Our 54-yard drive at the end of the game set up Mike Cofer's 23-yard field goal with 57 seconds left, tying it at 17–17 and sending the game into overtime.

This was only our fourth overtime game in the last ten years. Montana marched us 75 yards to set up the game winner, another Cofer 23-yard field goal, 6:12 into overtime. The Bengals walked off the field with their heads down. Losing a game in the final minutes is the most devastating kind of loss, and this was just another chapter in our series of cliffhangers with the Bengals. Prior to this game our last three meetings with the Bengals were determined on a Montana TD pass in the final two minutes:

• January 22, 1989, Super Bowl XXIII—Montana 10-yard TD pass to John Taylor with 34 seconds left;

• September 20, 1987—Montana 25-yard TD pass to Jerry Rice with no time left;

• November 4, 1984—Montana 4-yard TD pass to Freddie Solomon with 1:39 left.

The Bengals had played hard the whole game and thought they were going to win, but I suspect they knew when the game was close that they didn't have what it took to put us away. Emotions ran high in the Bengal locker room. Strong safety David Fulcher accused us of being cheap-shot artists.

"Those guys do things that people don't see as far as punching and trying to stick you in the eye," Fulcher told the media. "I'm assuming people are looking past all their cheap shots because of how good they are. This team is running down on kickoffs, clipping in the back, holding guys, punching guys, doing everything they want to do. The officials aren't calling it. And soon as we do one little small thing, and it isn't even a hold, they call holding on us with three minutes left. . . .

"Everyone puts them on a pedestal. They walk around on top of their toes. They're big-time. This was like a rich high school playing a poor high school. We don't have no marching band. They do. We got uniforms made out of towels, and they've got glowing uniforms."

If Fulcher wanted to call us cheap-shot artists because our guys continued to block after the ball had been caught and the whistle had blown, then, yeah, I think he's right. But when he refers to fingers in the eye and blocking below the waist and from behind, well, shit, special teams are all about being crazy. If I played on special teams, I couldn't imagine myself running downfield and worrying about proper technique. I would act insane. By the way, Fulcher didn't happen to mention the time the Bengals pounced on Montana after a tackle or when the 49ers were at the Cincinnati 35 and Montana was called for intentional grounding. We probably would have scored a touchdown on that drive if the official hadn't thrown the flag.

It's ridiculous to believe that the 49ers get any breaks from the officials. They certainly don't put us on a pedestal. Being labeled the hardest hitter in football hasn't helped me at all. If I put a late hit on somebody, the officials call it every time. People who play hard don't necessarily work within the rules. But to make a blanket statement that the 49ers are a bunch of cheap-shot artists isn't fair. Maybe Fulcher should play against more NFC teams. Then he wouldn't mind facing the 49ers every week of the season.

WEEK 14

The Battle of Wounded Knee

After returning from Cincinnati, I had another MRI taken of my left knee. The results confirmed that my sprained medial collateral ligament had gotten worse. Dr. Michael Dillingham told me I would be out of action for at least three weeks and that there was a chance I might be back for the playoffs in January. Hearing his diagnosis made me crazy and confused. In the past two weeks, the left knee had gone from a first- to a second- to a third-degree sprain. Now there was even talk about surgery. I wasn't sure what to believe. I wondered if Dillingham was telling me everything. Just give me the best remedy to heal my knee and get me back on the field.

With all due respect to Dillingham, I decided it was time to get a second opinion. In the past I had been thankful for a second and even a third opinion. After Dillingham performed arthroscopic surgery on my right knee in 1987, he said I would only be able to play two more years. I then sought out Dr. Robert Kerlan in Los Angeles, and he concurred with Dillingham. Finally I visited Dr. Richard Steadman, who had reconstructed the knees of some of the best United States Olympic skiers. Steadman told me that if I strengthened my quadricep I would be able to play pain-free for many years. He was right, and I have had no problems until now.

On Friday morning I flew to Los Angeles to see another doctor whose specialty is making diagnoses. He examined my MRIs and told me that I absolutely did not need surgery, but he advised me not to play until next season. Knowing surgery wasn't necessary eased my mind, but I refused to accept the opinion that I shouldn't play again this season. I returned home later that afternoon.

I really wished I could have stayed in the Los Angeles area because I would have to fly back again on Sunday for our Monday Night Football game against the Los Angeles Rams in Anaheim. Our road trips this season have been strenuous. I can't remember ever being greeted by so many fans. The hotel lobbies are packed with people of all ages who wait for hours to have their pictures taken with us or to get our autographs. I credit some of our popularity to being four-time Super Bowl champions, but I also think it is due to the boom of the sports memorabilia business and the recent interest in football trading cards. The thought that my autograph is actually worth money is surprising and repulsive. When somebody hands me a dozen Ronnie Lott cards to sign, I will only autograph a couple because I figure somewhere down the road this collector will cash in on my name.

The number of fans isn't the only change I have noticed since my early travel days with the 49ers. In the beginning some of our departures were delayed because a local restaurateur had rushed to the gate with pots of Italian food. In those days we stayed in downtown hotels, sharing a room with a teammate. Now we travel in luxury. We fly on jumbo jets, and we are served specially prepared meals. It's better than normal airline food. We stay in nice hotels away from the city scene, and some players have their own rooms. There is always a complimentary fruit basket in our room and, of course, containers of an energy drink called Power Burst made by a company belonging to Eddie DeBartolo, Jr. We have at least two security guards on our floor at all times.

We have won an NFL record seventeen straight road games. There has always been a no-nonsense approach to playing on the road that we learned from Bill Walsh. Instead of traveling on Saturday mornings like most NFL teams, he insisted we leave on Fridays to get acclimated to changes in time zones and weather.

"This isn't a family vacation," Walsh used to say. "I don't want you spending your free time with your relatives, getting fat, and not being able to run Sunday. You're here to play a game. They have to understand that. You're on a business trip. You're in business for yourself."

On the road, I tend to isolate myself in my hotel room. The 49ers have our hotel block calls to our rooms after 11 P.M. The rest of the time I do the screening.

"Is Ronnie Lott there?" the caller asks.

"No, he's not here," I reply. "Who's calling? I'll let him know."

Although I have been a bachelor my entire 49er career, I have never attracted groupies the way Joe Montana and Dwight Clark did in the early '80s. When they were single, they were like rock stars. The current hot ticket is backup quarterback Steve Young. I have met so many women who want to be introduced to him. My fans tend to be the more motherly types who send cookies, cakes, or brownies up to my room.

Occasionally I will share a meal on the road with a teammate, but most of the time I order room service and eat by myself. It always becomes a scene walking into a restaurant with Montana. Heads quickly turn. All eyes are on you. On the way to our table I'll hear people whispering, "There's Joe Montana. There's Joe Montana." That will be followed by "And that's Jerry Rice," or, "And that's Roger Craig." I guess people never expect Montana to dine with a defensive player.

Without a doubt, my favorite road trip came in 1988 when we traveled to London for a preseason game against the Miami Dolphins. At the hotel, hundreds of kids flocked around the entrance. We quickly learned that rock superstar Michael Jackson was in town for a concert and staying at the same place.

Charles Haley went nuts. He is such a big Jackson fan that, in tribute to him, he will wear only one glove while playing in games. You haven't lived until you've seen 6-foot-5, 230-pound Haley and his size-16 shoes moonwalking. Turner met Jackson's manager and arranged for tickets to one of his concerts in Wales. We were ushered backstage before the concert, and Jackson appeared in black leather pants with buckles up the seams. He nodded when introduced to us. We were speechless.

"My brothers would really like to meet you," Michael said, referring to the other members of the Jackson 5, as we posed for pictures.

"I met your brother, Jackie," I blurted out. I could not contain myself. I felt embarrassed by my outburst. A couple of days later Prince checked into the hotel. Feeling more bold, I tried to get together with his drummer Sheila E. but no dice. When I was finally introduced to her I froze.

I always enjoy our trips to play the Rams because it really doesn't feel like a road game. My family and friends drive to Anaheim for the game, and I always bump into old high school or college friends. For this game, I left tickets for my parents and they also brought along my sister Suzie and my son, Ryan.

Because we lost to the Rams three weeks earlier, I worried that a rematch so soon would give them a psychological advantage. The Rams knew they could beat us. We needed to win this game to clinch the home-field advantage for the playoffs, and the Rams needed it to help salvage what had been a disappointing 5–8 season. I noticed signs in Anaheim Stadium that read "Sweep. Sweep. Sweep." and "Keep the Fat Guy," a message to the Rams management not to fire coach John Robinson who had failed to guide them to the playoffs for only the second time in eight years.

Standing on the sideline, I could tell the intensity level was high. There was more jawing than in any Rams game I could recall, which I took as a sign of their frustration and our desire for revenge. We controlled the game for most of the first half. There was a 15-play, 76-yard 49er touchdown drive that took 9:03 to complete. But nothing was more satisfying than watching Montana connect with Jerry Rice on a 60-yard touchdown pass, putting us ahead 16–0 in the second quarter. Rice had scored for the first time in five games, his longest scoreless stretch since his rookie season in 1985, and when he crossed the goal line, he spiked the ball between his legs, and with his fingers fired bullets from imaginary pistols. For that show of celebration, we were penalized five yards on the kickoff, but I don't think anybody cared. It was good to see Rice so happy.

During the week prior to the game, Rice had vented his frustration to the media.

"I think we really have gotten away from the past," he said. "George Seifert has a different philosophy and I just work here." Rice had also said that he had been a nonfactor in our victory over the Giants, contributing only one reception for 13 yards.

I didn't ask myself, "Why is Jerry saying that?" I looked at the remark and wondered, "What would Walsh have done? How would he have handled the situation? Why isn't Rice more productive?"

To begin with, if Walsh were still here, chances are that Rice never would have complained publicly. Walsh always emphasized the word team, and he cautioned us about sounding off to the media. He impressed upon us that members of the media are not our friends. He didn't want players to say things like, "I'm not getting the ball enough," because when that happens the team starts to draw ranks. It can make the quarterback mad or the other receivers angry, and it gets the media dredging up hard feelings that have nothing to do with winning or losing. Face it, players always want instant gratification. It's hard for us to look at the big picture.

The Rams finally scored when quarterback Jim Everett hit Derrick Faison on an 8-yard touchdown pass with 1:32 left before the half. Everett had a bad night, completing only 17 of 35 for 232 yards. He was also intercepted twice. The Rams could only muster one more field goal, a 21-yarder by Mike Lansford in the third quarter that made the score 19–10. Our rookie running back Dexter Carter broke the game open when he raced 74 yards for his first NFL touchdown early in the final period, and we ended up winning 26–10. It was the longest touchdown run in an NFC game this season and our longest run in a regular season game since 1977.

Afterward some of my teammates were grumbling that we hadn't tried to score again with 16 seconds remaining. Rookie cornerback Eric Davis had recovered a Pete Holohan fumble and returned the ball to the Ram 4. A personal foul moved the ball to the 2, but Montana dropped to his knees to let the clock wind down. Why hadn't we gone for the jugular, considering the Rams had rubbed our faces in it several times in the past?

I am sure some fans and media wondered why Montana stayed in the game at all with a 16-point lead in the fourth quarter, especially since six starting quarterbacks, four from teams headed to the playoffs, suffered injuries in games on Sunday. Jim Kelly of the Buffalo Bills sprained ligaments in his left knee. Phil Simms of the New York Giants sprained his right foot. Jim Harbaugh of the Chicago Bears dislocated his right shoulder. Steve DeBerg of the Kansas City Chiefs badly shattered a finger on his left hand. Anthony Dilweg of the Green Bay Packers suffered a strained left arch. Bernie Kosar of the Cleveland Browns jammed a thumb on his right hand. Not since week nine of the 1977 season, when five teams lost starters, had there been such a devastating day for quarterbacks.

To be honest, protecting Montana for the playoffs was the furthest thing from anybody's mind. This was a 49ers-Rams game, and we wanted blood. In this fierce rivalry, if Robinson had innocently tried to shake Montana's hand at the end of the game, three mean and nasty 49er offensive linemen would have been right in his face.

When I returned from Los Angeles, I made the decision to step up my treatments on the left knee and to assess my progress from week to week. For the next few weeks I received acupuncture every other day from Bo Elliott, John Steinke, or the old Chinese man I had met at an herb store in San Jose. Jennie Winter gave me regular massages. Each day I took several sugar tablets for energy and two tablespoons of an amino-acid food supplement to help bring oxygen to my muscles.

One evening I had the pleasure of working with the Reverend Virginia Cantle, an auditor in the Church of Scientology in San Francisco, who helped me to heal myself in a two-hour "assist" session in my living room. The creed of the Church of Scientology says that the spirit alone can save or heal the body. Cantle's mission was to put me in control of my knees by directing my attention to the injury and, believe it or not, actually communicating with my knees. She insisted that I remain alert and focused for the session, stressing that if I fell asleep as I did during my other healing treatments, our assist session would be useless.

First she put me through a touch assist to clear out any congested energy. I lay on my sofa, and Cantle touched various parts of my extremities on the right side, then on the left side, as well as points up and down my spine. Each time she paused and asked me to tell her when I felt her fingers.

"Do you feel my touch?" she asked, touching my left foot.

"Yes, I feel the touch. I feel energy in my left foot."

"Do you feel my touch?" she asked, touching my right foot.

"Yes, I feel the touch. I feel energy in my right foot."

Next she had me roll over on my stomach for a nerve assist. She fanned her fingers and ran her hands from the top of my spine to the tip of my tailbone three times, then worked in the opposite direction, from bottom to top, three times. With injuries, Cantle explained, the nerves can get confused and send pain to unrelated parts of the body. The nerve assist, she told me, would reprogram my nerves and redirect my energy flow.

Finally Cantle put me through what is called "hellos and okays," which may sound a little crazy at first. By creating a dialogue with the injured body part, this procedure speeds up healing.

"Say hello to your knee," Cantle began, "and have your knee reply with okay." Then she said, "Have your knee say hello to you. And then you say okay to that."

When I first tried talking to my knee, I have to admit I laughed out loud. But Cantle said that reaction was typical. She told me she had treated many intelligent, sane people who had done the same thing, but when they got rid of the inhibitions and spoke to their injured body part it almost became human. At one point during the hellos and okays phase I got so quiet that Cantle softly said, "What's happening, Ronnie?" And, believe it or not, I answered, "I'm in a deep conversation with my knee."

Cantle's assist session reminded me of the guided imagery techniques I've heard that cancer patients have used to slow down or cure their disease. In our two hours together I concentrated on breathing and letting my body relax. At times I felt as though I were floating on air, I was so in touch with myself. I visualized a Ronnie Lott that was completely well, without any discomfort in his knees. I talked the pain out of my body for those two hours. I don't think I have ever been so focused in my life.

Each night after that I spent at least fifteen minutes before bedtime guiding the positive energy to my knees.

"Are you listening?" my fiancée Karen would say, helping to keep me focused and awake. "Are you conscious? Are you focused on your knees?"

Working with the minister also enhanced my other treatments. In the past, I would listen to Golden State Warriors games on television during my massage treatments, but now I preferred soft music on the FM dial, and as Winter massaged particular areas I focused on relaxing those muscles into her hands. During my acupuncture treatments, I concentrated on the needles being inserted into my muscles and visualized positive energy flowing through my bloodstream to my knee.

Regardless of my mindset and the number of treatments I received, speeding up Mother Nature's timetable proved to be impossible. There were many days I felt as if my knees were getting better, and just as many when they seemed to be more painful. There were moments I had peace of mind because I was extending myself to the limit to better my health, but those would be followed by feelings of helplessness and frantic behavior when I realized I had no control over the situation. How do I get healthy? What do I do? What can I do? I tried sleeping more. I changed my diet. Cut back on fast food. Ate lots of fruits and vegetables. Drank ginseng tea. Tried different combinations of herbs. I burned moxa sticks over my knees and shins, and I covered my leg with Chinese herbal casts. I had a finite amount of time to get back on the field. The clock was running out. There were days when I was so emotionally drained that I wanted to forget about my knee altogether, but concerned friends of mine and my fiancée would phone with advice and my worrying started all over again.

I kept wondering how much I had put my career in jeopardy when I insisted on returning to the Giants game for the final two series, and I kept telling myself that I was no different from daredevil Evel Knievel, who made national headlines for more than two decades performing motorcycle stunts. He leaped over trucks and as many as twenty-one cars lined up side by side between two ramps. In the process, he fractured some fifty bones. I have always believed in living for the moment because I feel the moment will never present itself again.

WEEK **15**

Life Isn't Always Fair

This week I was named to the Pro Bowl for the ninth time in ten years. I was chosen at cornerback from 1981 through 1984 and at safety beginning in 1986. This is a great honor, and it puts me in select company. The only other defensive back named to more Pro Bowls was Ken Houston, who was voted to ten while playing with the Houston Oilers and Washington Redskins from 1967 to '80. Although I am thankful to have been recognized once again by my peers, I must admit that I have mixed emotions about going to Honolulu for this Pro Bowl.

Singling me out as the best free safety in the NFC in 1990 was probably not that difficult a task. There just aren't that many outstanding players at free safety anymore. In the beginning of my career, most teams put their best athletes at free safety and let them roam the field from sideline to sideline to capitalize on their instincts. These days, with offenses using tight ends to catch passes, as well as three wide receivers, defenses seem to rely more on their strong safeties. The responsibilities of a free safety have been reduced to staying in the middle of the field and intimidating receivers with big hits.

I would like to think that other NFL teams put as much thought into Pro Bowl selections as the 49ers do, but I am not convinced. I have often been disappointed that the players who I believe have had the best seasons don't always get voted to the Pro Bowl. In fact, if they are recognized at all, it isn't until the following season. I spend at least a half hour with my teammates studying stat sheets and discussing performances I have seen throughout the year either on the field or while watching game films or TV games. The NFL forbids us to vote for teammates or players from within our own division.

Let me share my firsthand experience with the inequities of Pro Bowl voting. In 1984 I had missed all or parts of seven games because of injuries, but my reputation had a lot to do with being selected to the NFC team. When I found out my teammate, cornerback Eric Wright, who had given up just one touchdown that season, hadn't been voted to the Pro Bowl, I was embarrassed. I publicly said I would give up my spot for

Wright, but the NFL contacted the 49ers and said I could not do that. I certainly wouldn't have handed my spot to anybody other than my teammate and close friend. Fortunately, another defensive back had to relinquish his spot because of injury, and Wright was placed on the team.

The following year, Wright made the Pro Bowl and I didn't. I had led the 49ers in interceptions with six, and my 104 tackles ranked second to linebacker Riki Ellison's 106. I figured I hadn't made the team because I had been moved to safety prior to our fifth game, and perhaps my peers had viewed it as a bad move. My friend Dennis Smith of the Denver Broncos theorized that I had talked myself out of the selection.

"You were telling everybody the year before how Eric should have made the team and you shouldn't have, and a lot of players remembered what you have said," Smith said. "When they voted for the Pro Bowl the next year, they said, 'Ronnie Lott's not playing great anymore.' And they didn't vote for you."

Players must have performances that scream out from the television screen, and that's not always easy for those of us in the defensive backfield because we are seldom in the picture. My best games in 1990 were on Monday Night Football—my combined statistics were 14 tackles, 2 interceptions, 4 passes knocked down, and 1 forced fumble against the New Orleans Saints and New York Giants—and I'm sure those vivid pictures were more on the minds of the voters than the times I was burned for touchdowns or the three games I have been sidelined to this point with injuries. Other than Chicago Bear rookie Mark Carrier, there are no other free safeties in the NFC who had an outstanding year. Over the years I have felt sorry for the young, rising talents on the 49ers. Because Bill Walsh insisted on promoting himself—and he instructed the 49er public relations department to do so—the media repeatedly claimed that we had a finesse team, on both offense and defense. Our defense wasn't supposed to be tough. Therefore, when it came time for Pro Bowl voting, most players around the NFL believed what they heard. They disregarded our quality defensive players and concentrated on our offensive stars. We canceled each other out in Pro Bowl voting. For example, nose tackle Michael Carter, cornerback Don Griffin, and former 49er Tim McKyer should have gone to the Pro Bowl earlier in their careers, and defensive ends Kevin Fagan and Pierce Holt deserved to be there after the 1990 season.

At times I have worried that the Pro Bowl might be a popularity contest. Many of the other Pro Bowlers have expressed the same concern to me. I suspect players vote for their friends, and it is not out of the question for guys to vote for alumni from their colleges. Some days I think that once you're in the Pro Bowl clique, you're set for the rest of your career—unless you were hard to get along with in Honolulu. As Matt Millen says, "Once you're stamped a Pro Bowl player, you're stamped."

Pro Bowl voters also fall back on past greatness, and I have to admit I am as easily swayed by that criterion as the next voter. The Bay area media complained after linebacker Mike Walter, who led the 49ers in tackles in 1987 and 1988, didn't make the Pro Bowl either of those years, and I agreed. That is, until I took the field at Aloha Stadium with Lawrence Taylor and Mike Singletary. I looked at them and said, "You can't overlook great players even if they haven't had their best years." Taylor was selected in 1990 for the tenth time, and even though the media harps that L.T. doesn't have the skills he had as a young buck, he still ought to be in Honolulu because he is the best linebacker who ever played the game. (If only you could study L.T. on film, I guarantee that he would dazzle you. While he may not be out-of-this-world on every single play, L.T. still does things that others can only dream of.)

My first trip to the Pro Bowl after the 1981 season was an intimidating experience. I wasn't sure I fit in. It reminded me of my freshman season at USC when I felt out of place with all the older, more established players. I sat in my Honolulu hotel room a lot more than I did in later years, and because I remember feeling so uncomfortable I now make it a point to speak to the rookies and say, "You had a great year." As a rookie Pro Bowler, I remember introducing myself to Dallas Cowboy defensive tackle Randy White, whose mere presence intimidated me. I told White he scared me, reminding him about our dialogue during warm-ups before the NFC Championship Game a few weeks before. I was resting in between drills, studying the Cowboys' quarterbacks and receivers, when White barked, "Number 42. Get on the other side of the 50-yard line!" I was taken aback. Whatever you say, Mr. White. I quickly backpedaled a few yards. White laughed when I told him how scared I was, and teased me about it for the rest of his career.

Some of my best recollections of past Pro Bowls are of L.T., who is one of my favorite players of all time. I love his passion for football. The entire week in Honolulu he doesn't stop singing his rendition of the Mickey Mouse Club theme song. "Who's the leader of the club that's made for you and me? . . . Da da dah . . . Da da dah . . . Da da dah . . . L.T." We have traded Pro Bowl jerseys, and I once found myself in the middle of a heated debate between L.T., Hugh Green, and Rickey Jackson. The topic? Who is the best linebacker in the NFL.

"All you do is rush the passer," Jackson said to L.T.

"All you can do is cover," L.T. told Jackson.

"They just give you free rein," Green said to L.T.

"Hey, I can't go wherever I want to go," L.T. said. "Tell me, what is it that you two do?"

There is really only one honor I have ever wanted to win, the Len Eshmont Award, and I never have. This award is given annually to the 49er player who best exemplifies "inspirational and courageous play." Eshmont, a halfback from Fordham University, played on 49er teams from 1946 to '49, and he later coached at Navy and Virginia. He died in 1957, and the first recipient of the award that year was quarterback Y. A. Tittle. The Eshmont Award is important because it is chosen by a secret ballot of the players. Only two players have won it twice since I've been with the team: Joe Montana in 1986 and 1989 and Roger Craig in 1985 and 1988.

This week our public relations staff solicited our votes for the Eshmont. They explained the criteria and reiterated what a prestigious award it was. I have always wondered why our head coach or the previous winner haven't been the ones to speak about the importance of the qualities of courage and inspiration. When the votes were counted, there was a five-way tie on the first ballot, so we voted again. That time, Charles Haley and Fagan were declared the winners. The Eshmont stands for the principles I have prided myself on all these years. I had always thought I was being inspirational and courageous, but apparently I wasn't touching enough people.

For the third straight week, my injured knees kept me out of action. Montana joined me on the sideline after he discovered a bruise the size of a dime underneath his testicles while he was getting dressed. Montana said he thought he hurt himself against the Los Angeles Rams when a lineman fell on top of him, and although the area was tender, it hadn't hampered him in practice during the week. Montana acted unfazed by the bruise, but I insisted he have our medical staff check it out. It was in too private an area not to pay attention to it.

I knew Montana's goal had been to start every game in 1990 and to pass for 4,000 yards, but I didn't want him to overlook his health in the process. Montana showed the bruise to the doctors and trainers, and after they all conferred with George Seifert, the decision was made to have him sit out our upcoming game with the New Orleans Saints. Seifert announced that backup Steve Young, who had only attempted one pass all season, would start in his place. It would be Young's first start since December 17, 1989.

"Steve's going to be running the show today," Seifert told us. "We have been in situations like this before, where people have gone down and others have taken their places. I want to see people playing with enthusiasm. We've got to get the job done."

We have a lot of confidence in Young. When he came to the 49ers in a trade with the Tampa Bay Buccaneers several days before the NFL draft in 1987, he didn't have great quarterback skills. He would drop back, look for his primary receiver, and if that man wasn't open, Young would take off scrambling. Because he had received so much fanfare in 1984 when he signed a $40 million contract with the USFL's Los Angeles Express, everybody expected Young to be the second coming of Joe Montana, that he would waltz right in and make an immediate impact. In the past few years, Young has developed patience in the pocket as well as a good understanding of the ins and outs of the 49er offense.

That is the same patient attitude Young displays when asked about having to wait in the wings as Montana's backup. He has only started ten games in four seasons. Against the Cleveland Browns on October 28, he was used as a receiver on two third-and-long plays. He maintains his composure, remains dignified, and shows restraint. However, let's not kid ourselves. Young is such a competitive person—we are one of the few NFL teams to carry a third quarterback (Steve Bono) because Young takes half the snaps in practice and will not play scout team—that I have seen him pout at times of frustration. I don't think Walsh ever meant for Young to be Montana's caddie for so long. I believe he originally acquired Young as trade bait, because the team never held a big press conference to announce his arrival. I was somewhat surprised when Walsh kept Young and traded Jeff Kemp to the Seattle Seahawks in 1987. Walsh put the team through an emotional roller coaster with the Montana–Young controversy in 1988, but if he hadn't retired after Super Bowl XXIII I am sure he would have continued to work Young into the lineup. In my opinion, he would have phased out both Montana *and* me after our third Super Bowl championship.

The reason Young seldom complains about his predicament is because he is one of the rare athletes who can see life's larger picture. He's a devout Mormon and the great-great-great grandson of Brigham Young. I was touched by a comment he made to Lowell Cohn, the *San Francisco Chronicle* columnist. Cohn had been up all night with his sick son and remarked how tiring raising children can be. "Sure," Young replied, "but having a child is the only miracle we're allowed." Young feels lucky to be making a reported $1.1 million a year as a backup quarterback. For years he cruised around in a run-down 1965 Oldsmobile nicknamed the Cardinal, which had well over 200,000 miles on the odometer and tons of fast-food wrappers in the backseat, and when he moved in with right guard Harris Barton, Young had to be the only multimillionaire in the NFL who slept on a sofa bed. He lives in faded blue jeans. In the off-season he attends Brigham Young University Law School. I love his aggressive on-field demeanor: I think he wants to prove to everybody on the team that having the reputation of a smart, squeaky-clean, All-American guy in no way makes him a wimp.

Beginning with our opening drive against the Saints, Young showed his aggressiveness in our no-huddle offense and moved us 67 yards in 14 plays for a touchdown. He completed passes to Jerry Rice, John Taylor, Brent Jones, Tom Rathman, and Dexter Carter. Rathman scored on a 1-yard run to give us a 7–0 lead. Saint quarterback Steve Walsh brought New Orleans right back on a 77-yard drive, which included his 18-yard scramble on second-and-eight from the San Francisco 35, and he connected with tight end Greg Scales on a 5-yard touchdown pass. Walsh had been traded from the Cowboys in early October, and he didn't seem completely comfortable with the Saints' offense. Part of being a good quarterback is feeling relaxed. Throwing passes is just like shooting free throws. The more relaxed you are the better you play. Once Walsh completes a training camp with the Saints, he'll find his comfort zone.

The 49ers' following series, Young strung together another drive, hitting three straight passes, highlighted by a 16-yarder to Rice. On first down from the San Francisco 45, he handed off to Dexter Carter, who sprinted off tackle and fumbled the ball. Carter scratched and clawed for the recovery, but the Saints'

Vince Buck came up with the ball. Eight plays later, Morten Andersen booted a 30-yard field goal, and New Orleans took a 10–7 lead into the locker room at halftime.

Our nose tackle Michael Carter had been asked to leave the game in the first quarter to clean himself off after the officials noticed Vaseline on the football and then discovered Carter's jersey was lathered with the slippery petroleum jelly. That didn't seem to discourage our linemen because early in the second quarter a CBS Sports camera documented nose tackle Jim Burt, who wasn't dressed for the game, spraying silicone on the jersey of nose tackle Pete Kugler. Burt had hidden the aerosol can inside a white towel, but when he finished applying the silicone he realized he had been on television the entire time. He was so surprised, he looked as if he were going to fall off the bench.

When it comes to using illegal substances, the linemen are usually the biggest culprits. They'll use anything to keep opponents' hands off them. They buy silicone spray at art stores and raid the training room for Vaseline. The illegal substances are odorless and colorless, and officials don't see them unless the players are absolutely soaked in the stuff. We caught Green Bay's offensive linemen using Vaseline earlier in the season after the ball was too slippery for their center to handle. Packer guard Billy Ard tried to get the officials off Green Bay's tails.

"Ref, they got it on their jerseys! They got it on their jerseys!" Ard yelled, pointing to the 49er line.

"No. No. No," a couple of our linemen shouted. "They're the ones."

"No, we're clean," Ard said. "It's them. It's them."

One official walked over to Ard, inspected his jersey, and said, "You're out of the game." Then he walked over to our linemen and began touching their jerseys and determined they were clean. We hadn't broken any rules. Sometimes I wonder if these substances really help or whether they are just psychological tools.

On our opening series of the fourth quarter, Mike Cofer kicked a 30-yard field goal to tie the score at 10–10, but on our next possession we committed our third turnover of the game. Young hit Jones over the middle for a 14-yard gain, but Buck forced a fumble and inside linebacker Vaughan Johnson pounced on it at the New Orleans 40. Eight plays later, Andersen kicked a 40-yard field goal to give the Saints the lead.

We got the ball back at midfield three series later with 2:11

remaining. Young moved us to the 20 in four plays, completing two passes and scrambling for yardage two other times. With 53 seconds left, he handed off to Carter who fumbled again. The ball squirted loose, and Rickey Jackson recovered as the Saints held on to a 13–10 victory, which kept their playoff hopes alive. In our two losses this season, we made a total of 10 turnovers, and I blame it on lapses in concentration.

I hope Carter will be open-minded enough to learn from both of his fumbles. After the first one I encouraged him by saying, "Don't lose your cool. Play hard and they'll give the ball back to you." On the second one there was nothing to say. Carter came to the 49ers with a chip on his shoulder, and it seemed as if somebody somewhere had told him that veterans dog rookies in the NFL. The 49ers have never hazed rookies. We want them to contribute as soon as possible. I had stressed to Carter all season that hard work will lead to acceptance among his teammates, but he had a tough time understanding.

The Saints were not too pleased that Montana didn't play. Linebacker Pat Swilling said after the game that the 49ers did not respect the Saints, and free safety Gene Atkins called it "a slap in the face." In our locker room, several players claimed that we had suffered a letdown without Montana. Although I didn't make my feelings known, I was pretty ticked off about our lackadaisical performance. A team in search of three-peat should not make four turnovers. If you're a true professional, you should be able to bring forth the rage, no matter what is at stake. Granted, you might not play with the same intensity every time out, but you still have to be pissed off to some degree and smell that dog doodoo under your shoe. And you should never have to walk off the field embarrassed by your performance.

WEEK 16

Wrapping It Up

"Bring it up!" coach George Seifert yelled as he gathered the team for our pregame prayer in the locker room before the final game of the regular season against the Minnesota Vikings.

I was standing in the back in my street clothes, and I could see that the majority of my teammates were just moseying along in their own little worlds. Either they had not heard Seifert or they had chosen to ignore him until they were finished with their own business. Their attitude for today's game seemed to be, we'll get through this and then we'll turn it on in the playoffs.

The lethargic scene came as no surprise. This season it took us forever to come together, beginning with the pregame prayer. The enthusiasm of years past was noticeably missing. We hadn't played well as a team since beating the New York Giants, and Seifert knew the Vikings would challenge us. His face started to turn red and his eyes got as wide as silver dollars. Uh-oh, I thought, here it comes—

"Bring it up, goddammit!" Seifert screamed. "Bring it up! I can't believe this lack of professionalism. I will not allow you to embarrass yourselves or this organization. I don't give a damn if it's the last game of the season, and I don't give a damn that it doesn't mean anything. We have to play up to a certain standard."

All eyes in the locker room were glued on Seifert. I had seen him go into a tirade only one time. That happened at halftime of a Monday Night Football game against the Chicago Bears in 1987 when he was our defensive coordinator. We were leading 20–0 at the time, and to keep us fired up, he kicked a chalkboard and probably wished he hadn't. He broke his toe. But you could say his outburst worked because the final score turned out to be 41–0. In the two years Seifert has been our coach, he has pretty much kept his emotions under control. One time Seifert swore at outside linebacker Bill Romanowski for hitting Bubba Paris in the back of the head and ordered him to leave the practice field. Another time he chewed out a group of linemen for fighting among themselves and risking injury. He called them chickens. This season, he gave us a good tongue-lashing after our 30–10 loss to the Seattle Seahawks, which concluded a dismal 1–3 preseason. We deserved it—the last time we had a losing preseason record was in 1983, and Seifert vowed to tighten the reins.

"Goddammit! This isn't a players' team anymore," he hollered at us that day. "This is my team!"

I was glad to see him raise his voice before we came on the field to play the Vikings. He shouldn't hold back. Kick some ass. It was long overdue. Seifert sensed, and rightfully so, that after we committed four turnovers last Sunday against the New Orleans Saints there were a lot of wandering minds. A part of me wondered why he hadn't yelled at us sooner.

Our adviser Dr. Harry Edwards then brought Seifert's point home.

"I've seen a lot of games over the years, and I've been able to call most of them right on," Edwards said. "I can tell if you have been ready or not. We need to tighten up this ship. Everybody should realize the importance of this game. These guys aren't ready. If you go out and take them right away you'll win. If you let them hang around, the way you have been doing most of the season, I promise you they'll give you a run for your money. They'll fight you all the way to the end.

"Hit them right away. As quickly as possible. You do, and you'll be able to walk away from this. Act like professionals. Go out and do your jobs."

I thought about saying a few words to stress a sense of urgency and get across the point that we couldn't lose the last two games of the regular season and expect to head into the playoffs with much confidence. But I chose not to. I was feeling frustrated and complacent. On Monday I had dressed for practice, hoping to persuade Seifert to let me play against the Vikings, but he told me to leave the field and continue rehabilitating my left knee on an exercise bike. It was an emotional moment for me. I thought I was ready to play. For the past month, my teammates had acted as if I had a disease and the coaches had little to say to me. If I stood up now and started expounding on Edwards' theme, the players would ask, "What ship did you sail in on? You're not even a part of this game today."

Once we came on the field I realized that Seifert was delivering a mixed message. It would be hard to convince anybody that we desperately needed to win when Seifert had already decided that Joe Montana would be at quarterback the first half and Steve Young the second. Also, why would Seifert give a fiery speech about playing to a certain standard, then purposely allow plays to be called so that Jerry Rice could get exactly nine catches to finish the season with 100 receptions? I understood that the feat had only been accomplished by three other players in pro football history, but since when have records taken precedent over winning for the 49ers? Our game plan also included four catches for Brent Jones so he could break the 49er season record for receptions by a tight end. As long as the 49ers' hierarchy was so concerned about statistics, I wondered why nobody worried about giving Montana a shot at reaching 4,000 yards passing, a milestone he desperately wanted and might not come close to again.

We trailed 10–0 at halftime, and I could tell that Montana was unhappy about having to stay on the sideline in the second half. He had completed 10 of 20 for only 88 yards. The offensive line had allowed him to be sacked twice. Two passes were tipped, and he had to hurry a handful of others. Montana finished the season with 3,944 yards passing, just 56 shy of the goal that he had set for himself at the start of the year. If the coaching staff was so concerned about statistics, they should have worried about this: In Montana's last five games, including this one, he had thrown five interceptions and only four touchdowns. Why not let him build some momentum going into the playoffs?

As much as I wanted Montana to play in the second half, I couldn't fault the way Young performed. He drove us inside the Vikings' 20 two times, resulting in Mike Cofer field goals, and then found Rice on a 14-yard touchdown to put us ahead 13–10 with 6:23 remaining in the fourth quarter. Our lead, however, didn't last long. On the next possession, Viking quarterback Rich Gannon handed off to running back Alfred Anderson who scored from the 1 to make it 17–13. With 3:14 left, Young took charge, directing an 80-yard, 10-play touchdown drive. He completed 6 of 7 passes and carried twice, and John Taylor caught the 34-yard game-winning touchdown pass with 29 seconds left. We defeated the Vikings 20–17.

I left Minnesota with a sense of satisfaction, knowing that we had gotten our act straight in the second half and pulled together to win. We had finished the season the same way it started—with a fourth-quarter comeback in the final minute, a sigh of relief, and a lot of pride. (Oh, by the way, both Rice and Jones got their receptions records.) I took home another pleasant memory from the afternoon, the sight of Viking middle linebacker Scott Studwell being introduced for the 202nd and final time in his fourteen-year career. More than 51,000 fans in the Metrodome gave him a rousing ovation. Studwell, who was voted to the Pro Bowl in 1987 and 1988, finished as the Vikings' all-time leading tackler with 1,969. Although I only knew Studwell from Pro Bowl practices, I had always admired his hard-working style. What a great feeling it must have been for him to have played his entire career for the same team.

It got me thinking about how much I missed NBA superstars

John Havlicek, Bill Russell, and Jerry West after they retired, and how I will never see another third baseman like Hall of Famer Brooks Robinson. I didn't realize how special they were when I was watching them play, but once they were gone I felt empty because I missed their greatness. I wondered what my last game would be like. I don't need a special ceremony, and it doesn't even matter if I'm introduced at all. I just want to be able to pull on my red number 42 jersey, buckle up my chin strap, run onto the field at Candlestick Park and play football.

I compare retirement to the end of a long marriage. No matter how bitter you may feel about the divorce, love doesn't just evaporate overnight. You can't forget about all the time that has passed. Too few players admit their bond with the game as being a kind of love, and they spend their days away from football asking themselves, "Why am I struggling with retirement? Why can't I deal with this?" They have to realize that their love began as young children, and they have probably formed no closer bond with anything or anyone than with their sport. What else have they known for as long a period of time? Someday I am sure it will be difficult for me to walk away from the game. My biggest fear about retirement is that I will never find anything that I am as passionate about as football.

Keith Fahnhorst, an offensive tackle with the 49ers from 1974 to '87, had stopped by our practice at the Metrodome on Saturday morning. Fahny, now a stockbroker in Minneapolis, helped to build the 49ers into a winning organization with all his heart and soul. He was one of the most unselfish players I ever met. His first year and a half out of football, he felt like locking himself in a closet. Almost thirty years of his life had been devoted to the game, and he had defined himself through football. When he retired he worried that his wife Sue, who had only known him as a football player, wouldn't love him anymore. There was such a gap in his life he felt as though someone close to him had died. He said Sunday's game would probably be his last on the sideline with us because he finally felt able to cut the umbilical cord to the past.

I will try to learn from Fahny's retirement experience just as I have filed in my memory banks all of the obstacles other teammates have encountered at the end of the road. Active players avoid retired teammates like the plague because they don't want to know what life is like without football. So many times Bill Walsh's secretary would tell me how the retired 49ers would call and say they couldn't bear to have anything to do with the game. Each time I heard another sad story, I asked myself, "How can I learn to deal with retirement now?" That is why I made sure to pay attention to the pride and heartache of the aging veterans.

I saw the frustration in strong safety Carlton Williamson, who retired because of injuries after the 1987 season and then found out that being a former 49er and a college graduate didn't open any doors in the Bay area in urban planning. I felt heartbroken that defensive end Fred Dean, one of the most important men on our first two Super Bowl teams, has been forgotten by the 49er organization. He runs an auto body shop in San Diego and hasn't attended any of our Super Bowl reunions. And then there is linebacker Jack (Hacksaw) Reynolds, who went through such a tough retirement that I wanted to close my eyes at times so I wouldn't have to see him suffer. Walsh told Reynolds to retire after Super Bowl XIX and suggested he try coaching after fifteen years on the field. He brought Reynolds to our 1985 training camp as a defensive assistant. Immediately I sensed how miserable Reynolds was. He watched young players make mistakes that he never would have made. Reynolds grew quiet and depressed. Through the years, I had counted on him to answer all of my questions about defense, but now I was too afraid to bother him. I could tell that he knew in his heart he could still play. After a few weeks Reynolds walked out of training camp, flew home to Florida, and never returned to pro football.

I have found myself looking around our locker room the last couple of weeks of the season asking myself whom I can trust. I grew up with a certain group of players who are no longer with the team or who aren't playing that much. I see linebacker Keena Turner sitting in front of his locker, seeming detached and distant because he isn't playing. And my friend Eric Wright is sidelined with a knee injury. I ask myself, what will I be without football? And I wonder, will I even be playing in 1991?

Sometimes I have felt as though I am losing it physically and mentally. It's funny how I have gotten the same chills, felt the same nerves, and had the same insecurities before games in 1990 that I had before my first game at USC in 1977. I have even asked myself the same question: can I do it? It's the natural progression of life, I guess, and I sense that I am about to come full circle. You crawl, you walk, you ride a bike . . . you go to college, get married and have children . . . The only thing that is different is that in football you know approximately when your last day will come; in life you don't.

I try to visualize what retirement will be like, but I will never truly know until it happens. It's like saying, what will I do when my parents die? I try not to think about those days, but I cannot avoid them. It's a part of life.

THE PLAYOFFS

Destiny Awaits

On Monday December 31, 1990, the day after our victory over the Minnesota Vikings, we congregated at noon in the large meeting room at the 49er facility. The atmosphere was all business. Our minds were already fixed on our playoff opener—thirteen days away—against the winner of the Washington Redskins–Philadelphia Eagles game. Coach George Seifert stepped to the front of the room. Today he was in a positive frame of mind.

"You guys have done a great job. A 14–2 record is remarkable," Seifert said. "You are facing a once-in-a-lifetime opportunity to win an unprecedented three consecutive Super Bowls. That is something no other team has done. You should be proud of what you have accomplished this year."

I have always believed that playoff teams should pause at the end of the regular season and reflect on their achievements. Since reporting to training camp July 28, we had worked hard for five months to win more games than any team in our division and thereby assure ourselves a first-round bye for the playoffs. As we began our final push in our quest for three-peat, it would be important to let the tension roll off our shoulders and pat ourselves on the backs. In the next few weeks we would be under more pressure than we had ever experienced. From my seat in the back of the meeting room, I had the urge to put the 1990 season in perspective. Seifert could speak in superlatives all afternoon, but his words might not be as meaningful as those coming from a player.

"This is one of the greatest teams I have ever been associated with," I told my teammates. "No other team could endure what we have endured. All season we have been sailing in uncharted waters. We defended more than our Super Bowl championship. We defended ourselves. Whenever we picked up the newspaper we read we weren't playing great. It wasn't enough to win games, no, we had to be perfect. We endured. We fought back week after week. The season is over, and I think it deserves some recognition. You've got to take a moment to say, 'We're the NFC West Champions.' This is a great team. We can do whatever we put our minds to."

Trying to three-peat has been by far the toughest goal the 49ers have ever tried to accomplish. It has been mentally, physically and emotionally draining for everybody. In 1990 we had trouble scoring in the first quarter, won eight games by six or fewer points, and almost every week, because of our lack of a running game, Joe Montana had to be at his best to carry us to victory. Montana publicly admitted to being mentally exhausted, and who could blame him?

Considering the mood swings in our locker room, I wondered if we shouldn't have added a psychiatrist to our medical staff. Roger Craig, normally a happy-go-lucky guy, went through somber periods because of a torn ligament in his knee and the media criticizing him for having lost a step and being unproductive. The offensive linemen and running backs were testy because of the constant criticism about the running game. At times one group blamed the other for the problem, and they lost confidence when the coaches called for passes on third-and-three. Jerry Rice got upset because he wasn't catching enough passes. And even Seifert, who has never been outspoken, seemed more withdrawn than usual. He drove himself so hard that I seldom saw him smile. In 1989 he had been just a coach, but this season he had to be that plus a cheerleader, confidant, psychologist, and motivator, often wearing all the different hats in the same week. He raised his voice more than ever, and there were many days he looked dog-tired. He placed an emphasis on having fun—which I didn't agree with—but Seifert didn't heed his own advice. He clearly didn't seem to be enjoying himself during most of the 1990 season. Although he was another year removed from Bill Walsh, Seifert couldn't step out of his shadow. Walsh still had a visible presence in his job as a commentator for NBC Sports. A widely quoted expert on the 49ers, Walsh in the preseason predicted that the 49ers would three-peat, and that prediction hung like a cloud over Seifert's head all season. I am sure that Seifert knew when he stepped into Walsh's shoes that it wouldn't be an easy fit, but some days, as I watched him agonize over our running game, I wondered if those shoes might be filled with cement. Unlike Walsh, who also had a keen defensive mind, Seifert's strength was limited to defense. Yet he spent a lot of time motivating and critiquing the offensive line and running backs. Some afternoons at practice I felt he was totally consumed with proving the critics wrong. He took the criticism too much to heart. Every unflattering story or negative statistic sent him through the roof. He made the public relations department compile statistics on our running game from past seasons that he would then use to answer the critics. None of the players cared about statistics. It didn't take a brain surgeon to figure out the 49ers have never emphasized the running game, at least since I've been on the scene. Walsh primarily used the running game to protect our leads. The main reason we weren't running well in 1990 was because that part of our offense wasn't drilled in practice. Some days we only spent fifteen minutes on it; that isn't nearly enough.

You would think after all the success the 49er organization had in the 1980s that we would not allow any internal or external pressure to get to us, but I am convinced that we wanted to win a third consecutive Super Bowl so badly that it altered our approach to football. We tried too hard. We became overly critical. We didn't have a strong psychologist as our coach, a guy like Walsh who had a knack for turning negatives into positives. Not only didn't Seifert know how to let the stress and criticism roll off his back, but he never figured out how to eliminate it from our lives either. He wasn't good at communicating one-on-one with players or balancing the fragile chemistry of a locker room. I think Walsh would have more quickly defined the team's identity—its strengths and weaknesses—and not let external forces puncture our spirit or derail us from our mission of three-peat.

The playoffs are the time of year that champions love. This is the moment when we turn up our intensity another notch and garner all the passion we have inside of us. It should make no difference if games are played at Candlestick Park or on the streets of San Francisco. That's how strong the competitive juices are flowing. I knew that each 49er player had to look inside himself and ask, How badly do I want it? It was important for him to visualize himself as a one-man army and say, "I have to find a way to make a difference." We could not become overwhelmed by our mission. We had to ride our emotional waves like a good surfer and not try to fight the currents. We needed to reserve every ounce of energy. Cut back on media interviews. Turn down public appearances. Keep off our feet.

Get plenty of rest. And, most important, make sure everybody was on the same page.

Once we knew for sure that the Redskins would be our opponent—they defeated the Philadelphia Eagles, 20–6, in an NFC wild-card game—Seifert began to focus the team. On Tuesday he closed our practice sessions to all media, something he had not done in his two years as our coach. He announced his decision after someone was caught watching our morning practice while sitting in a eucalyptus tree at the 49er facility.

"You'll see a very paranoid coach this week about a lot of things," Seifert told the media. "I ask your indulgence from that standpoint. We're just trying to have it as secure as we can. It's a time when things could get out."

Seifert didn't have to resort to psychological tactics for most of the veterans. We knew what to do to get ready. After one of our practices I ran into right guard Harris Barton in the training room. Barton is such a gung-ho player that he has been known to practice his stance in front of a mirror in the middle of the night.

"How are you feeling, Harris?" I asked.

"Not good," Barton said with a stern face. "I haven't played my best game. I've got a lot to improve on."

"Harris, I was just asking how you feel, man."

"I know, Ronnie," Barton said. "I didn't want you to think that I was taking this game lightly."

I found Craig bouncing around the locker room with a big smile on his face and enthusiasm in his step. "I'm ready! I'm ready to explode!" Craig bubbled. "I can't wait for this weekend. Let me at these guys!"

Montana sits in the middle of the emotional spectrum during the week before a big game. He never gets too high or too low, and he would be the absolute last person to scream that he couldn't wait to play. Montana shows his determination and desire by making very few mistakes on the practice field, and in the locker room he keeps his banter light and comical. I congratulated him for being named the NFL's Most Valuable Player by the Associated Press for the second straight year, and he thanked me half apologetically, adding that he felt Houston Oiler quarterback Warren Moon deserved the award. Instead of talking about the Redskins, Montana teased me about a request he had received from my fiancée Karen, who was in France with his wife Jennifer on an antiquing expedition. "Karen asked me to give you a kiss, Ronnie," Montana joked. "How about it?"

As fond as I am of Montana, I was too preoccupied with my playoff preparation to laugh, much less think about puckering up. I hadn't played in a game since our December 3 meeting with the New York Giants and our playoff game on January 12 would be my first physical contact in six weeks. Our doctors insisted that I wear a brace on my left knee for protection on the practice field. I was not supposed to do too much running, so I concentrated on getting my timing back. I crouched in my stance, then rolled out or backpedaled against imaginary opponents. I worked on my balance, keeping my weight low for as long as I could. To recondition my body and mind to deliver hard hits, I put on my shoulder pads and slammed into heavy tackling bags. I worked out in the weight room. The explosion and tension in my muscles that I feel during lifting is similar to the way my body feels when I uncoil and drive through an opponent.

Although I believe a defensive player has an easier time engaging in contact after a long layoff than an offensive player has—because he is inflicting blows rather than receiving them—the pain in my knees told me I wasn't going to be 100 percent against the Redskins. I was worried that I might embarrass myself. There was nothing wrong, however, with my adrenaline flow when I got upset at rookie wide receiver Ron Lewis for loping through a pass pattern.

"Hey, come on, run that pattern hard!" I yelled. "Give me a good look!" When I was informed that Lewis was only executing the route the way he had been told, I felt bad about what I had said. It had been mistakenly written on the coaches' miniature playboard as an 8-yard route when it should have been a 20-yard pattern.

Another time I laid in to Wesley Walls, a backup tight end, for failing to make a catch across the middle. One of our defensive players had hit him in the stomach with a helmet and he lay on the ground for a moment to get his wind back. "Get up. Get up, baby," I hollered. "Let's go."

I was revved up and trying to encourage Walls but I guess he thought I was implying he wasn't tough.

"Man, I was hurt," he said.

"I wasn't being derogatory," I replied.

"It sounded like that."

"Gimme a break, Wesley. If I knew you were hurt, I'd never tell you to get up."

I had so much pent-up aggression from my six weeks on the

sideline that I was bouncing off the walls, both on the practice field and at home. I was so pumped up that I felt the way I did the few times I tried ingesting ginseng or caffeine pills to pep me up before a game. Instead of being wired at game time, I had already blown an engine. I had to caution myself about peaking too soon and pooping out before the playoffs.

Even though we weren't required to dress in pads, there was an emphasis on intensity and precision. The tempo of our drills was crisp. Barton slapped his hands each time he made a mistake. On running plays, Craig pranced like a show horse. His feet barely touched the ground. Montana threw with pinpoint accuracy. There was lots of chatter about the Redskins game being "a money game" and the quest for three-peat as "the dash for the cash." The pressures change throughout the year, but when you get to the playoffs, the only pressure is winning the game. It doesn't matter how you do it. You can win ugly. You can win great. You just have to do it.

Seifert had to remind us every day to protect each other from injury and not to get carried away.

"We've got a lot of enthusiastic guys out here as well as a lot of players with fresh legs," he said. "Let's not get so hyped up that we injure each other. We're the good guys, they're the bad guys. I don't want you to get so excited that you peak before Saturday. Just stay sharp and keep focused."

Although we were deeply immersed in the game plan, none of us was oblivious to the escalation of American troops and the growing tension in the Persian Gulf. The television in the players' lounge, which is normally tuned to soap operas, music videos, or ESPN, carried round-the-clock reports from CNN that pointed to the distinct possibility of war. Stanley Walker, one of my childhood friends I grew up with in Washington, D.C., was stationed in Saudi Arabia, and that worried me. A couple of friends asked me for copies of a music highlight video I had produced about the 49ers called "Team of the '80s" to ship to soldiers. On Thursday, Seifert shared a letter with us from a helicopter squadron specializing in rescue missions who were on their way to the Gulf. They extended their support and good wishes to the 49ers for success in the playoffs. "People like that are rooting for us, and we're providing them inspiration," Seifert said. "Let's feed off them the way they're feeding off us."

The NFL had ordered decals of the American flag to be placed on the back of our helmets and, as a military brat, I was proud to wear the red, white, and blue. However, I was also disappointed that the NFL had not made the decals mandatory from the first day our soldiers landed in the Middle East. I wished the league would allow me to put a flag on my helmet any time I wanted. I am not pro-military because my father was a career Air Force man. Rather, I believe in defending freedom and democracy. I can understand the strain on the people who have relatives in the Persian Gulf. War is a possibility every military family lives with.

In case any of us were feeling uneasy or guilty about playing a football game while American soldiers worried about their fate, our adviser Harry Edwards counseled us about where he thought the upcoming game fit into the scheme of life.

"Sensitivity of playing games in the face of war is important, but normalcy and continuity are also important to extend and reinforce the sense of vitality in our system," Edwards said. "You are recognized as the team of the decade, not because of some poll taken, but because milk is delivered, bread is baked, shoes are made, the sun rises in the east and sets in the west, and the 49ers kick ass at playoff time. That's what's normal in American society."

I picked up on Edwards' kick-ass theme after a light workout on Friday morning. Tight ends Jamie Williams and Brent Jones had both been bugging me for days about giving a pep talk. "We need to hear one of your speeches," Williams said. Seifert had gathered us at the edge of the practice field and told us not to play as if we were defending our championship but rather to go out and grab the victory. A defender, Seifert explained, would have the tendency to hold back and wait for the other person to snatch the game away. We had to attack.

Then it was my turn to speak:

"If you noticed, in the other playoff games, the team that didn't get the big play quit. We've got to play four quarters of football. Ride through the ups and downs. Let's take a cue from Sanjay Beach. He has given his heart to the team this year. He's only on the practice squad, but every time he steps on the field he gives us the best he possibly can.

"Even though he's not wearing a uniform on Sunday, he's out there with us. He has helped make all of us better. We are an extension of one another. If we don't give it 110 percent we're cheating ourselves and guys like Sanjay Beach. He has busted his butt. That's what it's going to take. Four quarters of tough, hard football, and we'll be back here next week."

"On the beach!" Williams shouted. "We'll be back next week on the beach!"

I spoke spontaneously and with conviction. It wasn't that I felt Sanjay Beach had more intensity than my teammates. I just wanted to conjure up the image of pure self-sacrifice. I scanned my teammates and saw confidence radiating from their eyes.

On Friday evening we assembled at our team hotel, and I immediately sensed that the kick-ass attitude had disappeared. During the showing of our weekly highlight film, featuring the top plays from our preceding game, guys often hoot and holler or make sarcastic comments to pump themselves up. This time there was silence. There were a lot of tight buttholes. We were a bundle of nerves. This was the start of a new season. I was somewhat concerned, but I wasn't about to deviate from my pregame routine. I had to devote myself to getting ready.

And that meant I had to have my favorite treat, a bowl of vanilla ice cream with chocolate sauce and fresh coconut flakes. I returned to my room about 9:30 P.M., and Fred Tedeschi came by to hook my legs up to an electronic machine to soothe my muscles. After that I phoned John Steinke, one of my acupuncturists, who had a room at our hotel, and I went to see him for a 30-minute treatment. Steinke inserted needles into my arms and legs. The pain in my knees diminished, and I went from a relaxed state to one of complete calmness. Back in my room, I lay on my bed, closed my eyes and began visualizing the Redskins. Keeping in mind that Washington coach Joe Gibbs left no stone unturned, I flipped through the different plays our opponents had used to attack weaknesses in our defense. I heard Gibbs had slept at the Redskins' facility three nights, and I knew he would pick up some minute detail from our game films to gain an edge. I pictured wide receiver Ricky Sanders running toward me up the seam and wide receiver Art Monk blasting over the middle. I reminded myself to play within the framework of our defense. I had to stay in the middle of the field and not be too aggressive. I'm just one of eleven players on defense. I had to stick to my responsibility.

I thought about Sun-tzu's book *The Art of War*. Prior to the 1989 playoffs I had used a passage from the book in an effort to psych our defense: "If you know the enemy and you know yourself, you need not fear the result of a hundred battles. If you know yourself but not the enemy, for every victory gained you will also suffer a defeat. If you know neither the enemy nor yourself, you will succumb in every battle."

If you're prepared and you know what you're going to do before you get on the field, then you're already halfway to victory.

After breakfast on game day, I received more acupuncture treatment in a corner of our main meeting room where the trainers were taping players. Dr. Jeff Saul, an associate of Michael Dillingham, placed needles in my knees, and I sat on the table for fifteen minutes and read the morning newspaper. Craig sauntered past and exclaimed, "Yeah. I think I'll get a little of that too."

Montana came by. "How are you feeling?" he asked. "Feeling all right? Ready to go?"

"I'm ready to go."

This was the first time I had had acupuncture on game day in 1990. I didn't think I was going overboard with my knees. I knew I would be playing on sheer guts and, to help reduce the pain, I wanted to create a peace of mind that I had taken care of my knees right up until the last possible moment. My knees felt pretty good, but I knew I hadn't come close to putting the kind of stress on them that a game would with its running, jumping, turning, twisting, and diving. The thought of having to wrap my arms around a ballcarrier, hold on for dear life while trying to plant my feet, and then wrestle him to the ground made me grimace. I told myself to pretend that I had been dropped into the middle of the wilderness without a map or a compass. The only way to make it back to civilization—to survive—was to have a calm, rational state of mind. It was time to simply suck it up.

Determined not to break my focus, I quickly cut a path through the throng of 49er fans in our lobby, jumped into my jeep by myself, pushed an L.L. Cool J cassette "Mama Said Knock You Out" into my tape deck, and listened to rap music on the way to Candlestick Park. My mind was solely on the game. . . . *You've got to stay deep in the middle, Ronnie. They might try a play-action pass, look you off hoping you'll bite, then throw down the middle, knowing you can't get there with your ailing knees. You've got to be patient. Play hard for four quarters* . . . I worried about a statistic I had heard on ESPN that morning, how every time the Redskins had played a defending Super Bowl champion in the playoffs, they had beaten them. . . . *This can't be the day for them to continue their streak. We can't let them.* . . .

As I drove into the players' parking lot at 9:45 A.M., I could feel the wild energy of some fans who were tailgating. Candlestick is always noisier at playoff time. "Stick it to the Posse!" somebody yelled, referring to the Redskins' receivers. "Terminate the Posse!" It is a myth that 49er fans are refined white-wine drinkers. They want blood the same as we want blood. Walking into the locker room, I sensed a mixture of confidence and nerves. Tackle Bubba Paris, with a glassy-eyed glare, was praying softly to himself. Montana was studying his playbook. Nose tackle Jim Burt, his T-shirt wet with perspiration, was pacing. "This team will not give up," Burt announced to anybody who would listen. "I played the Redskins twice a year when I was with the Giants, and I promise you, they will not give up."

The Redskins had played as well as any team in the NFL since the beginning of December. During that stretch they had a 4–1 record, which included victories over the Miami Dolphins, Chicago Bears, and Buffalo Bills. All three were headed to the playoffs. The Redskins were winning because they had made a commitment to the run with Earnest Byner averaging 28 carries and 123 yards in his last six regular-season games. We had rolled up 487 yards and had beaten the Redskins, 26–13, on September 16 in what turned out to be our best overall game in 1990. But these Redskins were playing so much better. While watching game films our defensive coordinator Bill McPherson had counted the Redskins in more than fifty formations. They were using shifts, putting players in motion, and going on quick counts. Anything to cause confusion and create mismatches.

Before the game, former Pittsburgh Steeler quarterback Terry Bradshaw, a commentator on the CBS Sports NFL pregame show, came into our locker room and sat down to talk to defensive end Kevin Fagan. Montana wanted his privacy, so he took off to our auxiliary locker room to watch television. I was headed there too when Pat O'Brien, another CBS commentator, stopped me.

"They're going to attack you," O'Brien said.

"Yeah, good," I replied. "They're supposed to attack me."

"Are you worried about it?" O'Brien asked.

"Not at all."

I wondered why O'Brien would say something like that to me right before kickoff. I figured he must have gotten some information from the Redskins.

In warm-ups, I made a point of running and lifting my knees high, to send a message to Redskin quarterback Mark Rypien and the Posse—as well as to myself—that I wasn't concerned with my knees. I wanted them to see I wasn't wearing a brace. Then I joined our other defensive backs on the 40-yard line to study Rypien. He was throwing the ball extremely well, although I did notice that the Posse (Monk, Sanders, and Gary Clark) were having trouble with their footing because the field was wet in spots.

Back in the locker room, Charles Haley was the only player to speak before our pregame prayer.

"It's time for this team to meet destiny," Haley said. "We've got to go out there and take it. You've got to play with your heart and give it your all."

Our offense roared onto the field during the pregame introductions. Craig was so fired up as his name boomed over the public address system that he jumped three feet off the ground, kicking his feet and flailing his arms. Fullback Tom Rathman let out a loud yahoo. Montana shot his fist in the air. I stood a few feet away, stretching my hamstrings and torso. I was lost in my own world and refused to get caught up in the excitement. Meanwhile, we had no idea that President George Bush was about to hold a press conference. The Congress had voted to give the President the power to declare war on Iraq if Saddam Hussein failed to withdraw from Kuwait within three days, and the kickoff was delayed four minutes.

The Redskins scored on their first possession. Rypien threw a 31-yard touchdown pass to Monk. As expected, the Redskins lined up in a number of different formations on their first series. They used three tight ends in one formation and four wide receivers on another. I could tell the Redskins were brimming with confidence, and we were too.

We came back on an eight-play, 74-yard drive, with Rathman tying the game at 7–7 on a 1-yard touchdown run. The quick comeback gave us a big lift because in twelve of our sixteen games in 1990 we had failed to score a touchdown in the first quarter. It made us believe, right from the beginning, that we were in the game, and it was especially important for our confidence because the Redskins followed with another good drive that ended up with Chip Lohmiller kicking a 44-yard field goal.

The second quarter belonged to Montana, who showed once again why he is in a class by himself. On our two scoring drives, Montana was marvelous, pulling off breathtaking plays that were determined by a matter of inches. Take the touchdown that put us ahead 14–10. We had a third-and-goal on the Washington 10. At the goal line, Rice encountered cornerback Darrell Green and free safety Todd Bowles. He got away from them at the back of the end zone, and Montana made a perfect throw to Rice under the outstretched arms of Green.

Only Montana would take a chance like that. His timing on the pass to Rice had to be absolutely perfect. Green is a Pro Bowl cornerback with tremendous speed. He has been timed at 4.1 in the 40-yard dash, which is mighty impressive, and he has won the NFL's Fastest Man contest two of the past three years. It looked as if there was no place to put the ball. But leave it to Montana to say, "Hey, I'm going to see if I can stick it." I have never seen a quarterback spot an open receiver faster than Montana. He simply has a knack of getting the ball to the open man at precisely the right moment. Montana never gives defensive backs a chance to relax. I would hate to be a linebacker and have to read his eyes. He can look one way and flick the ball the other way. He can throw across his body, underhand, overhand, and on the run with a defender in pursuit. Montana has made throws like the one to Rice that only he can make.

Is Montana-to-Rice the best passing combination ever? I sure think so. This touchdown was their twelfth in ten post-season games since Rice became a 49er in 1985. They have a sixth sense about each other. Montana will nod his head or Rice will flick his hand and the next thing you know it's a touchdown. They rate right at the top with Johnny Unitas to Raymond Berry, Dan Fouts to Charlie Joiner, Dan Marino to Mark Clayton and Mark Duper, Terry Bradshaw to Lynn Swann and John Stallworth, and Joe Namath to Don Maynard.

There was another key play on that series that deserves a tip of the hat. On first down at the Washington 34, Harry Sydney, a former wishbone quarterback at Kansas, took a handoff from Montana and lofted a quivering "ugly duck" pass in the direction of tight end Brent Jones who made the catch with one foot out of bounds. However, the officials ruled that Alvin Walton, the Redskins' strong safety, had shoved Jones out of bounds and the play counted for 28 yards. Three plays later Rice scored.

Montana performed his magic again on the second touchdown drive. On first down from the San Francisco 11, he rolled to his right and lofted a high-arcing pass to Craig who leaped to make the catch for 32 yards. Seeing the play unfold, I thought Montana was going to throw to Rice, who was open downfield. But Montana never looked at Rice. He saw Craig along the sideline in front of the 49er bench, where Craig made a hell of a catch.

Two plays later, Montana connected with Jones for 47 yards down the right sideline. Jones had beaten Redskin rookie linebacker Andre Collins who looked the wrong way at the last second. A running play lost a yard. Then Montana threw to wide receiver Mike Sherrard for eight yards in the right corner of the end zone for the touchdown that put us ahead 21–10. We were happy for Sherrard. Millen and assistant trainer Fred Tedeschi rushed to the end zone to congratulate him. The crowd gave him a standing ovation. The day before, Sherrard had been activated from injured reserve after missing the last nine games of the season with a broken right leg. He deserved to be saluted for playing with so much courage. In fact, Sherrard was so elated about the touchdown, he chucked the ball into the stands. I'm sure he'll be fined $100, but so what?

Right before halftime we had a scare. With about half a minute left, Montana was popped by 290-pound defensive end James (Jumpy) Geathers, who had gotten by Ricky Siglar. Siglar was filling in at right guard for Harris Barton, who had gone to the locker room a few plays earlier with a bruised right shoulder. It took several minutes for Montana to get back on his feet. He knelt on the field, his head bent over, trying to catch his breath. Having the wind knocked out of you feels like being caught underwater without oxygen in your tank. Backup Steve Young took the final snap of the half, and the coaching staff laid into the linemen in the tunnel on the way to the locker room. They were livid about the sack.

At halftime, McPherson and defensive backs coach Ray Rhodes drew formations on the blackboard to show us some adjustments we should make when the Redskins line up with three wide receivers to one side or four spread out wide. I was angry at myself about my tentativeness. I was playing too cautiously. Sitting back on my heels. Staying in the middle of the field. That is what I had been told to do, but I didn't feel comfortable. It wasn't me. My game is to attack. I needed to come up with the big play, the crushing hit that sends a message to everybody. But who was I kidding? My left knee was throbbing with pain. I was worried that the knees might get to the point where they hurt so much I just couldn't play anymore in this game. I lay on the floor in the locker room and kept the knees elevated. I sent positive healing energy to the tender areas and said a few prayers.

As it turned out, I didn't need to do much more than protect the middle. Our defense gave up more yards—the Redskins outgained us 441 to 338—but three key plays in the second half kept the Redskins from scoring. All three plays were made by the 49ers' rising young defensive backs I call the Pepsi Generation.

With about seven minutes remaining in the third quarter, the Redskins had a third-and-goal on the San Francisco 7. Monk got open for a few seconds in the left corner of the end zone, but Johnny Jackson sprinted over to pick off a Rypien pass that was underthrown. This could have been the play of the afternoon, because a touchdown here would have made the score 21–17. It possibly changed the momentum of the game. Jackson's responsibility on the play was the middle "curl zone." But he saw Monk open and quickly realized that rookie cornerback Eric Davis wasn't back far enough in the deep zone. He made his break even before Rypien had thrown the pass. If he had waited any longer, he would not have gotten there in time.

Then, early in the fourth quarter, the Redskins had a first down on the San Francisco 15. Sanders ran a corner route but slipped at the 5, and Rypien's pass wobbled toward Darryl Pollard. There were no receivers in sight. Pollard easily made the interception in the end zone.

Finally, on fourth-and-five from the San Francisco 14, Rypien threw to Clark in the left corner of the end zone and Davis bumped him, which appeared to be pass interference. But was it? I told myself at the time, "I just hope Eric looks back for the ball, then we won't get flagged." The rule states that a defensive back is allowed contact with the receiver if he looks back for the ball because that indicates he is trying to make the interception. Davis turned his head. The pass fell incomplete. There was no penalty. It was the right call.

Not to take anything away from these three plays, the one I'll remember years from now is the 61-yard interception return for a touchdown by our 6-foot-2, 325-pound nose tackle Michael Carter with 57 seconds left. It made the final score 28–10.

What a sight as Carter rambled and rumbled toward the end zone! The silver medalist in the shot put in the 1984 Olympics, Carter is one of the biggest, strongest, and toughest men on the 49ers. He kept his arms and legs pumping, imitating his former Olympic teammate Carl Lewis, and he managed to outrun a pack of Redskins that included Monk. When he crossed the goal line, he spiked the ball and was mobbed by a dozen of my teammates. It was his first touchdown since high school, and the first scored by the 49er defense all season. It had taken him what seemed like forever to make the mad dash, and in the process he wiped my 58-yard TD interception return, the longest in 49er post-season history, from the record books. But that didn't matter. We were on our way to the NFC Championship Game.

As the game ended, the crowd began chanting loudly. . . . Three-peat! Three-peat! Three-peat! . . . I was caught off guard because our fans hadn't chanted it before. . . . Three-peat! Three-peat! Three-peat! . . . I stood in the middle of the field to soak it in, turned toward the 49er bench and threw my arms into the air. . . . Three-peat! Three-peat! Three-peat! . . .

How could I have known then that this would be my last victory in a 49er uniform?

EPILOGUE: SAYING GOODBYE

SAYING GOODBYE   On Tuesday January 22, 1991, less than forty-eight hours after our 15–13 loss to the New York Giants in the NFC Championship Game, Dave Rahn, a 49er public relations assistant, phoned me at home to say that George Seifert wanted to see me in his office early that afternoon. I didn't give the call a second thought because over the years Seifert often met with me at the end of the season to evaluate my performance and discuss ways to improve our defense. I was still too numb from the loss to the Giants to think there might be another reason Seifert wanted to speak to me. At 2 P.M., as I walked in the front door of the 49er facility, I saw Roger Craig coming down the stairs with a frantic look on his face.

"I've got to talk to you right now!" Craig said. "I can't believe this. I can't believe this."

"Calm down, Roger," I said. "What's wrong?"

Craig had been in such an emotional state after Sunday's game, I figured he was still upset and wanted to rehash what had happened. With a little more than 2:30 remaining, and the 49ers leading 13–12, Craig had fumbled the ball on the New York 40. Lawrence Taylor recovered, and seven plays later Matt Bahr kicked the game-winning 42-yard field goal as time ran out. Our chances of going to another Super Bowl, and possibly winning an unprecedented third in a row, had ended on a turnover. None of us blamed Craig. In fact, if I had to put my finger on the biggest reason for our loss to the Giants, I would place the blame on our defensive game plan. We never let our defensive linemen loose. The week prior to the Giants game, each one of them expressed their displeasure to me over the coaches' conservative approach. They even predicted defeat! At halftime, when I noticed a discouraged Charles Haley slumped in front of his locker, I spoke to Seifert about being more aggressive. But it was too late. The emotional damage had been done. The fumble marked a bitter end to a frustrating season for Craig. He had only eight carries for 26 yards and three receptions for 16 yards against the Giants. On top of that, he had had a bad knee for most of the season which caused him to finish with a career-low 439 yards rushing and only one touchdown. On Sunday I had consoled Craig as he came off the field after the fumble, and then later when I had seen him teary-eyed in the locker room. "We love you, Roger," I said. "Don't worry about this."

Seifert had not called Craig in to talk about the fumble.

"He just told me the team was going to make me a Plan B free agent," Craig said. "This is too much for me to handle. My head's killing me. Why tell me something like this after we've just lost the biggest game of our careers?"

Craig was the last guy I expected the 49ers to leave unprotected during the Plan B free agent period that would begin on February 1, 1991. (Each team in the NFL can protect thirty-seven players. The rest are designated Plan B free agents who are free to negotiate with any other team through April 1.) Craig had always set an example for the 49ers with his amazing work ethic. Sure, he hadn't had a great year, but neither had fullback Tom Rathman (318 yards, 7 TDs) or No. 1 draft pick Dexter Carter (460 yards, 1 TD). Part of the problem was our offensive line, which I believe did not play well. In particular, left tackle Bubba Paris was too overweight to be a full-time player. I also figured that Craig would be safe because of his loyalty and close friendship with Eddie DeBartolo, Jr. Haley liked to kid that whenever DeBartolo flew into town Craig would be the first person on the tarmac to greet his private jet.

Then it dawned on me. That must be the reason Seifert called me in. The 49ers were also planning to make me a Plan B free agent. I wondered how they could make a decision like this less than two days after such a devastating loss. Everybody in the 49er organization, from top to bottom, was in an emotional stupor. This wasn't very humane. When I walked into Seifert's office, he motioned for me to sit down on the couch. It was the same couch that had been there during the Bill Walsh era. The couch was built low to the floor. I remembered that I had always felt Walsh was talking down to me when I sat on the couch during our conversations.

"George, if you don't mind, that couch is uncomfortable," I said. "May we sit at the table?"

"Well, Ronnie, I'm not sure you'll feel comfortable sitting anywhere in this office," Seifert said, trying to be polite. "I've got some things to tell you that you won't want to hear. We're thinking about leaving you unprotected."

"Okay," I said, taking a deep breath.

"What would you do if we put you on Plan B?" he asked.

"I'd leave."

"What?"

"I'd leave."

"Well, I figured you would probably say that," Seifert said.

If I hadn't bumped into Craig, I probably wouldn't have been so quick with a comeback. Craig had prepared me for the jolt. The motivation behind my comments was simple. I wanted to put Seifert on the spot just as he had put me on the spot. I wanted to see him squirm.

Then I got serious.

"George, I have given my heart to this team. I have always played as hard as I can. We came within seconds—just seconds!—of our dream of possibly three-peating. To lose a game of that magnitude—and now you're telling me you're thinking of putting me on Plan B? I've got to do what's in my best interest."

I paused for a moment, trying to envision the 49ers without me. "Who are you going to start at free safety?" I asked.

"I don't know."

"You're going into the season without knowing who your starting free safety is?"

"Look Ronnie, you've missed a lot of games in the last two years. I don't think you can be a full-time player anymore. I'd like to use you in our nickel defense. The way you play the game, you just keep getting hurt. Dave Waymer and Johnny Jackson don't bang themselves up the way you do."

I laughed to myself when Seifert offered that explanation. The two times I had injured myself in 1990 had been the result of being run into by other players. The severely sprained ankle I suffered in 1989 wasn't my fault either. I had been clotheslined by a player from the Philadelphia Eagles while running back an interception that set up the game-winning touchdown. These injuries had forced me to miss ten games.

"And that's not the kicker, Ronnie."

The kicker? Seifert had never used that term with me before. "Okay, what's the kicker?"

"We not only want to make you a part-time player but we want to cut your salary in half."

At that moment I was so angry I knew I had better keep my mouth shut. There was no telling what words might come out. Taking a pay cut seemed so unfair. Carmen Policy, the 49ers' executive vice president, had told me soon after Super Bowl XXIV that DeBartolo wanted to reward me for all my contributions to the organization. In November 1990 I signed a new contract that would pay me a base salary of $1.1 million in 1991. Unlike previous contract negotiations, this one had been pleasant and easy. I had actually conducted negotiations without any help from my attorney, Leonard Armato. I had worked directly with Policy. When I signed, I felt that I really fit into the 49er organization, and that I was part of the DeBartolo family. Although we had had an acrimonious business relationship over the years, I had finally made it clear to DeBartolo that I only cared about one thing—winning.

Why wouldn't Seifert have to take a pay cut for not getting us to Super Bowl XXV? Would anybody in the organization dock him a couple of paychecks for not preparing us for the Giants' fake punt that had led to a field goal? Would Seifert have to give up a bonus for having Craig run up the middle at the end of the game when he should have called for a sweep, which is a safer way to protect the ball and run more time off the clock? I thought about what Chicago Bear defensive tackle Dan Hampton had said a couple of weeks earlier after he played the final game of his twelve-year career. Following the Bears' 31–3 defeat to the Giants in an NFC playoff game, Hampton said he had always hoped to go out with a Walt Disney movie ending. Instead he had been left with a train wreck. Well, I could hear my train rumbling down the tracks, and Seifert was the conductor, blowing the horn and turning our conversation to life after football.

"What about when your career is over, Ronnie, are you sure you want to be a coach? All those hours it takes . . ."

"I'm willing to do that," I said.

After spending the past ten years as one of my coaches, I couldn't understand why Seifert would question my commitment to the game. Just because I don't go into the office at 5:30 A.M. to watch game films didn't mean I don't immerse myself in football. I thought Seifert knew about the hours I spent trying to rehabilitate my body from injuries, that I had put my neck on the line going to bat for my teammates with management and coaches dozens of times, and that I had expended an enormous amount of energy on the field. I couldn't be more passionate about football or my team. I was at the 49er facility on draft day every year and made it a point to counsel the rookie defensive backs about the 49ers, the NFL, and life. I gave my heart and soul to the 49ers.

I swallowed hard. "George, let me ask you one last thing. Is this your decision?"

"It's part mine and part management's."

"Well, you've just gotta do what you've gotta do."

I walked back downstairs and found Craig in the locker room. "Roger, George told me that they're thinking about putting me on Plan B, too," I said. "There's nothing we can do about this, so there's no use in worrying."

I got into my jeep and phoned Armato at his office in Los Angeles. I told him that the 49ers were seriously considering putting me on Plan B. He was more outwardly emotional than I was about the possibility.

"Why are they talking about this now?" Armato asked. "The team just lost a very emotional game. You just signed a new contract. You've made All-Pro more than anybody on that team. You've been to the Pro Bowl more than anyone else. You are very involved in the community. I can't believe they're treating you like this."

I told Armato that I wasn't sure that I could financially, let alone emotionally, cut the cord with the Bay area. I didn't want to get caught up in my feelings because I needed to make a rational decision.

"Leonard, I've got to think about my future," I said. "I have a lot of business interests here. It's a business decision for them, a way to cut costs. I think it might be advantageous for me to stay."

Early Wednesday morning I phoned Seifert to tell him that if the 49ers left me unprotected I wouldn't leave. I wanted to play with his mind again.

"Oh, great! I hoped you would feel that way," Seifert said. "You can deal with the public relations end of it."

"Yeah, no big deal."

I also wanted to listen to his voice to try to determine if the 49ers were definitely putting me on Plan B. I couldn't tell that for sure. The conversation did make me begin to question Seifert as a straight shooter.

"Ronnie, I always felt that you deserved a day."

"What are you talking about?"

"I'd like you to have a Ronnie Lott Day at Candlestick."

A Ronnie Lott Day? Seifert had already envisioned hauling me out to the middle of the field and having me wave goodbye to the fans. This wasn't about Plan B and cutting my salary. The 49ers had made a decision on my future. They wanted me to call it quits. I was surprised that Seifert would presume that I would go along with a Ronnie Lott Day. I hadn't played the game for money, awards, or retirement ceremonies. I played for respect. When my career is over, I don't want anybody to say I didn't have the heart or that I didn't give it my all. When I leave football, I just want people to say, "That guy kicked some serious ass."

Seifert tried to sound enthusiastic about Ronnie Lott Day, but I felt ready for the old folks home for NFL players. The 49ers were not making me feel wanted at all. Prior to announcing unprotected lists, it was not unusual for NFL teams to make verbal commitments to some of their Plan B players, promising them bonuses or new contracts if they didn't negotiate with any teams during the two-month free agency period. But nobody had given me that option. It hurt me deeply to think that I wouldn't be one of the thirty-seven most needed players on the 49ers. As linebacker Keena Turner, who had been placed on Plan B after the 1989 and 1990 seasons, told me, "You'll know if they want you. They'll tell you in some way." In my mind, the 49ers were telling me how they felt. Loud and clear.

I had coped with the possibility of being put on Plan B pretty well, until I arrived in Honolulu on Monday, January 28, for the Pro Bowl. By this time word of the 49ers' intentions had been leaked to the media. I felt embarrassed and sorry for myself. There were eighty-four players at the Pro Bowl, and I was the only one who was about to be made a Plan B free agent.

"What's the deal?" asked Lawrence Taylor. "I don't understand this. I don't think the Giants would ever do something like this to me, after what I've meant to the franchise and the city of New York. I couldn't see myself playing for anybody but the Giants."

Philadelphia Eagle quarterback Randall Cunningham tried to make me feel better, "You can come play with us." And so did

Washington Redskin cornerback Darrell Green. "Look at this as a positive situation."

On Tuesday afternoon I bumped into 49er defensive backs coach Ray Rhodes at the hotel. He was in Honolulu along with Seifert and the rest of the 49er staff who were the coaches for the NFC team in this Pro Bowl game. I asked Rhodes if the 49ers were definitely going to put me on Plan B.

"I don't know, Bo," Rhodes replied. "If they do, I won't understand it."

"Ray, I've got to talk to George."

I finally met with Seifert on Thursday afternoon at the little bar on the beach at the Hilton Hawaiian Village. The bar is the focal point of all activity during Pro Bowl week. As I sat down I could never recall feeling so nervous around Seifert.

"What's going on, George? Are you going to put me on Plan B?"

"I told you we were."

"You said *maybe*."

"The decision has been made, Ronnie."

Unbeknownst to me, the day after we arrived in Honolulu, 49er general manager John McVay had sent a letter dated January 29 to my home officially notifying me that I would become a Plan B free agent. Here's the text of that letter:

Dear Ronnie:

This is to notify you that the San Francisco 49ers have designated you to be an unconditional free agent as of February 2, 1991. Beginning on that date and continuing through April 1, 1991 you have the right to negotiate and sign a contract with any other NFL Club, with the San Francisco 49ers maintaining no right of first refusal or compensation. If you do not sign a contract with another NFL club during that period, the exclusive contract rights currently in existence shall revert to the San Francisco 49ers on April 2, 1991.

Sincerely,
John E. McVay

But I hadn't yet seen the letter. Now, my heart sank. "Who are you going to protect?" I said, my stomach feeling hollow.

"We have a source who advised us to protect all of our offensive linemen because linemen are at a premium."

"Who is this source? An agent?"

"I can't tell you."

"Why offensive linemen?"

"The source says that's the consensus around the league. Offensive linemen are hard to find."

Seifert then stopped himself in midsentence. "Listen, this is really none of your business. I don't want to discuss this any further."

I was stunned. They were going to protect offensive linemen like Paris and long snapper Chuck Thomas over somebody who had given so much? "Why didn't you tell me for sure a week ago that you were going to put me on Plan B?"

"I wanted to ease you into it."

That made me angry. It was obvious that loyalties only went so far with him. If he had been straight with me I could have begun planning for my future. But left up in the air, I had spent every night since our first conversation rolling around in my bed, unable to sleep. "George, you've been straight with me on everything else in my career! You asked me to be straight with you in training camp, when I was acting quiet and moody and you wondered what I was thinking. I told you then that I was mad because I wasn't in good enough shape. I promised I would be straight with you, and I have been. Now what about you?"

Seifert didn't respond to that. He took a deep breath and said, "I feel better now that we've had this man-to-man talk."

I didn't feel better. I felt worse than ever. "Are you still going to cut my salary, George?"

"Yes."

I wanted to stay with the 49ers. They were like family to me. I knew I didn't want to settle anywhere else. I had recently built a house and I was part owner of a restaurant called Sports City Cafe. I had also invested in a new health club in San Jose. I decided to go out on a limb and make a proposition to Seifert without checking with Armato.

"Look, George, I'd be willing to agree to a $200,000 pay cut." That would bring my salary in 1991 to $900,000, which was about a $100,000 raise from 1990.

"Well, I'll tell Carmen [Policy], but I think you'll need to take a bigger pay cut than that."

Then I got upset. "Can't you talk to them for me? I don't want to leave. I don't want to go through the embarrassment."

"Look, Ronnie. Eddie and Carmen think you're against them."

They thought I was against them? What was that all about? I

had always tried to treat DeBartolo with the utmost respect. I have never been a player who thinks management is perfect, that everything the front office and coaches say is right. I wouldn't have credibility as a team leader if I did. I could only think of one incident that Seifert might have been referring to. In May, I had skipped the first day of minicamp to help the homeless in the Bay area. I had been under the impression that the opening session of minicamp was optional—flanker Jerry Rice hadn't attended either—but the media quickly surmised that I was staging a walkout to protest that the 49ers had put my friends Eric Wright, Keena Turner, and Riki Ellison on Plan B earlier in the spring. Seifert jumped to the conclusion that I was unhappy with the way my contract negotiations were going. And DeBartolo flew off the handle, saying I had better get my ass into camp or he'd trade me. When I reported to minicamp the following day, I was surprised at how the whole situation had been blown out of proportion. I kiddingly said that I thought DeBartolo had been drinking too much vino when he had made his statement. I wasn't implying he was a drunk, and I didn't mean for it to be taken as an insult to his Italian heritage. In all honesty, I had been a little taken aback that he had been so harsh with me.

"George, I'm not against Mr. D, you know that. Please explain that to him. Talk to Mr. D and Carmen for me. Please. I don't want to leave."

As I left the bar and walked back to my room, I thought about how I had been the one player who supported Seifert when he was named the 49er coach on January 26, 1989. Many of my teammates had asked me if he would be a good head coach, and I responded with a resounding yes. Even though he had been our defensive coordinator since 1983, he hadn't made a major impact on most of the defensive players. He had spent so much time in his office, drawing up intricate defenses, that none of them knew much about him. Wright and I were the two remaining defensive backs he had coached in the early '80s. I guess I had believed that somewhere down the road, Seifert would fight for me. He had not seemed sentimental about me at all. What happened to the good old days, the days of the rookie defensive backs and the Great Santini? Clearly Seifert was looking out for his own butt rather than concerning himself with allegiances. I knew I would soon find out if that was true because the following day, February 1, NFL teams would announce their lists of Plan B free agents.

As for how DeBartolo felt about me, well, I never had been one to get involved in office politics, and I guess that was now working against me. Those invitations I had turned down over the years to his shopping mall openings and to his home in Youngstown, Ohio, DeBartolo had mistaken for snubs. I should have walked into his office at the 49er facility a long time ago and explained that I felt uncomfortable socializing with him because he was my boss. I would have been better off telling Mr. D that I was intimidated by his wealth and his position. But I had been too shy to say that. If I had talked to him, maybe I wouldn't be a humiliated Plan B free agent in the twilight of my career.

My spirits were down. I placed a call to Armato, who besides being my attorney, is one of my dearest friends. He cheered me up with the news that he had called the Washington Redskins and they had indicated they'd be interested if I was left unprotected. Knowing that at least one team wanted me made me feel a little better. Then Armato told me about a conversation he had with Policy, which made me upset and angry all over again.

"Carmen said the 49ers will protect you if you agree to play for *one year* at a salary of $550,000," Armato said.

"Leonard," I said, softly, "why are they doing this the day before Plan B is announced?"

"I don't know."

They were hoping I would make a quick decision, that I'd grovel and say, Okay. Whatever you want. Please, I don't want to be embarrassed by Plan B. But I was stronger than that. I had my dignity to protect.

"Tell the 49ers to go ahead and put me on Plan B, Leonard. There is no way I will accept their offer—give into their stipulations—especially with less than twenty-four hours to think about it."

When I hung up the phone, I felt empty inside.

February and March were filled with some of the most emotional days of my entire pro football career. Many nights I lay in bed thinking, why did they treat me like this after I played my heart out for them? Why don't they want me? Meanwhile the Green Bay Packers, Phoenix Cardinals, Kansas City Chiefs, Minnesota Vikings, Los Angeles Rams, and Los Angeles Raiders all inquired about my interest in playing with them. Their questions were similar. Are you still interested in playing? What is the condition of your knees? They were all under the impression that I would need off-season knee surgery, which wasn't the case.

I talked on the phone with Redskin coach Joe Gibbs a couple of times. He said he wanted to sign a free safety quickly, and he asked me to come to Washington as soon as possible to meet defensive coordinator Richie Pettibon. I loved the idea of playing for my favorite childhood team. But I explained to Gibbs that I was getting married on March 2 and could not fly to the East Coast until after my honeymoon a week later.

"I can't wait that long," Gibbs said.

"Well, I'm interested in speaking with you," I said, "so I hope you can wait."

"Sorry," Gibbs said.

Next I met with Ram coach John Robinson at Armato's office in Los Angeles. For the first fifteen minutes of our conversation, Robinson spoke to me like a friend and not as a coach. He stressed that I should be gracious and respectful of the 49er organization. Robinson always had been more in touch with the human side of football than any other coach I had known. He understood what it was like to be a player. He knew how humiliated I felt without my saying it.

"I'm more concerned with how you go out of this game than whether you decide to play for the Rams," Robinson said. "You have always respected the game, respected yourself as an athlete, and respected your place in history. Don't be bitter. It would be an easy time to unload on the organization, or individuals, but don't do anything that tarnishes what you have accomplished in your career."

When he switched into his role as a coach, Robinson told Armato that he couldn't afford to get into a bidding war for me, and he suggested that I meet with Jeff Fisher, who had recently been hired as the Rams' defensive coordinator, before we talked seriously about salary. Fisher, thirty-three, who had been the Philadelphia Eagles' defensive coordinator, had played in the same defensive backfield with me at USC in 1980. I met Fisher for breakfast one morning at a hotel at the San Francisco International Airport. I felt I could fit into his defensive scheme, but I decided that playing for Fisher would put too much pressure on both of us because of our USC connection. I admit that the thought of finishing my career with Robinson was very appealing but I didn't want to put myself through the emotional drain of playing the 49ers twice a season.

Two days after my wife Karen and I returned from our honeymoon in Hawaii, Armato and I flew to Minneapolis to meet with Viking coach Jerry Burns and defensive backs coach Jerry Brown. I felt comfortable with Brown. He had been one of the first to attend Bill Walsh's black coaches fellowship program at 49er training camp in the early '80s. The Vikings and I would be a good match. The team had been Super Bowl caliber for the past several years but had failed to put it together, in part because of a lack of leadership and salary squabbles between the players and the front office. I felt Minneapolis would be a great place to live and raise a family. But the Vikings imposed a strict deadline. If I didn't make up my mind in a week, they would sign safety Felix Wright of the Cleveland Browns. I wanted to take my time to thoroughly research my options. The Vikings ended up with Wright.

The Raiders would be the last stop on my Plan B journey. My meeting with managing general partner Al Davis and coach Art Shell was unlike any of the others I had had. We talked about football. Why teams win and lose. The greatest moments in Raider and 49er history. The key moments in Super Bowl XXV between the New York Giants and the Buffalo Bills. Davis didn't promise me that I would start nor did he say I could play for two more years. He only promised to give me the *opportunity*. I liked the idea of coming home to finish my career. Playing for the Raiders in the Los Angeles Memorial Coliseum would give me a feeling of having come full circle, and the move would give my parents and my twelve-year-old son Ryan the chance to see me play in person.

In the end, my decision came down to the Raiders and 49ers. I agonized every day for a week, seesawing between the two. Forty-niner fans had approached me in shopping malls, restaurants, and on the street to let me know how much they would miss me if I didn't stay. That always made my eyes fill with tears. Joe Montana told me to do what I felt was right for me. "That's what I would do," Montana said. It was hard for me to think in those terms. Ever since I was a kid, it had never been I, always we. Marcus Allen raved about playing for Shell. Hall of Famer Joe Morgan, who left the Cincinnati Reds as a free agent toward the end of his career, assured me that if I handled the situation well, I could return to the Bay area without any hard feelings. "Don't be bitter," Morgan said.

Some of the best advice came from Ahmad Rashad, who was blunt with me. "Think of the consequences of your staying," he said. "By putting you on Plan B and asking you to take a pay cut the 49ers have admitted they think you're depreciated talent. The Bay area media see you that way now, too. Will you be able to handle them constantly criticizing you for the slightest mistake? Will you be able to deal with them saying over and over that you can't play anymore?"

I also sought the advice of Bill Walsh. Since he was friendly with Davis and remained on good terms with the 49er organization, Walsh declined to tell me which team to sign with. He did say, however, that money shouldn't be the issue.

"Ronnie, you've got to feel good about your decision," Walsh said. "Don't make it based on emotion. Be rational and clear headed. Otherwise you'll second-guess yourself."

I flashed back to my rookie season in 1981 when I returned three interceptions for touchdowns. I flashed to 1986 and our game against the Packers in Milwaukee. We were behind 14–0 when I shifted into overdrive and snared two interceptions to bring the team back to a 31–17 victory. I played most of that game with a hairline fracture of my right shinbone. I flashed to 1990 and our season opener at New Orleans and December 3 against the Giants. And, finally, I flashed through each one of our four Super Bowl victories. Those were the best times of my life.

Did I want to go out giving up my starting job on the 49ers to somebody else? Would I be content playing in the nickel defense? Could I deal with the humiliation of being replaced in front of the Candlestick Park fans if I got beat on a touchdown or a long pass?

At that moment, I looked in Walsh's eyes and I knew that it was time for me to say goodbye to the 49ers. It would hurt me too much to be less than the Ronnie Lott of old, especially in my home stadium.

"Look at the big picture," Walsh said. "If you truly want to play longer, than make sure you give yourself that opportunity."

Dr. Harry Edwards helped push me to make my final decision, although I don't think our meeting at a Golden State Warriors basketball game five days before the Plan B signing deadline had been designed with that in mind. Edwards reiterated that the 49ers would cut my salary to $550,000 in 1991, and the following year I would become an assistant coach for $75,000 to $100,000. He said I could possibly sit on the board of the

DeBartolo Corporation. Under no condition, Edwards said, would the 49ers allow me to play more than one season, period.

I was crushed.

My life as a 49er was over.

I refused to allow the 49ers to put any limitations on me. I couldn't believe they were so adamant about my playing only one year. I was going to suggest a major pay cut in 1992 but they never gave me an opening to do so. I wanted to have a say in when and how I would end my career. Hall of Fame cornerback Mel Blount, who played with the Pittsburgh Steelers from 1970 to '83, once told me that I should try to play thirteen or fourteen years, and so I had always kept that in the back of my mind as a goal to strive for. Forty-niner broadcaster Wayne Walker, who played linebacker for the Detroit Lions for fifteen years, once said not to let anybody tell me when to leave. I was certain of only one thing when I left Edwards at the Oakland Coliseum Arena that night. I would go out like former 49er Jack (Hacksaw) Reynolds—kicking, screaming, crying, and fighting it. Nobody would tell me when and how I should end my career.

On Sunday March 31 I flew to Los Angeles to sign with the Raiders. My two-year contract would pay me $800,000 in both 1991 and 1992, and I would receive a $100,000 signing bonus. I felt confident and upbeat on the hour flight, but when I stepped off the plane, something grabbed my heart. While driving to the Raider facility with Armato, I mentioned how uneasy I felt and how scared I was.

"Something inside feels funny, Leonard."

"What do you mean?"

"I can't explain it. My stomach feels really weird."

"Things will be okay, Ronnie."

When you put your heart into something and it doesn't turn out the way you had hoped, it can be devastating. I had put my blood, sweat, and tears into making the 49ers The Team of the '80s. What a monument we built! I was going to miss watching Joe Montana work his magic with Jerry Rice, and I knew no locker room would ever be quite the same without Charles Haley's endless debates and pranks. As we turned into the Raiders' parking lot I took a deep breath. I told myself, if I've done it before, I can do it again. The football is still brown. The grass is still green. And my heart is still pure. As pure as the first day I walked into the 49er offices—innocent, ready to give 110 percent, and willing to do whatever it took to win.

"Are you ready to sign?" asked Steve Ortmayer, the Raiders' director of football operations.

"Yes, I'm ready."

ACKNOWLEDGMENTS

I would like to gratefully acknowledge the assistance of the following people whose work, memories, and insights contributed to putting this book together: David Black, Ken Norwick, Leonard Armato, Joel Fishman, David Gernert, Chaucy Bennetts, Roy and Mary Lott, Chuck and Eva Young, Carlton Williamson, Keith Fahnhorst, Matt Millen, Tom Holmoe, Jack (Hacksaw) Reynolds, Charle Young, Eric Wright, Fred Dean, Freddie Solomon, Keena Turner, Charles Haley, Mike Walter, Darryl Pollard, Dr. Harry Edwards, Jeff Fuller, Spencer Tillman, Dave Waymer, Mike Wilson, Lindsy McLean, Michael Zagaris, Jerry Attaway, Dennis Thurman, Eric Scoggins, Don Lindsey, Bob Toldeo, Marv Goux, Stan Morrison, Tim Tessalone, George Chung, Dr. Vincent Pellegrini, Jennie Winter, Bo Elliott, John Steinke, Virginia Cantle, Navy Lieutenant Commander Chuck Franklin, Navy Lieutenant John Foley, Bill Christopher, Mike Mayne, Dick and Marilyn Cardosi, Mickey Pfleger, Linda Wachtel, Peter Hirdt, Denise Bomberger, and Wordflow, Inc.

Special thanks to Roger Reupert, athletic director at Eisenhower High School, and Dave Rahn, public relations assistant with the San Francisco 49ers, for their time and patience during the fact-checking process; to Mark Mulvoy, Peter Carry, John Papanek and Paul Zimmerman at *Sports Illustrated* and Gil Rogin at Time Warner for their interest, encouragement, and support, and to Larry Klein for his wisdom and wit.

And much heartfelt appreciation to Jerry Klein, the managing editor of this project from Day One. His line-editing, reporting, interviews, and ideas were invaluable. I couldn't have done it without him.

—JILL LIEBER
New York City